Eight Setbacks That Can Make a Child a Success

Also by Michelle Icard

*Fourteen Talks by Age Fourteen: The Essential Conversations
You Need to Have with Your Kids Before They Start High School*

*Middle School Makeover: Improving the Way You
and Your Child Experience the Middle School Years*

Eight Setbacks That Can Make a Child a Success

What to Do and What to Say to Turn "Failures" into Character-Building Moments

Michelle Icard

RODALE

NEW YORK

Copyright © 2023 by Michelle Icard

All rights reserved.
Published in the United States by Rodale Books, an imprint of Random House, a division of Penguin Random House LLC, New York.
RodaleBooks.com | RandomHouseBooks.com

RODALE and the Plant colophon are
registered trademarks of Penguin Random House LLC.

Library of Congress Cataloging-in-Publication Data is on file with the publisher.

ISBN 978-0-593-57866-7
eBook ISBN 978-0-593-57867-4

Printed in the United States of America

Book design by Andrea Lau
Illustrations by Haley Weaver
Jacket design by Anna Bauer Carr

10 9 8 7 6 5 4 3 2 1

First Edition

For Travis, Ella, and Declan. Always.

There is no other choice.

CONTENTS

Introduction

Most of us try hard to be successful. And when we can't be, we try harder to make sure no one notices.

We all have our own ways of hiding our shortcomings. My favorite is avoidance. I, for example, have "been busy" the past four times my friends have invited me to their cardio funk class on Sunday afternoon. It's not because I'm bad at scheduling (*this class happens at the same time every week*) but because I have the irregular, awkward, sputtering rhythm of an old car running out of gas on the highway and my friends can still break it down to Missy Elliott like former Fly Girls. I don't want to look like an idiot next to them, but I also don't want them to stop asking me, because then I'll really feel like a loser. Plus, I keep thinking maybe I'll be brave and say yes next time! Or, I don't know, maybe the time after that?

Avoidance is a popular technique for sparing ourselves pain or embarrassment. Masking is another. Masking means still showing up but using coping skills to hide inabilities. That could be finding a spot in the back corner of the dance room (*except that the instructor makes everyone turn around and face the back during some of the routines—I've already tried that one!*) or taking water breaks whenever the choreography becomes tricky. Sometimes people take it even further, bending the rules or cheating to avoid looking bad. (*How does one cheat at cardio funk? Send me a DM if you know.*) This one probably doesn't happen in the basement of a local rec center class, but for sure it happens in actual dance competitions when money and reputations are on the line.

Avoiding, masking, and bending rules aren't ideal ways to respond to the stress of potential embarrassment or humiliation, but they are normal. We'd all be better off if we could just face our self-doubts with our heads held high, laughing off our flubs, dancing (and failing) like no one is watching. We're just not that enlightened. So, we call on our coping skills—good, bad, ugly, and even immoral sometimes—to spare ourselves from painful experiences.

Our children are no different.

Except in two huge ways.

The first is that they lack our general freedom of choice to avoid doing the things we find most humiliating. Sure, I have to do plenty of things I don't like as an adult, but I can get out of most of what's embarrassing or painful. I still have the recurring nightmare where I have to sit for an exam in a math class I never showed up for all semester, but, thank goodness, when I wake up in a cold sweat, I slowly realize I will never take a math class again in my life. Our kids, on the other hand, face being terrible at things all day, every day. Whether it's talking to people at lunch, or giving a presentation in front of the class, or running laps in gym, their days are filled with opportunities for social and emotional failures.

The second difference is that we adults have decades of experience with failure. Kids do not. Missing an easy pass in a game or being ignored by someone they don't even like that much might seem like something your child should be able to blow off. But because they haven't accumulated enough perspective to know what's a real threat to their social safety and happiness, and what's just a temporary letdown, they feel these slights in big ways.

Feeling like a failure isn't just an uncomfortable part of growing up; it's a necessary and valuable experience. It's how kids learn to cope. It's how they gain perspective. It's how they become more capable, confident, and discerning versions of themselves, not to mention better family and community members. That doesn't make it easy to watch. But knowing what to do and say *does* make it easier, for you and them. We'll get there, but the first thing we need to agree on is this: For kids to learn from their failures, they must trust adults enough to stop hiding them from us. And for that to happen, adults must stop judging kids for messing up in the first place, on every level, from minor setbacks to major f-ups. We need to minimize our own avoidance, masking, and rule bending to protect our kids from the discomfort of their mistakes and embrace what failure can teach us all.

Uhhhh. In an unrelated epiphany, I'm going to need to go to that cardio funk class, aren't I?

Impression Management

But how is it that some people don't seem to worry about looking like fools at all? They proudly post their latest burned-food fiasco on Instagram, or tell all their co-workers about that time they tripped on the stairs and spilled coffee down the front of their crotch before a big presentation, or laugh off being a total slob before anyone can comment on their messy outfit, car, or house. Maybe these people are self-actualized heroes, truly at peace with their shortcomings. These people do exist. And maybe sometimes there's more than meets the eye to this kind of "keeping it real."

Deflection can be another effective way of avoiding what failure wants to teach us. Regularly sharing little blunders or mishaps can distract people from seeing what you fear are your *real* failures. Like a magician's sleight of hand, you draw everyone's eyes to the charbroiled cupcake you just posted online so no one looks too closely at your real insecurities: your relationships, your career, your debt, your self-worth, or any of the imperfect aspects of your messy, normal, human life that many of us try to keep hidden.

I'm not saying you're under any obligation to broadcast your failures, or your child's, out to the world. It would be weird if you did. But I *am* saying that the harder we work to build secrecy around the normalcy of a messy life, the worse we feel. And the worse we feel, the more we fail. Screwing up is nothing to be ashamed of; however, failing to deal with our failures in ways that help us learn and grow has bad consequences.

This drive toward projecting an appearance of infallibility will carry into your parenting, not only because your child's failures will be less endearing than a burned cupcake, but also because of what you worry those failures might say about you, as much as them. Parental angst is often complicated by fear: first, your fear that their missteps or troublemaking will harm them irreparably *and* then your fear that children's failures are more than a reflection on them, but also an indictment of you, the parent. We feel as though we wear our kids' failures like a scarlet *F* on our chests for our community to judge us by. I hope this book will change that.

When your kids are in elementary school, the stakes are a little lower (because you've got more time on the back end to work things out before your child heads off on their own and you're still able to shape outcomes through your rules). If your nine-year-old struggles with getting into fights, you can still make them talk to a counselor (or, at least, sit in a room with a counselor), or you can still physically remove them from dangerous situations.

By middle school, as kids start gaining more autonomy, their setbacks begin to feel higher in stakes. A kid who gets into fights in seventh grade, with more strength and less emotional regulation, projects a scarier feel. Not to mention middle schoolers (and their parents) are less forgiving when kids make bad choices or lack the regulation their peers have achieved.

By high school, adults and other teens can be extremely judgmental of kids (and their parents) when they screw up. As the stakes grow higher, our ability to ration out grace and compassion seems to in-versely decline. It may be that our tolerance wanes when teens don't achieve success, social, academic, or otherwise, because they face inde-pendent living in just a few short years, or it may be that we fear that they'll do damage to themselves or others in ways they can't come back from. Either way, kids experience the *very* normal, natural challenges of growing up, driven by defiance, impulsivity, insecurity, or inexperience, and parents are left craving a judgment-free zone to talk about it all.

Without that, what can we as parents do? *Oh, hey! See this burned cupcake with goopy frosting? LOL I'm* such *a mess. Please keep your eyes on this* weird *cupcake only!*

Reader, the cupcake is never just a cupcake.

The cupcake is an example of a theory known as impression man-agement, conceived by the sociologist Erving Goffman. Impression management explains how people perform aspects of their life for vari-ous audiences. I am a parent and I perform that role for Ella and Declan. I am a writer and I perform that role for you. I am a friend and I per-form that role for many people I love. I am a wife and life partner and I perform that role for Travis. And so on. Each of us performs for vastly different audiences throughout our day. And the performance is a way to manage the impression we make on each different audience.

Where this becomes more fascinating, and relevant, is *why* we do this. Goffman's impression management theory stipulates that we do these things not just to impress other people but because we develop our sense of self from taking in how others see us. Our audience re-sponds, and we learn about ourselves. Sometimes what we learn is af-firming. Your child draws a family portrait with hearts around it, and you take in that you are a good parent. Your partner texts you a sweet thank-you for handling a household issue, and you take in that you are a good spouse.

Sometimes what we learn is less fun, but nevertheless constructive. That joke didn't go over well, or you got too loud after you had a few drinks and people were annoyed. Impression management isn't just doing a song and dance to make others feel good so you feel good. Goffman says impression management is how we learn who we are by seeing ourselves reflected back to us by our audience. Our sense of self is contingent on, and formed by, how others react to us.

Redirecting your audience to look at the wonky cupcake isn't just a ruse to curate a pleasing image of near perfection. It's a fundamental part of our human nature to set up our audience so they can reassure us that we aren't failures in any greater way than a botched baked good. And when you're feeling like a failure in a bigger way, that's exactly when the cupcake photo goes up.

A sitcom moment I often call back to is when Ray Barone on *Everybody Loves Raymond* complains to his wife about having to clean up before people come over. "Come on! Ow! Why do you always do this? Every time we have people over we spend all day making the fake house."

Making the fake house is a little like making the fake life, spending our energy stuffing all our unsightly failures under the bed or into the closet so no one sees them, instead of dealing with them in the first place.

Adolescents are masters of the craft of impression management, or at least they're working hard on their apprenticeships. Social media has become the ultimate tool for this job, but teens have always done this regardless of what technology was at their disposal. In her brilliant book *It's Complicated: The Social Lives of Networked Teens,* Danah Boyd writes about the ways kids tried to manage what others thought about them long before Instagram or Snapchat came onto the scene. From the gossip mill to handwritten letters or notes, or from bathroom wall graffiti to going person to person pressing for needed information, teens have always made it a priority to know what others think of them.

Though parents and teens alike fear what damage a public failure could do to their impression management plan, the reality is that anytime a child fails before leaving the nest is a good time to fail. Try as they might to project an air of perfection, kids don't learn anything by living perfect lives, no more than they learn from the polar opposite, experiencing trauma. There is a sweet spot between the two where kids learn from experiencing the pain of setback and then figuring out how to overcome. I'll explain that fully in chapter 1. For now, feel better knowing your child will experience failures in a variety of ways that will feel confusing, embarrassing, and scary to you (and often to them, too, though I find usually the parents take these things harder). This is good! Because at the core of each failure is a lesson. This book will teach you how to uncover those. You'll learn how to recognize the raw material, see the potential beneath the grime, and welcome failure as an opportunity for growth. I'm offering you tools to help transform rocky situations into polished stones on which your child can move forward.

We owe it to ourselves and our kids to stop thinking about failures as conclusions and begin to frame failures as character builders. Because here's the thing: Failure isn't the worst thing that can happen to your kids. Often, it's one of the best. Young adolescents learning how to become adults need to figure out their own boundaries, values, and motivations. Failing is a great way to do that.

We owe it to ourselves and our kids to stop thinking about failures as conclusions and begin to frame failures as character builders. Because here's the thing: Failure isn't the worst thing that can happen to your kids. Often, it's one of the best. Young adolescents learning how to become adults need to figure out their own boundaries, values, and motivations. Failing is a great way to do that.

Your Reaction to Failure Predicts Future Growth

I happen to be privy to a lot of failure in my line of work. In addition to writing parenting books and articles, speaking at schools and organizations on raising adolescents, and managing leadership programs for tweens and teens, I run a Facebook parenting group called Less Stressed Middle School Parents where moms, dads, and grandparents gather in search of support, advice, commiseration, and inspiration for raising tweens and teens. (The group name has become a misnomer because we have a large percentage of high school parents who've stayed in the group and share their wisdom throughout adolescence.) Because it's a safe, private space with members from all over the world, it's often where people come for help figuring out how to respond to their child's latest experience with failure in its many iterations: failed friendships, failed tests, failure to follow the rules, and so on.

Take, for example, a mom I'll call Ellen who posted about her eleven-year-old daughter's recent foray into self-expression and problem solving. Her daughter, whom I'll call Sophie, had begged for permission to add streaks of purple to her hair. Ellen agreed if only to make Sophie happy or quiet (good choice, I think, because it's only temporary and hair color is fun). Neither Ellen nor Sophie anticipated how quickly the color would fade, going in just six weeks from purple to blue to a faded grayish color. When Sophie complained about how terrible her hair now looked, Ellen encouraged her to have patience. It would grow out eventually. Not satisfied with that timeline, Sophie took the situation, and a pair of kitchen scissors, into her own hands, chopping off large sections near the roots. I picture the "after" look as Björk meets sad baby bird.

We've all been there, either as the plucky tween who reached for the scissors because really, *how hard can it be to give yourself bangs?* (SO hard), or as the appalled parent who found out about the botch job too late. The response to this post in my group was divided. Many touted *natural consequences* and *now she will learn to live with a terrible haircut,* while others said, *Actually, she had a problem and she tried to solve it,* and *Let's applaud her initiative.* And lots of people said *hats.*

But was the home haircut a failure? By salon academy standards, absolutely. For Sophie having to go to school the next day? Oh yes. But as a moment of learning or problem solving? Depends on what Ellen does next.

If Ellen yells and punishes Sophie for something that has already kind of punished her, it's a fail.

If Ellen laughs it off and hurts Sophie's feelings: fail.

But if Ellen understands that what she does in that moment can both help Sophie *now* and help her *grow,* it's a success.

Your response to your child's failure can be the difference between your child getting stuck in failure and your child using that experience to push back onto the road toward success.

Because failure is such a subjective concept, we've all lost a little sleep worrying about whether we should worry or not. *Was today's fiasco a foreshadowing of bigger problems down the road? Or just a blip best ignored?* Hair is one thing because it grows out, but underage drinking, lying, losing friends, getting bad grades . . . are these things we can just patiently wait for our kids to outgrow, too? Not only will this book teach you what to do and say when your child fails, but it will help you assess what falls in the normal range of adolescent mess-ups (most of it, I promise).

Having worked with adolescents, their parents, and their teachers for nearly two decades, I know some things to be true about kids and failures:

- All kids mess up.
- All parents mess up.
- Your child is amazing.
- Your child is also annoying.

- All tweens and teens fail in all kinds of ways.
- Failure is a great way to build better character.
- With proper guidance and patience, most kids can learn to feel successful after failure.
- Recovery and future success hinge on removing shame from adolescent failure, for child and parent alike.

For this book, I interviewed parents who were in the midst of, or had recently been through, what felt like failures with their children. Their stories are woven into these chapters, but because the details belong to the children who experienced them, all identifying information has been changed to protect their anonymity.

I didn't have to look hard to find parents who were eager to share their experiences with you, and every parent I spoke with told me the same thing: The single most helpful decision they made was to finally share their experience with a few trusted people. When they stopped hiding the failure was the exact moment they could finally move past the humiliation and uncertainty, begin to feel optimistic again, shed some stress, and start to find the solutions they needed. I agree that this is the key. Even my own child's story is somewhere ahead in these pages, scrubbed like the others, but offered as my testament that every adolescent experiences failures, even those with a "professional parent" as my kids' friends used to call me—as in, *Dude, your mom's a* professional *parent. That suuuucks.*

How This Book Works

A note on wording: This is a book about overcoming childhood setbacks. With hindsight, it makes sense to characterize most of our children's struggles this way. When you're in the middle of a breakdown, though—of communication, friendship, trust, or confidence—it feels so much bigger than a setback. It *feels* like failure. So, you'll notice I primarily use the word "failure" to describe the experiences in this book, because until you break through the breakdown, failure better expresses the magnitude of fear, frustration, and confusion both parents and children undergo.

The first five chapters of this book will explain why failure is crucial to growth and development: if, that is, we enable kids to process and learn from it. You'll learn how failure ignored, shamed, or internalized can stunt personal growth as well as how the right words, reactions, guidance, and behaviors can help your child bypass that into personal growth. I'll also introduce you to *Your Child's Bill of Rights,* an important document I completely made up (though it is based on almost twenty years of practical work and research) and hope you'll ratify in your homes to support your child's continued growth and success. I'll introduce you to ways you can follow a three-step process to overcoming failure—*Contain, Resolve, Evolve*—and give you plenty of examples throughout the book of how you can put those steps into practice.

The second part of this book contains eight chapters, each covering a different kind of failure experience, with guidance on how you can coach your child through it so they are more likely to learn from it instead of getting stuck. Obviously, there are more than eight ways your kid can mess up between now and the next ten seconds to a lifetime. If I tried to write a book that covered every potential scenario, not only would you need a crane to get it home, you'd have to ask your kid to move out to make room for it.

By categorizing teen failures into wider contexts, this book will give you a flexible framework to handle any of the multitude of mess-ups that will come your way, along with easy-to-reference lists and pullout summaries you can use when facing your child's specific failures. The eight failure chapters cover the most common areas in which nearly all adolescents fail at some point. They are following the rules, taking care of their bodies, performing well in school, showing concern for others, connecting with peers, handling their feelings, getting along with their families, and believing in themselves. It's in these chapters that you'll hear from other parents like you and be reminded that you are not alone and that, no, your child is not a capital *F* Failure just because they face-planted or just because they *keep* face-planting when you think they clearly should have learned their lesson by now.

In this section you'll learn from eight families whose children faced a failure of sorts, and you'll see how the *Contain, Resolve, Evolve* methodology I explain in part 1 plays out in real life.

So, who are these faces of failure? I like to think of these kids as eight teenage archetypes. You may see your child in one or several of these "types" all at once, or they may jump between types over time. Maybe you'll even recognize your own childhood experiences in some of them.

THE CREW
The Rebel (Failure to Follow the Rules)
The Daredevil (Failure to Take Care of Their Body)
The Misfit (Failure to Perform Well in School)
The Ego (Failure to Show Concern for Others)
The Loner (Failure to Connect with Peers)
The Sensitive One (Failure to Handle Their Feelings)
The Black Sheep (Failure to Get Along with Their Family)
The Benchwarmer (Failure to Believe in Oneself)

Even if you don't relate to the exact archetype or anecdote featured in a chapter, by following along as we put the three phases of working through failure into practice, you'll become increasingly competent at helping your child handle *whatever* failure presents itself in their life. I've ordered the chapters so they move from the most concrete, and therefore easiest to understand, to the more nuanced ways in which our children find themselves socially and emotionally adrift that can be harder to wrap our heads around. But, just like my other books, once you've read the opening chapters that set the foundation for the process, you can skip right to the chapter that serves your immediate needs, or you can take them in the order presented. As always, I favor a choose-your-own-adventure approach to reading my books.

An Important Note on Mental Health

What isn't a failure? A mental health diagnosis.

I have worked with adolescents, their parents, and schools for more than twenty years, but I am not a physician or a psychologist, so if your child is struggling with a medical or mental health condition, this book will not provide the expert support that can only come from your own assembled team of doctors and counselors. Nonetheless, this book has some practical strategies every parent might benefit from, like techniques around communication and self-care. And most parents will find comfort and solidarity in peeking behind the curtain of shame parents hang around their child's circumstances to witness the ways that every child goes through times of gut-twisting tests and trials on the way to becoming an adult.

I've focused on the kinds of common failures parents tell me have temporarily derailed their children throughout middle and high school, the kinds that keep parents up at night spinning smaller worries into bigger catastrophes. "Does the fact that my child argues with me about every little rule mean we won't spend time together when they are an adult? Are they going to leave and never call once they turn eighteen? Oh my God, will I even get to know my grandkids?"

Life Is Messy. Let's Help Each Other with That.

Though I loved raising my two children through their tween and teen years, I fully recognize that being a parent to a young adult is hard, unpredictable, unappreciated work much of the time.

Staying up late waiting for a new driver to come home. Watching a long friendship unravel into heartache. Week-old oatmeal stuck in bowls under beds. Moldy towels. Days on end of receiving the silent treatment. Bashed expectations. Broken promises. Big fights. From sad to gross to scary, raising children to adults is a long lesson in learning to tolerate discomfort.

I'm here to say that the sooner we accept this—really *accept* it in practice, not just theory—the sooner our burdens will lift. It's a big ask and a hard thing to do, but the more we resist, the worse we'll feel. As long as we keep hiding our experiences with failure from plain sight, we're just like our teens shoving those crusty oatmeal bowls under their beds. Let's bring the dirty dishes into the light of the kitchen window and start scrubbing together.

PART I

Getting Comfortable with Failure

CHAPTER ONE

Understanding Failure and How It Functions

You, I, and every other reader bring to this book a different take on what it means to fail and what it means to succeed. Difference in perspective is surely a good thing because we need all kinds of ambition, goals, and talent to make the world we live in interesting, industrious, safe, and innovative. But we need to reframe failure and success, at least for this book to make sense; we can't have a meaningful conversation about failure and success unless we wrangle the concepts down to a certain degree.

Speaking of reframing failure, if you skipped the intro and jumped straight into chapter 1, I don't want you to miss one important point on wording. This book's title refers to setbacks, which is how I'd categorize childhood struggles once we have the hindsight to learn from them. In the thick of it, when your child is experiencing a breakdown of communication, trust, confidence, or relationships, it feels like a failure. In this chapter, we'll do a deep dive into the importance of childhood failure in relationship to adult success.

Success, as I see it, has less to do with a young person meeting measurable, enviable outcomes and more to do with a child becoming personally fulfilled, developing competency in an area of interest, and finding a community in which to participate.

Success, as I see it, has less to do with a young person meeting measurable, enviable outcomes and more to do with a child becoming personally fulfilled, developing competency in an area of interest, and finding a community in which to participate.

Of course, this is highly subjective, meaning what I find personally fulfilling you might not—unless you're also weirdly into binge-watching TV shows, then buying wigs and dressing up as your favorite characters for your tiny Instagram following? Probably not, but that's my point. Societally, our definition of success has become way too narrow, and the pressure on parents to mold "perfect kids" begins mounting from day one.

I bet one of the first things someone asked when they met your new baby was, "How are they sleeping?" It's not a rude question, per se, and I know for sure I asked many new parents the same thing. Recently, though, Kristin Daley, PhD, a psychologist who served as chair of the Society of Behavioral Sleep Medicine, pointed out how stressful this question can be. It signals to new moms and dads that the parent community is ready to assess them right out of the gate.

Our own mothers likely never asked each other this question because (a) who cares? (b) they could probably guess the answer—*not great, Gladys!*—and (c) books, podcasts, and Facebook groups weren't needling our parents about the urgency of sleep training. Asking about sleep has become one of our first ways of gauging parental proficiency. And from there the questions never stop. Is she walking yet? Any teeth? What reading level is he on now? What height percentile? Boyfriend yet? Girlfriend yet? Is he moving up to a travel league for sports? Is she taking the advanced or honors classes next year? What colleges are they applying to?

When a parent can't answer success-related questions with enthusiasm, it can make them feel anywhere from alienated to annoyed to angry. Spend some time observing online parent communities, and you will notice a desperation for understanding and acceptance from parents whose kids aren't on the same predictable path toward "success." They don't know how to answer these questions without feeling as if they're disappointing people. I'm not suggesting that you shouldn't take an interest in your friends' children, but questions aimed at *assessing* their success might be better replaced with curiosity about feelings and interests, either the child's *or* the parent's.

If parents are feeling alienated, annoyed, and angry, imagine how children are processing things. Our kids know their success is being monitored and measured nonstop by both their peers and the adults in their lives, and it's unequivocally hurting them. The American Psychological Association reported a rise in perfectionism among college students, finding that parents who held their children to high standards caused their children to develop perfectionist tendencies resulting in depression, anxiety, self-harm, and eating disorders, *even more so* than parents who expressed criticism of their children. When parental expectations feel hard to meet, young adults are far more likely to experience what's known as "socially prescribed perfectionism," or the sense that other people, and even society as a whole, require them to be perfect.

To be clear, having expectations for our kids is natural. I expect my children to be polite when meeting someone new, for example. But having standards our children can't meet, or that they must suffer to meet, is not only cruel but futile. You are no longer the parent in the swimming pool taking another step back each time your gasping child almost reaches your outstretched hands. Setting benchmarks for success just beyond our adolescents' reach doesn't encourage them to pull harder. It causes them to sink.

Parents are yearning for a new way to think about success and therefore failure. We're ready to throw off the impossible burden of raising perfect kids and find relief in a community that accepts failure as not just part of being a human but a way of becoming an even nicer, smarter, happier, and more inclusive one.

We live in an era when all our decisions feel increasingly public, thanks in large part to our ability to share all aspects of our lives online: what we're eating, how we voted, where we vacationed, whether we donated, whom we invited, when we last exercised. The pressure to please and impress our families, neighbors, followers, friends, and frenemies alike is crippling.

A copy-and-paste post that regularly goes around social media says this:

> A big shout out to all the kids who didn't win an award, make honor roll, and barely made it through the school year. A big hug to the moms, dads, grandparents, caregivers, and foster parents that stuck by them as they maneuvered the school year.
>
> To the kids that didn't get invited to the prom, didn't get a scholarship to college, and perhaps have to go straight to work out of high school. . . you are still worthy of a pat on the back and a Facebook post with people talking about how amazing you are.
>
> Some kids have to work twice as hard as other students just to get a C. Their achievements deserve recognition.

Don't forget those kids.

Kindness, creativity, and generosity. . . . those attributes sadly don't get the accolades they deserve.

The original post above was written by the educator Dana Chavis, and I see it shared widely, often with tweaks or new takes, and parents commenting in ALL CAPS gratitude for the message that success isn't one size fits all.

If you're feeling antsy because your child isn't churning out post-worthy accolades left and right (or maybe they are and they're *still* bugging the crud out of you at home with snark, disorganization, lethargy, and ungratefulness), don't waste another minute worrying what that means for their future or yours. This book will bring you peace of mind that your child isn't the only one derailing from the fantasy you once envisioned. In turn, it will unburden your child from the constraints of those expectations and allow them to find success in new and meaning-ful ways. Once you've realized why *not* being perfect is so key to their future success, you'll learn the language you need to work through whatever circumstances your child faces as a team so that you can both emerge stronger, content, and more connected on the other side.

A Little Perspective Might Help Throughout This Process

When it comes to thinking about our kids' failures, which we often then absorb and take personally, it helps to keep as much perspective as possible. Here is a story about how I try to do that.

In 2000, I gave birth to my first child. That was also the year I real-ized I could never watch another episode of *ER* again.

Each episode, set in the fictional emergency room of a Chicago hospital, introduced me to a new, more brutal, more mysterious condition that I projected onto my own life and realized might afflict my own baby. Is that bump a developing tumor? Was that quiver a sign of seizures to come? Did that blink seem slow to anyone else?

The journalist Elizabeth Stone wrote, "Making the decision to have a child—it is momentous. It is to decide forever to have your heart go walking around outside your body." I think that might have literally happened on an episode of *ER* once.

Anyway, I remember holding my newborn, staring at my tiny heart outside my body, and thinking, *This is too much good fortune. Something bad is going to happen. No one gets this much perfection without a price.*

Other parents of babies confirmed we weren't going crazy. They thought about it, too, all the ways this might end. If we didn't worry about the most infinitely small possibilities, weren't we tempting fate? Better to let the universe know we were on our guard, sleeping with one eye open, knuckles cracked, and poised to google any symptom or hunch.

No parent should live in that state of perpetual anxiety. Particularly not as those vulnerable infants become toddlers without fear, then bigger kids without judgment, and then suddenly they're middle schoolers without impulse control and teenagers without experience, and they're asking to go hang out at someone's house you don't know or to borrow the keys to your car. We must learn to cope with fragility and risk at the same time that we train ourselves to keep it all in perspective.

What helps me through the uncertainty of it all? You might be surprised. It's thinking just a *wee* bit about the concept of death. Much like the cheerful people of Bhutan, who are widely considered the happiest people on earth, I cope by reminding myself that things can almost always be worse and that just being alive is a thing to be treasured. If I start to feel paralyzed by my problems or those of my children, I actively seek perspective. Most of the time, even the saddest, most worrisome, fearful circumstances are not finite, not the beginning of the end. As my favorite little singing orphan reminds us, tomorrow is "always a day away," and a lot can change when the sun comes up again.

Nurturing Isn't Enough

Are you a plant person? If you were an adult during the pandemic of the early 2020s, chances are good you became one. Plant ownership allowed us to easily care for something living, to nurture, to tend, and to feel a sense of purpose, all of which we desperately needed in our lockdown as evidenced by the 65 percent increase in houseplant sales during the pandemic.

So what can we learn about parenting children from parenting plants? For me, the biggest metaphor crossover is that it's not enough to give plants fertile soil with the right nutrients, plenty of sunshine and water, protection from the elements, and even little pep talks, as 70 percent of plant parents admit to doing. Nurturing isn't just about being nice to something. Greenhouse gardeners know that for plants to grow hearty and healthy, they need exposure to harsh conditions, too. This process, called "hardening off" the plants, involves exposing tender young seedlings to harsh, freezing conditions outside the cozy greenhouse for increasing increments of time. This toughens the plants up so they aren't shocked to death by the real world outside the nursery.

Your delicate children need exposure to adversity, too, to become stronger. Consider opportunities to acclimatize to failure an essential way to help kids grow into healthy, stable, and resilient adults.

Failure Failure Failure Feeelure Feeler...?

You know how it is when you repeat the same word over and over and suddenly your brain jumps the tracks? You don't know if you're even pronouncing the word correctly anymore, much less what it means or if it's even a real word. I don't want that to happen to us with "failure."

Before we go any further, let's make sure we're thinking about the same thing, in the same way. Chances are we're all thinking about failure in a different way, and we can't begin talking this through until we know we're talking about the same thing. I advise parents to clarify meaning often during conversations with their tweens or teens, in part because words mean different things to different generations (see "catfish," "lit," "smash," "dating," "tag," and so on), but also because some words, like "failure," are loaded with an emotional heft that varies from person to person. Let's start by exploring that.

"Failure" is a broad term, and each reader has brought to this book their presupposed notions of what fits under its umbrella. Take, for example, chronic disorganization. This may feel like a kind of failure in the sense that it

(a) represents an unlearned skill,
(b) may be the cause of missed opportunities, and
(c) is bothersome to be around.

If you discover your son, for instance, who only spottily checks his email, has missed a deadline to apply for a college scholarship, you might say his disorganization represents a huge failure. In another family, where college may not be an option, a missed email from a university isn't much more than flattering junk mail. But in that same family, if that same teen who doesn't check his emails also has a wanderlust that pulls him toward the beach at sunset and away from the cash register of the family business? Now, that's a failure. To a third family, a child who gets all As and never misses a shift at work, but gets panic attacks about the *possibility* of missing emails from colleges, when that child develops an ulcer, we have a different kind of failure. It's difficult to define a term that is entirely subjective.

For this reason, let's adopt a broader definition for the sake of this book: An adolescent failure is an experience that leaves a child feeling unmoored, unhappy, unaccepted, or questioning their self-worth.

An adolescent failure is an experience that leaves a child feeling unmoored, unhappy, unaccepted, or questioning their self-worth.

You should know right off the bat that when your child experiences this kind of failure, it probably has little to do with your ability to instill grit or values, effectively discipline, or properly inspire your child. No one can raise a child to avoid failure in life. A teacher will publicly correct your child, a coach will embarrass them, a best friend will move on to a new group, a love interest will not reciprocate, dream colleges will send rejections, and there is nothing we, as parents, can do to change this. We're not superheroes who can spin the globe backward to reset time and prevent upsetting things from happening. We're more like medics, with no bearing over how the rest of the world treats our kids. We can only be prepared to offer some quality first aid.

I should also note that sometimes what presents itself with the characteristics of a failure is not *actually* a failure. I wanted to include a wide range of scenarios for this book, but sometimes that posed a moral challenge for me because I don't want to label normal parts of growing up, normal parts of being human, as "failures." For instance, some parents shared with me the challenges their kids faced because of a learning difference, or a spike in anxiety, or a struggle with their sexual identity. I would never call having dyslexia or anxiety or not being heterosexual a "failure." But what the parents in these situations were observing, before they understood the cause, *looked* like failing to them. Bad grades, withdrawal from family and friends, lack of happiness, health ramifications, loss of a sense of self—all made the parents question whether their child was starting to fail and why. So, in this book you will read about some scenarios that weren't ultimately failures at all but that *appeared* that way while the context was still unfolding.

How to Define Success

To understand failure in the broad sense, we also need a common understanding of what it means to be successful. I think the best definition can be derived from the work of the mid-twentieth-century psychologist Abraham Maslow. The list below is inspired by his work and centers on self-actualization, or as we might have more modernly put it, becoming the best version of yourself. I have slightly modified it to be more applicable to adolescents today.

Markers of success:

- Are you comfortable in your own skin?
- Are you comfortable being around lots of different kinds of people?
- Do you learn from your experiences?
- Do you feel hopeful about your future?
- Do you feel gratitude for what you have more than despair for what you don't?
- Do you form mutually respectful bonds with others?
- Do you have a sense of humor (specifically one that doesn't hurt others)?
- Do you like helping others?
- Do you like being able to take care of yourself?

This is a terrific list to help us keep perspective on success, as adults helping to shape the futures of children we love.

The Function of Failure

I've long been fascinated by the concept of learned helplessness, first coined and researched in the late 1960s by Martin E. P. Seligman. The concept explains why people give up in difficult situations and do so more frequently over time. In my first book, *Middle School Makeover: Improving the Way You and Your Child Experience the Middle School Years,* I wrote about this theory as it relates to the adolescent social world. Very quickly, a tween or teen can start believing they are socially helpless after even a small social failure, like wearing the wrong outfit and being looked at funny. The effects of this self-perception can last into adulthood. In a 2016 follow-up to his original study, Seligman discovered neurological evidence that helplessness is actually the brain's default mode when it experiences pain (physical or emotional). Overcoming this requires taking action to change the feeling rather than passively enduring it or waiting for it to pass.

To better understand this, consider a famous Seligman study involving the Pavlovian response of dogs to fear. I am a dog lover, and this is hard for me to write about and I'm sorry if it is difficult for you to read about, but let's press forward and hope these dogs got plenty of treats and belly rubs after this. In phase one of this experiment, researchers separated dogs into three groups and strapped them all to harnesses. The first group was not exposed to pain. The second group received electric shocks but faced a panel that, if they learned to push with their nose, would stop the shocks. The third group received shocks but did not have access to a panel to stop the pain sensation.

In phase two, all three sets of dogs were placed individually in small boxes that had electric shocks running through them. They were not harnessed. All boxes had a small wall on one side that, if the dog simply jumped over it, would allow them to escape the ongoing shocks.

Of the three groups, only the second group, comprising dogs that had previously discovered a panel to stop the shocks, jumped over the barrier. The first and third groups never tried, learning quickly how to succumb to helplessness even when given an obvious opportunity for relief.

This experiment shows us that helplessness is the default reaction to discomfort and pain, and not just in canines. Seligman went on to replicate the dog experiment with humans using loud noises, not shocks, and the outcomes were identical. The experiment also shows us that we don't learn when situations are easy or perfect (the first group in the experiments). We also don't learn when situations are traumatic (the third group in the experiments). But we *do* learn when we feel pain and then successfully figure out how to navigate past it (the second group in the experiments).

The study of learned helplessness reveals that only one thing can overcome our predisposition to giving up in the face of pain: a positive experience. Not blind hope, or a clever parable, or watching someone else's success. Personal, positive experiences with success are the only way kids learn to overcome hard situations. As children grow, their failures become increasingly painful and complicated, so this will be crucial for parents to remember; rescuing your child from a tough situation or manipulating a situation to help them avoid getting hurt doesn't serve your child best.

Rescuing your child from a tough situation or manipulating a situation to help them avoid getting hurt doesn't serve your child best.

Make Sure You're Not Modeling Helplessness

A woman recently posted to one of the online groups I'm in that she needed help coming up with a list of household items she should buy for her daughter's first apartment, postcollege. She started off strong, coming up with paper towels, toilet paper, Clorox wipes, shower curtain, detergent, laundry soap, and then she drew a blank. After six items. She mentioned living in her own home, though, so it had me wondering, How does this person not know what belongs in a place where you live? And will this daughter be able to say to herself, "Hm, my kitchen sponge is old and smells bad. I might need a new one. Can I figure out how to solve this problem?"

The issue here is not that buying your child household items is wrong nor is wanting to find connection with other parents in the same position. It's what feels to me like an artificial helplessness that gets passed down and around, among parents and their kids, that has me concerned. From what I've observed, many of the posts in parenting groups follow a familiar setup.

Step one: Feign helplessness. *I am such an idiot!*

Step two: Flatter others for being better equipped to solve your problems than you are. *Figured you much wiser mamas out there could help!*

Step three: Ask for help with a problem you could easily solve with a ten-second Google search. *I didn't realize my child has only sixty-two dollars left on their meal card. Now what??*

The obvious answer, you're thinking, is let the child starve to death. Bad luck!

I don't think parents are really this dumb, by the way. I think the first mom knows what items belong in an apartment, and the second can figure out how to keep her nineteen-year-old from eating dirt while she reloads the meal plan, or Venmos a hundred dollars, or tells her kid to stop wasting money and start looking for a part-time job.

Without even realizing it, many parents have bought into a pattern of communication that uses helplessness, instead of grit, as a personal safety net. When adults approach challenges this way, it feels safe to assume they aren't modeling for their kids how to deal with everyday setbacks. Instead, it seems as though parents are "supporting" their kids into a lifestyle of paralysis. Interestingly, research shows us that experiencing a crisis doesn't need to be crippling. In business and sports, it can be motivating. In corporations, crises open the path for innovation or what's known as a growth mind-set. In the same study, when researchers looked at how injuries affected the success of sports teams, they found that when a teammate sat out due to injury, the rest of the team played better. I feel certain that in families, too, when crisis comes knocking, if we don't model helplessness, we rise to a new level of improved support and success.

Will Strong Family Values Insulate My Child from Certain Failures?

No.

But having strong values can be a great tool for your teen to use when overcoming failure. I'm speaking about their values, though, not yours.

Elvis Presley once, apparently, said, "Values are like fingerprints. Nobody's are the same, but you leave them all over everything you do."

Since I cannot find proof whether this gem is made up or real, I'm going with it, even though I have a hard time picturing the Pelvis himself pontificating like a human Successories poster. What I like about the quotation is that when he says we all have different values, he means everyone, and yes, that means every member of your family. The King has spoken.

A funny thing about values in our families is that they feel vital to us and yet we never really articulate them. Can you say what your parents' top five values were? Can you be sure you're right? Maybe. Some of you might have grown up in homes where your parents explicitly discussed their values with you.

Many of us did not, though we gleaned what we could from context clues. For instance, *My mom must value hard work, because she spends a lot of time and energy on her business,* or *My mom must value family to-getherness, because she spends a lot of time preparing family meals.* These clues might lead us to correct assumptions, or we may simply be equating "time spent on *x*" with "valuing *x*," and that can be misleading.

A friend of mine grew up in a family that went to church every Easter. They were not members of the church they attended annually, but it was a historic and beautiful building, and it drew a big crowd, especially on that day. To her, going to church felt more like an opportunity to dress up and participate in a community event. When my friend had a family of her own, she casually mentioned to her father that she was not raising her children in any particular faith. To her surprise, her father was hurt. Religion was a meaningful foundation of his life, and his grandchildren's exposure to Christianity was important to him. The lack of time spent at church in her own childhood had led her to believe otherwise.

If it's important to you that your children know your values, you'll need to do two things. First, know your values. Many of us have a soft list of things we believe in, but we rarely take the time to purposefully sit down and ponder the full range of values we might attach ourselves to, and then more deeply consider our points of connection to the ones we're drawn to most. Second, articulate your choices to your children. Label your values, define them, and talk about when and how you use them.

Having said this, I must acknowledge that living your values clearly in front of your child is no guarantee they will share your beliefs. One of the realities of your child moving into adulthood is that they get to make choices about what they value and how they want to center that in their lives. You might not agree, you might wish their beliefs or self-expression were different, and yet part of letting your child become an autonomous, well-functioning adult is allowing them the space to figure out what aligns with their soul and how to articulate that as well as giving them the space to stand in those beliefs in full view of the world.

When Values Conflict

Generationally, values change in response to both our own childhood experiences and what is happening in the world. Maybe your parents valued stability and saved reliably for early retirement, but you value adventure and don't mind putting a family trip on the credit card for the opportunity to show your children other parts of the world. That's your fingerprint, and that's okay. Your child, having grown up seeing lots of the world, might share that value or feel as if they've had enough exposure and instead value the comfort of a quiet life at home. This might be less fun for you, and you might be sad when they don't want you to take the family on a road trip for the kids' birthdays, but it's not a personal affront, just a bummer and an opportunity to reframe your expectations.

Sometimes, though, your values will feel in conflict with your child's. Perhaps, like my friend's father, you value religion, and your child has embraced atheism, or you value education, and your child has decided not to go to college. When you find your values conflicting, take a deep breath. One of the other realities at work here is that your child will develop their own value system, even without your permission. So, get curious. Don't just discuss with them what you believe, but open a two-way dialogue for them to explore what they believe out loud, without your fears or judgments leaking in. That's about *all* you can do. Being open to an exchange of ideas may make your child less resistant and more respectful of your values, but if not, at the very least you will be teaching them how to coexist among difference, and that is something we dearly need in our families and our larger communities, too.

A final bit of murkiness to cloud this already complicated issue is whether and how our own values as parents might actually *limit* our children. I'll use a silly example: Let's say you value health, and as such you are committed to the benefits of exercise. It brings you great joy and comfort, and you are certain it plays a crucial role in your mental and physical resilience. Because you love your child and want them to be healthy, it's important to you that they also benefit from regular exercise. You articulate your values by talking often about how great exercise makes you feel, you invite them to exercise with you every evening, you model your commitment by exercising openly in front of them, and you create a reasonable daily exercise requirement of thirty minutes for your child, because you understand that values are best practiced and not just theorized and, more to the point, that exercise becomes easier and more fulfilling over time.

Your child, however, hates exercise. Every time you require them to get up and move, they seem to value being sedentary even more. Their body is changing, they are uncomfortable in their own skin, and movement feels like being exposed. It's not a source of energy or comfort. You push, knowing what's best for them, and they resist. The next time they jog around the block to fulfill their obligation to you, they do so angrily, miss a curb, trip, and twist an ankle. Now they are nervous to navigate the crowded hallways of school on crutches, afraid they might trip again and people might laugh. They get stomachaches in the morning and won't go to school, so they set up with a tray and laptop on the couch, flipping between online class and YouTube until the ankle heals. They are experiencing the total opposite of intended mental and physical benefits from exercise.

Well-intentioned parents can want what is truly and undeniably a good thing for their child, and that can end up backfiring in unexpected and frustrating ways. We believe values are inherently good;

therefore, they can't also create trouble, when really, they can be as duplicitous as anything else in life.

Often, what we want for our child most of all is for them to be protected. Doesn't this feel like our number one task as parents? We all remember the moment we first brought our child home, no matter how or when they arrived in our families, and that overwhelming feeling of responsibility mixed with doubt: *Can I really keep this little person alive when an entire world full of sharp edges, serial killers, fast cars, and mutating diseases is conspiring against me?*

Safety is a baseline value, resting on an equally baseline assumption that this is something we can control, especially for our emerging adults with their heightened impulsivity and emotionality. Anyway, what could possibly be bad about valuing safety? It's almost as absurd as suggesting that valuing exercise could be harmful to your child. Wink, wink.

Yet when parents value safety above independence, experience, learning, and growth, kids suffer. Don't allow your urges to keep your child safe—even if that need is also grounded in your morality—to override their need to experience a life of exciting, if scary, challenges. It's that experience only that will teach them to overcome failure and not curl up in learned helplessness.

What's at Stake When We Don't Let Kids Fail?

Why should we care whether kids today are failing hard or hardly failing? This seems to be a big debate among parents of adolescents. Some say we should get out of the way and let teens figure life out on their own. Natural consequences and so forth. Others say it's our job to protect teens and letting them fail is to willfully compromise their safety, endangering them and essentially turning ourselves into failures as parents. If you've read my other books, you probably already know what I say: How about we meet in the middle?

I like the middle ground, in part, because I don't think it's possible to protect teens from getting hurt while still giving them the space they need to grow. Clinging to the adage "Work smart, not hard," I'd rather spend my energy teaching kids how to overcome inevitable setbacks than trying to predict problems and putting up arbitrary defense shields. For me, it's not just the easier approach now but the one that pays off down the road.

What happens when a generation of parents, incredibly loving if also highly protective, denies their teenagers the opportunity to really blow things up for themselves every once in a while? At what cost comes our impulse to rescue?

Fixing problems, overcoming embarrassment, developing coping skills—these things take practice. When we deny kids the opportunity to have bad feelings and practice working through them, we set them up to be incapable, insufferable adults.

Parents of little kids, your primary job is to protect your child from hurting themselves. Parents of tweens and teens, your primary job is to give your children practice protecting and taking care of themselves. You'll still need to step in, providing feedback, expectations, and restrictions from time to time. But if you take away all opportunities to learn these valuable skills, your kids will enter college, the workforce, and adult relationships at a huge disadvantage.

Parents of little kids, your primary job is to protect your child from hurting themselves. Parents of tweens and teens, your primary job is to give your children practice protecting and taking care of themselves.

Practice is a sloppy thing, and that makes it hard to tolerate. You may recall the mixture of pride and dread you felt when your toddler wanted to start doing things for themselves. Those wobbly arms hoisting that giant carton of juice, pouring some into a plastic cup but most onto the floor . . . remember those days? What a mess! But if you never let them do it badly, they wouldn't learn how to do it well.

Our kids' happiness and self-confidence are at stake here—to say nothing of their ability to earn a living (or pour a glass of juice).

"Failure to launch," the phenomenon in which adult children struggle to transition into adulthood and independent living, is steadily on the rise. The Pew Research Center reported that in 1964, 8 percent of people aged twenty-five to thirty-five lived at home. In 2000, that grew to 10 percent. And in 2016, it reached 15 percent, though 2016 also had the highest employment rate of the three, so a lack of jobs wasn't the issue. Diagnoses of clinical depression in adolescents have increased by 37 percent since 2005, and diagnoses of anxiety among people aged eighteen to twenty-five doubled between 2008 and 2018, though some upsurge may be due to increased awareness and availability and acceptability of therapy. And certainly, some kids stay at home longer to care for family members or to be cared for by them. Sometimes that's a cultural norm, and sometimes it's just what that family needs for its members to thrive. And then of course, we can't downplay COVID and what a serious damper that put on young people's ability to graduate, get jobs, or stay healthy, as they might have intended and planned. Exceptions like these aside, I'm concerned that these numbers indicate a rise in young people who can't figure out how to live independently and parents who are so afraid of their offspring trying and failing that they rescue them into dependency.

For parents, the prime directive may always be protection and preservation of their offspring, but the way to assure success isn't through isolation. It's through exposure. It's our responsibility to let kids experience failure so they may strengthen their ability to cope with mistakes and messes, and so we may open the door and escort these young adults comfortably across the metaphorical threshold of adulthood and the literal threshold of our parental homes. By denying teens the chance to experience and learn from failure, we deny them the chance to grow, and we deny ourselves some well-earned independence later in life, too.

Still, Be Nice

There are many myths about what constitutes good parenting, and one of them is that kids won't learn how to be independent unless they figure it out all on their own. At one of my school talks, a concerned parent asked me if she was being a micromanager to her teenage daughter. Micromanaging, if you've read my previous books, is something I strongly discourage. Specifically, she said, her daughter was overwhelmed with schoolwork, and her room was becoming so cluttered it was difficult to move around in. The mom saw that the mess of the room was a burden to the daughter, so she tried to encourage her daughter to set aside thirty minutes to clean and organize, saying, "A clean space will help you find a calm mind." But the daughter simply couldn't. One day, while her daughter was at school, the mom went into her daughter's room and organized it herself. When the daughter came home, she was grateful.

"Have I set her up for failure?" the mom asked me. "I don't want her to think I'll always do this, and I know she needs to learn to manage these things herself."

My response was simple. "I think it's nice to be nice." All of us need help from time to time, and all of us know what it feels like to be overwhelmed. Occasionally helping each other out of a bind or easing someone's load is a kindness and a wonderful way to show love and support to someone who is under pressure.

This mom didn't want her daughter to think she would always be there to, quite literally, pick up her messes, but I assured her that this was unlikely. In fact, all she had to do to avoid that outcome was *not* do it every time.

Pain is inevitable. Comfort is necessary. Growing teens need increasing responsibility and opportunities to learn, including learning how to cope with discomfort, and they also need empathy and support. Just like us.

CHAPTER TWO

How Communities Benefit from Letting Children Fail

I was in the sixth grade in Cambridge, Massachusetts, and walking with my new friend, Heather, through Harvard Square when she asked me if I had ever seen a *boynton*. Not wanting to let on that I had no idea what she was talking about, I mumbled, "Yeah, maybe . . ." while I struggled to imagine what could *possibly* be a *boynton*. Was it a ghost? A TV show? A penis?! I had no idea!

Heather pulled me into the nearest drugstore saying I *had* to see one. She darted to the greeting card section, grabbed a card, and showed me. It took me a moment to decipher the message: *Hippo Birdie Two Ewe!*

"Get it . . . ??" she asked with delight. "It's a birthday card!"

I got it! And sweet relief it was not a penis. Sandra Boynton, I learned that day, is an artist who creates adorable illustrations often featuring word puns and lovable animals. Though I didn't know it when I was twelve, she was prolific, and you may, in fact, have had stacks of her board books in your child's nursery, like *The Going to Bed Book*. We eventually did. Though most of my Boynton memories are purely positive, when I reflect on one of the biggest mistakes of my high school life, I can't do it without picturing one of Sandra Boynton's more famous images: a massive elephant slumped on the ground with six turkeys casually posed on his back, and underneath them all the caption "Don't let the turkeys get you down."

How the Turkeys Actually Did Get Me Down

Fast-forward six years to when I was a junior in high school. I applied for, and had been accepted into, a semester-long boarding program at a combination working farm/private school in Vermont. There, along with students from around the country, I went to class six days a week, studying a rigorous curriculum of classic literature, environmental science, U.S. history, math, art, and French until lunchtime, when the day turned to farmwork. The school's "eat what you grow" organic farm philosophy had me digging potatoes, harvesting carrots, and milking cows, along with activities such as washing dishes, cleaning cabins, hiking, and orienteering.

Through the mental and physical strain of my days, there were moments that stuck out like miracles. I lay with friends in a field at night, far from the city, staring at the brightest stars I'd ever seen, and had a sudden epiphany of perspective: that I was infinitesimally small in an incomprehensibly huge world, and that it wasn't scary. It was liberating. I happened upon a baby cow being born in a pasture and watched it take its first few impossible wobbly steps. I spent three days and nights on a solo in the woods with nothing but a journal, a map, a bag of food, a sleeping bag, and a saggy tent I made from tarp and rope. I kissed a cute boy during a light snowfall behind a barn.

I learned and grew so much during that semester. I'm sure of it.

I'm sure of it because that is a list of astounding things I just shared with you and it seems as if a person would *have* to learn and grow from all of that, doesn't it?

But I can't actually say exactly how those things have shaped me with any certainty, other than I know they were good for me. I know they broadened my horizons, and they gave me new experiences and knowledge. And these are unequivocally Good Things.

However, nothing that happened during that semester taught me more, or remained a part of me with such clarity, as the biggest mistake I made while I was there.

Daily chores were a requirement of both farm life and communal living, and we students were assigned these on a rotating schedule. For two weeks at a time, students might have to clean bathrooms, or serve breakfast, or scout the fields for broken fences in need of repair, for example.

About halfway through my semester, I landed turkey duty. Before the sun rose, it was my job to bundle up against the freezing Vermont morning air, trudge the aptly named Turkey Hill in the dark, fill a bucket with grain, and then scatter that grain across the frozen grass so the turkeys could have breakfast. It was not particularly hard, except for the bright-and-early necessity of it. I did the chore halfheartedly for less than a week and then . . . I slept in. I got away with it once. Then twice. But on the third day, I woke to a screaming farm manager at the door of my cabin. "How could you do this to those turkeys? To the community? Do you know what happens when turkeys go unfed? They become cannibalistic is what happens! What's wrong with you that you think you can sleep in while everyone else pulls their weight and those turkeys turn on each other? How could you behave this way?"

I need to let you know that the turkeys had only *started* to have a Donner party. They survived. But still. They had begun down a dark and peckish path. Yes, pun intended. Even now, as I admit this to you, I feel nervous. If the animal lover Sandra Boynton is somehow reading this today, she hates me.

Why had I done such a selfish thing? I don't know. I didn't think it through? I was tired? I was cold? I put my needs before those of others? I thought no one would notice? I didn't know turkeys could be cannibals? I was sixteen?

Being exposed in front of my peers was embarrassing, and afterward I retreated. Already a shy teen and worried I didn't fit in with this group of high achievers, I grew increasingly self-conscious and quiet. I corrected my behavior around chores, but I felt as if I were faking my way through the rest of the program as someone who didn't naturally have what it took to be there.

Are You There, Farm Manager? It's Me, Michelle.

How *could* I behave that way? With hindsight, I see my disappointed manager's question as exactly the point of adolescence: to figure out—at least loosely—why we do the things we do and what that says about who we are. But *how* do we do that, the figuring out of it all? As teenagers, we don't have the clarity to know how the process works, but the beauty of youth is that we figure it out anyway. We're like newborn sea turtles who instinctively know to rake back the sand and head toward the water, even if we don't know anything about the science of tides or moonlight, the dangers of flashlights and racoons. As teens, we put one foot in front of the other toward an unknown future despite countless setbacks of awkward, embarrassing, angry, and painful moments.

That instinct to keep moving forward fuels the way in which we learn best: through trial and error. Well, trial and error and error and error, to be more accurate. Whether by boldly making risky choices or falling backward into unintended mistakes, we learn what hurts and what doesn't. We calibrate our internal scales over and over until we find how much pain is bearable and how much tips us into despair.

Do you remember the first time you learned how to impress your friends by snuffing out a match or a candle wick with your bare fingertips? Kids ease into playing with fire like that until they develop enough confidence to really get burned.

For me, the cannibalistic turkey situation taught me more than reading Thoreau, using a compass, or conjugating the pluperfect in French ever would. It was painful, but that pain became the portal through which I emerged a better version of myself. Knowing I never wanted to make a mistake of that caliber again, I made an important vow to myself: For the rest of my life, I would avoid all situations in which I might possibly be asked to feed a farm animal.

I'm kidding. Mostly. What I really learned from that experience is that I disliked the feeling of regret much more than I liked the feeling of self-indulgence. I would do my best from then on to be sure that meeting my own needs was never in direct conflict with the well-being of people whom I cared for and who counted on me.

Later in this book, we'll look at the specific ways adults can help kids learn from moments of failure like this one. But for a little closure on this story, I'll share now the three things I think helped me from getting stuck: First, the farm manager never treated me differently after that moment. Any further guilt I felt came from inside my own head and heart, not from being continuously reminded of my shortcomings. Second, though I was mortified to be called out in front of my peers, they also moved right along. The fast pace of farm life and schoolwork helped ensure that no one lingered in the moment. And third, the semester ended. I was given the chance to move on and return to my high school, where no one knew a thing about any turkeys. I had a built-in escape valve. A change of environment gave me an opportunity to reinvent myself once more, an act that benefits most young people, and probably most adults, too, from time to time.

The Modern Rite of Passage

When I was a teenager, I assumed becoming an adult was just a matter of time passing, years being accumulated. One day I'd be drinking alcohol in public, dreading tax season, and enjoying discussing birds (turkeys even) or politics. Poof! Adulthood.

Thanks to a December birthday and a late kindergarten cutoff, I was the youngest in my grade for most of my life, and when I entered college at age seventeen, I felt like a little kid compared with everyone else. I couldn't even set foot into the Ruby Tuesday for so much as mozzarella sticks on Thirsty Thursdays because I wasn't eighteen yet. Woe was me. Being an adult still seemed out of reach, even as I lived eight hundred miles from home. But through some fascinating courses in education, psychology, religion, and sociology, I learned that becoming an adult was less of a poof and more of a path, one that is surprisingly predictable once you know where to look for the signposts.

It was in those classes that I learned about the importance of rites of passage to becoming an adult. Perhaps when you think of rites of passage what comes to mind are events that celebrate a child's transition into adulthood: bar and bat mitzvahs, sweet sixteens, quinceañeras, Holy Communions, debutante balls, walkabouts, or rumspringas. Just about every culture has a way of celebrating coming of age, some more frivolous and some more daunting than others.

Inuit girls, at the age of menstruation, are given face tattoos that take three days to complete before rejoining their families with adult status. Maasai boys are taken on lion hunting trips to earn their passage to adulthood, and in the Amazon, boys aged twelve of the Sateré-Mawé tribe must go into the forest to gather stinging bullet ants, weave them into gloves, then wear the gloves for a public dance performance while being stung. Each sting, by the way, is reported to be thirty times worse than a bee sting.

Oh, and did your child just throw a fit for being asked to put down their phone and throw their yogurt container into the trash before the dog eats it? Of course.

Before you think I'm a masochist, I'm certainly not advocating that you impose upon your child rituals that uphold traditional and problematic gender roles, *or* that would constitute torture under the Geneva Convention. It could make an interesting conversation, though, to bring rites of passage up over dinner one evening as a matter of perspective alone.

I'm not saying we should popularize childhood pain contests or, conversely, that it's overly indulgent to throw your teen a big party if you want. Simple rules: Don't torture children. Do have fun. But also, we need more than these two options. Somewhere between stinging ants and an all-you-can-eat candy buffet with a live DJ there lies a territory where I believe kids really *do* cross from childhood into early adulthood.

This liminal space is one where failure meets opportunity for redemption. It's the moment in a young person's life when they have an experience that is so uncomfortable, profound, and solitary they must figure out how to overcome it—by apologizing, by changing behaviors or beliefs, by making reparation, as just a few examples—and, in doing so, begin the metamorphosis to adult.

The liminal space between childhood and adulthood is one where failure meets opportunity for redemption. It's the moment in a young person's life when they have an experience that is so uncomfortable, profound, and solitary they must figure out how to overcome it and, in doing so, begin the metamorphosis to adult.

Many parents are so bothered watching their kids feel discomfort that they rush in to soothe or distract them before the child can (a) reasonably increase their tolerance of uncomfortable situations and (b) learn, like the dogs in Seligman's experiment, how to stop the discomfort on their own when it becomes too painful.

Your tween complains that adult conversations are boring, so you hand them headphones and let them watch a video during every meal. Your teen has a history of falling out with their friends, so you take them to get their nails done or let them download a game whenever they report a new conflict. Sometimes it's nice to do these things. But if placating pain is your go-to move every time your child is hurt, how will they ever manage to cope when you're not there to help them tune out?

The answer to this dilemma is rooted in the work of the renowned French-Dutch ethnographer Arnold van Gennep, who was the first to introduce the concept of universal rites of passage in 1909.

Van Gennep's study of societies across the globe led him to observe that the most successful way a person moves into adulthood is by passing through these stages:

1. separation from their group,
2. a time of being tested,
3. learning and growth as a result of the test, and then
4. return and reintegration with the group as a better version of oneself.[*]

Boiled down, a rite of passage is not so much the big celebration we think of today as a predictable, sequential process. As someone whose childhood was marked by uncertainty, I have always been drawn to predictability and patterns. They were a comfort to me as a child in the

---

[*] Van Gennep combined steps two and three, but for the sake of clarity I'm separating them into distinct steps.

midst of family turmoil, and later as a parent who watched my own children struggle with the regular discomforts of growing up just as you are watching yours.

I hope a high-level understanding of this process will bring you some peace, or at the very least a new knowledge that what shows up looking like failure in your adolescent's life may actually be step one in the age-old, universal process of becoming an adult.

When Theory Meets Real Life

Once you know the four stages to a rite of passage, you'll start noticing them everywhere. Any good coming-of-age story, from *Stand by Me* to *Star Wars* to *The Hate U Give,* follows this pattern. To simplify things, I've used my own story below to show you how real life lines up with van Gennep's work.

Theory	Separation from their group	A time of being tested	Learning and growth as a result of the test	Return and reintegration with the group as a better version of oneself
My Real Life	Going away for a semester to a farm school in Vermont, leaving behind friends, family, and known way of life	Facing new personal challenges like having to wake early and do chores, then failing at the chore of feeding turkeys	Learning a valuable lesson about self-indulgence and responsibility	Returning to my home school with a new understanding that I did not want to feel that embarrassment again, and resolving to be a better community member

In stage one, separation from the group can be physical, like going away on a journey, or emotional, like getting iced out by your friend group. It can start out optimistically, like being accepted into a cool farm program offered at another school, or it can begin negatively, like being suspended from school. Failure can be a trigger for this first event, or failure may not appear until the second stage of being tested.

When it comes to stage two, a time of being tested, it's important to remember that a test isn't much of one when it isn't challenging enough to risk failure. If I say to the Olympic swimmer Katie Ledecky, "I'm going to give you a swim test. Please swim the length of this pool," big deal. But if I myself had to take that test, it would be embarrassing. Add a couple more lengths and I'd be tempting death, but that's a story for another book about kids who never learned how to properly swim. The point is, a real test contains the opportunity for failure. If parents don't embrace this stage of growing up, they deny their kids the access to the last two stages where they become better versions of themselves and are celebrated for it. Then it's time for that party!

To be clear, I'm not asking you to let your kid suffer a little just because it's ultimately what's good for them. It's good for you, too. And me. And my kids. It's what's best for the entire community.

In Donna Jackson Nakazawa's excellent book *Girls on the Brink,* I learned of a parenting phenomenon known as the starling effect, named after the aggressive parenting techniques of starling birds* that do things like destroy other nests to give their babies a competitive advantage. Among humans, the starling effect describes when parents go to any lengths to spare their children discomfort, even manipulating circumstances to ensure their child has the best possible advantages despite how it affects other children in the same community. Those other children, though, they don't just receive fewer or lesser resources and ad-

---

* We are covering a lot of bird knowledge in this chapter! Turkeys are cannibals. Starlings are assholes. Who knew?

vantages. They also take in an unintended message: If other parents will do anything for what's best for *their* child, they won't do what's best for me. I am less safe now.

Nakazawa says we've moved from a parenting era when we valued what was best for society into a "my kid first" period that is ultimately harming us all. For more on how to break this cycle, check out Lenore Skenazy, who has been on the forefront of this concept with her non-profit LetGrow.org, ever since being nicknamed America's Worst Mom by the media for letting her nine-year-old ride the subway alone. What a rite of passage!

In summary, to grow up, your child needs to (1) pull away emotionally or physically, (2) go through a hard situation by themselves (mostly), (3) figure out what they can learn from this experience, and (4) rejoin the community a better, more grown-up version of themselves. If formulas like this bring you comfort, I have more good news. Your child and the universe will take care of the first two stages. You only need to get involved in the second two, and I'm here by your side to help with that.

So whether you picked up this book for confirmation that you are not alone, or practical advice on how to react to your child's failures, or perhaps you were just intrigued by the free can of stinging ants and child-sized gloves I'm offering with every hundredth purchase of this book, you're well on your way to finding the relief and practical answers you need, and with any luck perhaps changing the social stigma around adolescent failure so parents who come after have it a bit easier. We'll think of it as our generation's rite of passage, perhaps.

CHAPTER THREE

Keeping Children Safe as They Take More Risks

Featuring *Your Child's Bill of Rights*

Becoming independent is something that I like-slash-*need* to remind parents is an outcome we all want for our children. It is also an incredible act of *risk taking*.

Why would any young human consider leaving the parental home to strike out alone in this hard world, when doing so carries with it such uncertain conclusions? Taking care of oneself carries with it huge risks for failure, embarrassment, hunger, and isolation. Instead, your child could enjoy the simpler alternative of continuing to live under your roof, not paying rent or utilities, and enjoying all your magically regenerating groceries. With no way of knowing whether they're good at taking care of themselves yet, you might think this seems to be the smarter decision. And isn't it the *safer* alternative, too, since independence exposes them to so many new dangers, from their own poor decision making to victimization by others?

Lucky for you, teen biology works to override any desire to stay safe during adolescence. Womp, womp. It's not easy to appreciate a teen's drive to take risks when that drive shows up as, say, speeding to get to school on time, creating secret social media accounts, or drinking to look cool, but we do appreciate that exact same drive when it presents itself as trying out for a play, organizing a club at school, or starting a small business to earn money. Your teen's brain doesn't differentiate between what we adults think of as good risks and bad risks. It craves all risk equally, period.

That's the bad news. The good news is that your teen's brain is satisfied by all risk equally, too, and the more you encourage your child to do terrifying and exciting things without you, the less they feel the need to go behind your back to satisfy the urge for independence.

Your child's risk-taking years are going to include some good choices and some bad ones. Sometimes they'll make choices that scare them but are still socially acceptable, like riding a roller coaster or finding the guts to ask someone to the school dance. Sometimes they'll make choices that terrify you, like binge drinking, taking a dare to run through traffic, or sending a nude selfie. You can't control these choices, but your job is to stack the deck as much as possible toward the right ones. The way to do that is to fight your own instincts to overprotect your child from making mistakes, feeling scared, or getting hurt, and instead encourage tweens and teens to do *more* things that fill them with a mixed sense of nervousness and exhilaration. Plot twist: The way to keep your teen safest is to let them take more risks.

If the more you fear for your child's safety the more you tighten boundaries, you run the risk of signaling to them that the only way they'll be able to satisfy their biological need to take risks is to do it underground—where things get exponentially less safe. Might your child's pursuit of risk taking get them hurt? Made fun of? Humiliated? Yes. It's totally possible. But will they be safer for being allowed to take more risks out in the open? Without a doubt. Risk is highly personal and subjective, and you may be surprised what kinds of safe risks are enticing to your child. For this reason, you don't get to choose for them. Your job is to make peace with the need for adolescents to do scary things. If you're lucky, your child will test the waters by asking you for permission to take risks. Can I stay out later? Can I go by myself? Can I try? I tell parents to walk to the edge of their comfort zone, then tiptoe two *baby steps* further before they say no.

Avoid Failure Traps Along the Way

Avoiding failure is not the point of this book, but there are some traps that surround failure, much like quicksand, that can keep you stuck in a way that induces panic. Moving forward means learning the lessons from each failure, which will help you to become a better person. These are traps you—as the parent, guardian, or teacher of a young person—need to avoid.

Failure traps include the following:

- *Thinking you can avoid failure by micromanaging your child.* Sometimes parents who successfully help their kids sidestep a puddle inadvertently end up steering them right into a pedestrian holding a steaming cup of coffee. Guiding your tween or teen through life by the arm, literally or metaphorically, will sometimes be helpful and sometimes harmful. What it can never be is a surefire way to keep them from getting hurt or hurting others.
- *Believing failures are rare or shameful.* If you think your child's particular kind of failure is the worst, you're in good company. Most parents see their kid's "fall from grace" as uniquely awful (because it is, to them), but if you can pull back your scope to see that every family faces a different but daunting situation, you can uncloak your shame to find comfort in community.

- *Accepting that failure can cause damage without accepting that it can also create space for growth.* Think of failure as a tool and understand that no tool can be helpful without also being harmful. The stove that is hot enough to cook your dinner can also start a house fire. The knife that is sharp enough to cut an apple can also slice your finger. If we focus only on how failure can hurt us, we miss the point. Fear of failure, often commingled with fear of losing control, causes some parents to constantly harp on everything that *could* go wrong, catastrophizing ad nauseam. When you feel yourself snowballing into a long list of ways your child's failure could derail their life, pull back. Consider the ways in which failing can also be helpful. If you're at a loss for what the sunny side might be, keep reading this book.
- *Asserting that kids who fail don't have the right to* continue *failing.* This is the biggest trap of all, and the hardest to avoid, so we'll focus on this one for the rest of this chapter.

I know this last trap must feel counterintuitive to many of you. Good adults stop bad things from happening whenever there is a reasonable opportunity to do so. We call the city to report a fallen stop sign, or we warn friends to avoid a business that didn't deliver on its promise, or we sweep up glass from the street after recycling day. If we do these things for the safety of people outside our families, shouldn't we be at least that proactive for our own children? Think of this as protecting your child from *obvious or imminent* pain. If there is something you can do to immediately stop your child from getting hurt, take action. Sweep up the broken glass in your driveway after recycling day, of course! But don't keep your child from playing basketball in the driveway for fear they'll break a bone or be abducted by a child molester if you aren't vigilantly watching them every second. Those kinds of fears stagnate growth without a firm basis in probability.

Teens Who Screw Up Must Retain Some of Their Rights

Once again, as a frequent participant in online parenting platforms, my own included, I see parents regularly debating whether the answer to a worried parent's quandary lies in taking away the child's rights. When a parent posts a story about their child's latest blunder, mishap, or rebellion, comments like these always get a huge response:

> If you're under my roof, you don't get to act that way.
> If they are disrespectful like that again, the bedroom door should come off its hinges.
> If I paid for it, it's mine—that means the phone, the laptop, and the Xbox are mine to take anytime, for any reason.
> There is no such thing as privacy for teens.
> The world is too dangerous to allow my child to be out there without me.
> Their brains aren't fully developed yet. It's our responsibility to keep them from messing up.

I know people say things they don't mean, or haven't fully thought through, in online forums all the time, but given how often and fervently people agree with these sentiments, it seems reasonable to conclude that some parents think the idea of tweens and teens having rights, even after they've screwed up, is absurd.

There are rights we cherish as adults that many parents deliberately don't offer their adolescents—privacy, autonomy, freedom of expression, for example—and yet they then expect them to be good at managing these once they leave our homes. We want our children to be able to speak up for themselves, stick up for others, be critical thinkers, question authority, respect authority, and all the things we *value,* but we don't want them to practice these in our homes because practicing can be sloppy, hurtful, and upsetting.

I am certainly not suggesting your teen has the right to ignore your rules, say cruel things to you, or destroy family peace of mind or physical property. What I would like to explore, though, is whether taking away their rights as our go-to response after a failure serves them, and us, best. Sometimes, for safety's sake, the answer is yes. Often, for the sake of continued character development, the answer should be no.

Staying open to failure is a scary prospect when we could much more easily clamp down and remove opportunities for more you-know-what to hit the fan. If we are going to embrace the reality that becoming a good adult doesn't begin at the age at which a child leaves the parental home, but instead happens incrementally throughout adolescence, then we have to be deliberate about giving young people opportunities to practice.

If we are going to embrace the reality that becoming a good adult doesn't begin at the age at which a child leaves the parental home, but instead happens incrementally through-out adolescence, then we have to be deliberate about giving young people opportunities to practice.

Let's Get Civic-al! Civic-al!

(Olivia Newton-John beat starts building in the background . . .) Don't worry, you won't need to grab your one-pound hand weights and sweatbands for this section. I'm prepping you for more of a mental workout here, but by all means, if you want to jog in place and squeeze in a little cardio while we're at it, more power to you!

Okay. We all know the United States gives societal rights to adolescents on a sliding scale. A fourteen-year-old can't yet drive, and a sixteen-year-old can't yet vote, and an eighteen-year-old can't yet buy alcohol. I'll argue that in addition to these rights given by the state, all adolescents deserve a minimum range of basic personal rights, bestowed by parents—not the government—that can become broader in scope with age and experience, yet also reduced or temporarily revoked when real safety protocols have been violated.

The Bill of Rights in the U.S. Constitution overlaps surprisingly well with the adolescent need to construct adult versions of themselves (bearing of arms and quartering troops aside). Many of our constitutional amendments can relate to teen life today. From the Fourth Amendment: No unreasonable searches and seizures sounds like a good reminder not to read your kid's diary or overly monitor their texts. From the Fifth Amendment: No double jeopardy reminds me that when a young person screws up, we shouldn't keep convicting them of the same crime or asking them to prove their ongoing acceptability or worthiness to us.

Given the overlaps here, I've taken it upon myself to play the roles of Alexander Hamilton, James Madison, and Thomas Jefferson in this much anticipated performance of *Your Child's Bill of Rights*. I offer you a living document, much like the Constitution, that can grow with your child, your circumstances, and the world we live in, with the intent of protecting your teen's needs along with your family's, to serve as a guide for making decisions and rules that affect you and your child, and to clearly set goals and boundaries in otherwise unexplored territories.

Note: Every child is different, and sometimes those differences affect how and when they receive access to rights. You and other adults in your child's life, whether health-care professionals or friends and family who know them best, will need to evaluate your tween or teen's ability to maneuver through the world with varying degrees of independence and responsibility.

All adolescents deserve a minimum range of basic personal rights, bestowed by parents—not the government—that can become broader in scope with age and experience, yet also reduced or temporarily revoked when real safety protocols have been violated.

Your Child's Bill of Rights

ADOLESCENTS HAVE THE RIGHT TO:

I. MAKE MISTAKES AND HAVE OPPORTUNITIES TO FIX THEM

II. MAINTAIN SOME PRIVACY

III. TAKE RISKS

IV. CHOOSE THEIR OWN FRIENDS AND GATHER WITH PEERS

V. PRACTICE MAKING INFORMED DECISIONS ABOUT THEIR BODIES

VI. RECEIVE THE BENEFIT OF THE DOUBT

VII. NEGOTIATE AND SELF-ADVOCATE

VIII. DETERMINE THEIR OWN VALUES

IX. ACCESS ACCURATE INFORMATION FROM MULTIPLE PERSPECTIVES AND SOURCES ON ALL TOPICS

X. SEEK INDEPENDENCE AND NOT BE RELIED UPON BY THEIR CAREGIVERS FOR PERSONAL, EMOTIONAL, OR FINANCIAL GAIN

Adolescents have the right to

    I. Make mistakes and have opportunities to fix them

    II. Maintain some privacy

    III. Take risks

    IV. Choose their own friends and gather with peers

    V. Practice making informed decisions about their bodies

    VI. Receive the benefit of the doubt

    VII. Negotiate and self-advocate

    VIII. Determine their own values

    IX. Access accurate information from multiple perspectives and sources on all topics

    X. Seek independence and not be relied on by their caregivers for personal, emotional, or financial gain

A Closer Look at These Rights

Below, you'll find a short overview of each right, including why that right is vital to continued development; how kids get better at using, not abusing, these rights; and how parents inadvertently and occasionally get in the way.

Then, in each chapter where we dive deep into a specific adolescent failure, I'll call back to *Your Child's Bill of Rights* to explain which ones are most useful in helping a child begin to move past failure.

I. The Right to Make Mistakes and Have Opportunities to Fix Them

Let's mentally star this one. This is my favorite of the ten because it's the crux of this book's message.

Making mistakes is easy and fixing them is hard, which means it will take practice to become proficient. The fact that so many adults are bad at this is a sure sign that we need to start teaching this earlier. Mistakes can be embarrassing, painful, and infuriating, but they are also a part of the human experience. Pressure to be perfect comes at a steep price, including eating disorders, self-harm, depression, anxiety, and codependence. If we don't teach kids that mistakes are a necessary part of life, teens will hide their mistakes because they don't know how to handle the complicated emotions that come with them. If a child is spending their energy hiding something, they aren't using their energy to learn.

Teens practice getting good at this right by having the opportunity to apologize after they screw up. You can make this easier by teaching them what a good apology sounds like and then modeling this yourself when you screw up.

Parents get in the way of successful practice when they talk about mistakes as if they were always avoidable; are overly strict; focus too much on high achievements; shame or poke fun at others who make mistakes; embarrass (especially publicly) their kids for making mistakes.

II. The Right to Privacy

Developing an adult identity—a.k.a. figuring out what kind of adult you want to be—takes a lot of guesswork. Kids need to try on new beliefs and behaviors for size before they become part of the fabric of their character. If teens aren't given privacy to experiment with this, they may be unwilling to go through this experimentation publicly (too embarrassing) and will miss opportunities to firm up their beliefs, values, preferences, and other aspects of adult identity.

Teens practice this when they are allowed to do things like spend plenty of time cocooning in their room, communicate with friends without being constantly monitored, safely explore their community without an adult, and experience relationships without having to share full details.

Parents get in the way when they monitor every text or DM *in case* their kids are misbehaving, read diaries or journals without cause (a very good cause would be a child expressing suicidal ideation or an intent to run away from home), enter a teen's room without knocking, or remove a teen's door for rude behavior.

III. The Right to Take Risks

The adolescent brain undergoes extraordinary changes that ramp up a teen's need to seek out new, exciting experiences. This scares parents, but this new drive is also exactly what propels young people to take the kinds of positive risks they need to become independent. When we limit a teen's ability to do things they find exhilarating, the need remains unsatisfied, and teens tend to sneak around to scratch that developmental itch.

Teens practice doing this when they do things like learn how to drive or take public transportation alone, try out or audition for a team or program, launch an entrepreneurial venture like a small business, or engage in new relationships.

Parents get in the way when they overly restrict exploration of their community, constantly observe their child's social interactions, or repeatedly focus on danger more than opportunity.

IV. The Right to Choose Their Own Friends and Gather with Peers

Finding a friend group outside your family unit is a crucial part of feeling accepted, confident, and capable: key ingredients to adult independence.

Teens practice this when they do things like leave behind an outgrown or even toxic friendship, look for opportunities to meet new friends, and engage in what may appear to be mindless and unstructured hangouts with peers, whether in person or virtually.

Parents get in the way when they judge their kid's friends for being different, force friendships with people the child indicates they aren't comfortable with (even if they previously had a close relationship), put unreasonable limits on a teen's time to be in company with friends, or restrict access to friends based on reputation or assumptions alone.

V. The Right to Practice Making Informed Decisions About Their
Bodies

Though we're entrusted to care for our children's physical and mental
well-being, at some blurry point we must turn that responsibility over
to them. You may notice this transition starting to happen when your
child's pediatrician asks you to leave the exam room so they can talk
without you, or when your child refuses to hug a family friend, or when
your terrified-of-needles teen athlete opts out of an injection that will
help manage a sports injury. Kids who don't grow up practicing making
informed decisions about everything from consensual touch to medical
procedures do not make for adults who can reason well with other people's advances or boundaries.

Teens practice this when they do things like make or contribute to
decisions about their bodily appearance (hair dye and style, clothing,
ear piercing), debate the pros and cons of big medical decisions, and
feel safe communicating openly with others about unwanted physical
attention.

Parents get in the way when they establish strict dress codes, comment on "inappropriate" clothing choices that tie reputation or morality to appearance, force physical contact with relatives or friends, enforce
cultural norms like shaving, make unilateral medical decisions without
at least discussing and considering their adolescent's preferences.

VI. The Right to Receive the Benefit of the Doubt

Teens live in a state of emotional, physical, and social uncertainty,
which can make their reliability a little suspect at times. They say or act
one way and then completely change the next time you see them. This
isn't a character flaw; it's part of being in a developmental state of flux.
Their bodies won't cooperate, their heads are full of doubt about who
they are becoming, their brain chemistry is shifting, and the swirling

social pool of kids around them is utterly exhausting. Of course, adolescents will show us their exhaustion in a variety of unappealing ways, but it doesn't mean they want to be annoying. They need us to believe them when they tell us how they feel or what they think, even if they aren't quite sure yet of those things themselves.

Teens deserve this right even when they do things like refuse the lasagna you make that they used to love, do not want to pursue a sport or hobby you've invested in, change or reject religion, or do not like your politics anymore; these are not personal attacks—even if it feels that way. Assume teens aren't doing this to be jerks and instead are trying to figure themselves out as they become more socially, intellectually, and emotionally complicated beings.

Parents get in the way when they frequently remind kids of their shortcomings, respond to a teen's behavior with emotional outbursts, make negative comparisons to other people in the family, or deny basic needs as punishment for bad behavior.

VII. The Right to Negotiate and Self-Advocate

Being able to think for yourself isn't easy, especially for kids who are anxious, people pleasers, or just great at following directions. Learning to make your own decisions can have messy results, but how else do kids learn how to become better at finding resolutions? When they feel capable of making informed decisions and not just emotional ones, they become better equipped to care for themselves. This enables them to advocate for and negotiate on behalf of people who may need their assistance (including, someday, aging parents).

Teens practice this when they do things like approach a teacher about reevaluating their grade, ask for a raise or promotion at a part-time job, negotiate a new bedtime, or persuade a frenemy to treat them better.

Parents get in the way when they refuse to explain how they come to decisions ("because I said so") and when they don't allow kids to question them or engage in negotiations. This militaristic approach to parenting can be satisfying in the short term because you've induced compliance, but it will not teach your child to be skilled in either critical thought or cooperation.

VIII. The Right to Determine Their Own Values

Independence means, well, not being dependent on others to decide what's best for you. Adults often base their hardest decisions on how that decision affects their values. If kids aren't given a chance to fully explore their values outside the family's, they won't have a complete and reliable toolbox for future decisions. And since decisions only get harder with age, particularly after you have children of your own, early value exploration is a key right to healthy growth.

Teens practice this when they clearly communicate their own beliefs, engage in respectful discussions about other principles, and feel comfortable having values that don't align with their parents' or peers'.

Parents get in the way when they dismiss or joke about a child's values, or insist children believe what parents believe without room for discussion.

IX. The Right to Access Accurate Information from Multiple Perspectives and Sources on All Topics

Introducing a young person to accurate information from multiple perspectives and sources on all topics doesn't make them do bad things; it *reduces* their risk of injury. For example, talking about suicide openly and frankly with teens doesn't put it on their radar; it lowers the risk that they will consider acting on suicidal thoughts. The same goes for sex, birth control, illegal substances, vaccines, politics, war, poverty, and religion. Getting info from multiple sources teaches your child how to make informed decisions, instead of emotional ones, as they begin to navigate the world outside their parents' bubble.

Teens practice this when they research topics of interest, discuss politics and voting with information from more than one news source, volunteer for a cause that matters to them, feel emboldened to engage with adults on these topics, or share a meal or personal experience with someone who is different from them.

Parents get in the way when they block or disparage valid news sources; insist that people who think differently are bad people; refuse to acknowledge that experts in fields have more knowledge than the general public; never admit that they, as the parent, were wrong; dictate family beliefs and punish family members who feel differently.

X. The Right to Seek Independence and Not Be Relied On by Their Caregivers for Personal, Emotional, or Financial Gain

The classic child star trope comes to mind here, a Jennette McCurdy sort, for example, who was groomed by her mother for celebrity and then used for her mother's financial and emotional gain, despite the devastating effects on her daughter's health and happiness. But this right has a broader application, too. Even children in average families, without the pressure of early careers or stardom, can experience "enmeshment" in which a parent relies on the child for support or comfort that should come only from another adult.

Teens practice emotional independence when they are encouraged to spend time away from their parent learning or enjoying new things (for example, by going to camp, traveling with school or friends, sleeping over at a family friend's house), or make decisions that best serve their future—if not the parent's ideal vision for the future.

Parents get in the way when they ask a child to soothe their emotions, use a young person's income to pay for parent expenses that are not critical to the household, convey to their children that their happiness rests on their child's connection with them or on their child's appearance of success within their community.

Does Every Adolescent Experience These Rights the Same Way?

How a child identifies and presents in the world will sometimes dictate their experience with these rights. Racism exists. Homophobia exists. Xenophobia exists. Transphobia exists. Misogyny exists. Classism exists. Sadly, we can't feel confident that children who are marginalized will be treated equally by teachers, coaches, store owners, public servants, or bystanders. The parents I work with who are raising children in minority groups, whether by gender, sexuality, skin color, religion, mental or physical disabilities, or national origin, express a common and heartbreaking fear that their children will be denied their dignity, acceptance, or safety by the adults they encounter outside the home. My hope is that all of us can listen to their fears, affirm their concerns, and respond by stepping in as needed to protect children of all ages from harmful judgments or reactions from adults, as well as by reminding each other that *all* kids deserve the right to become adults through independence and exploration.

I hope you now feel buttressed with a better understanding of rights so that when you support a child you love through failure, you have a strong foundation from which to begin. Now let's get you prepped to start that work.

CHAPTER FOUR

Preparing Yourself for What's Ahead

If you picked up this book because your kid is metaphorically on fire, chances are you're inhaling secondhand smoke. So, before we get into how to support your child, let's tend to your needs first.

Assessing Your Response Style

When you become aware of something that could hurt your child—whether it's their own doing, someone else's fault, or plain bad luck—you'll need to step in and take some parental action. This can go a few different ways, depending on how you typically handle perceived threats.

Picture this: Your almost fifteen-year-old son, a freshman walk-on to the school lacrosse team, has always loved playing sports. Shortly into the season, though, you notice a distinct and disconcerting shift in his attitude. He only grunts when you ask him about practice. He seems angry all the time and erupts at family members for little to no reason. Now his best friend's parent has told you they've heard from their son that the team is ganging up on him and it's gone from what might be considered playful banter to more aggressive verbal attacks. Your son doesn't know that you know about any of this yet. What's your move?

When You Feel a Threat to Your Family, Do You...

Fight? You feel an instant rage and call the coach to give him an earful. When you see parents of other players, you make sure they know what's going on with the team and rally them to speak up to the coach, too. You're not above glaring at certain players you perceive to be the team alphas so they know you are aware of what's happening.

Take flight? That's it, you're pulling your kid from the team. You can take a family trip to the mountains this weekend and let your son know the team is not the right fit for him. For that matter, the whole school could be toxic for supporting this culture. Would homeschooling be a better option? You'll look into a community lacrosse program and never have to face those jerks again.

Freeze? This is a lot to take in, and your son doesn't know that you know. Plus, the sources might not have gotten the story right, or it might have gotten exaggerated over time. All kids get teased. It's a normal part of growing up, especially for athletes. Feeling overwhelmed, you decide not to do anything. Besides, if you do something, you could make it worse.

Fawn? You have a stomachache. The idea of your son being attacked fills you with a real sense of dread, and the key to fixing it is to smooth things over, pacify all the potentially upset people involved, and make everyone feel happy again so you can stop worrying and start untying the knot in your stomach. You buy three boxes of doughnuts and bring them to practice as a peacekeeping effort. Maybe if you can just warm up the feelings on the team, everyone will come to their senses. You'll show them what a likable guy your son is! You thank the coach, cheerfully yell out some encouragement to the team, and hug your son as he's walking to the car, telling him what a *great! amazing! unbeatable!* job he did out there.

Fight, flight, freeze, or fawn. It can be appropriate to have *any* of these four responses to a perceived threat. Your instincts are probably embedded in how you first learned to deal with danger as a child, and therefore are deeply rooted in your own childhood psyche, which means they've served you well before.

But just because they worked for you then doesn't mean they are your best tools now. It's time to Marie Kondo any habits that are no longer of service to you with a sweet kiss and thank-you for all the protection or comfort they brought you, then respectfully put them in the donate pile to make room for new ways to cope. No one can tell you what coping mechanisms will work best for you, but you might start to figure out yours by doing the opposite of what your instincts have told you in the past. If you avoid conflict, try jotting down how you feel, and then initiate an open and direct conversation about those feelings. If you are quick to flare up, try meditating and waiting a bit before responding to the person who angers you. Flipping your script can be a great way to see what works for you now that you're an adult.

If All You Have Is a Hammer, Everything Looks Like a Nail

This adage derives from the psychologist Abraham Maslow, who said, "I suppose it is tempting, if the only tool you have is a hammer, to treat everything as if it were a nail." It's a helpful reminder that we do our best with what we have, but if we don't pick up more tools, our responses will be limited. Your reflexive responses determine the course you follow as you approach (or retreat from, or ignore) problems, including the problems that you encounter when your child experiences failure. Being aware of your impulses may allow you to survey the land-scape more broadly and find an approach that best suits the problem instead of best suiting your feelings.

Threats to your child can send you spinning back to your own child-hood traumas, but as obvious as it seems, it's a good idea to remind your-self that you are a grown-up now. You've been through a lot, and you have many more tools than you did when you were little and still developing your survival toolbox. Watch your own responses and see if you detect a pattern, then consider whether you're picking the best tools you have available to you now. Focus on auditioning a number of ways you can react before choosing your go-to method every time. By not relying on age-old impulses, you can diversify your response portfolio.

It may also be worth exploring how your reactions change when the perceived threat is coming for you, not your child. What happens when it's not your son's lacrosse team that becomes aggressive, but your co-workers, neighbors, or Facebook acquaintances? When you feel person-ally attacked by someone's comments or actions, is your response the same as when your child is threatened, or do you go in another direc-tion? Do you become a keyboard warrior (fight)? Do you start looking at job postings, houses for sale, or new social groups to join (flight)? Do you call in sick and pull the blinds (freeze)? Do you apologize immedi-ately and befriend the attacker (fawn)?

It's worth examining how you react on your child's behalf, as well as on your own, and what effect your responses might have on the out-come. Don't expect to make quick changes to ingrained habits, but just pausing to be mindful about your choices will help you develop your skills over time so that you learn to choose the best response to a situa-tion instead of the first one that comes to mind.

You Can't Use Your Brain if Your Body Is on Fire

If the situation you face is causing you a lot of anxiety, anger, fear, or doubt, that's perfectly normal. Lots of good therapy has taught me that when you are in a state of stress, your body has a palpable, physical response. You may notice your brow sweating, muscles tightening, head thumping, and heart rate accelerating. Your ears may ring, and breathing may become faster, tighter, or less rhythmic.

When stress attacks your body, it can be scary and exhausting. If you know this feeling, you also know that it's very hard to persuade yourself not to feel this way.

Your mind races, desperate for a way to make your discomfort go away; then, having no luck, it becomes increasingly agitated, rushing faster and faster to the edge of panic. We humans pride ourselves on our rational, innovative problem-solving abilities, but our brains will flat-out abandon us during a crisis.

Your body, through the autonomic nervous system, will immediately begin pumping blood and releasing adrenaline at the first sign of a threat. It does this to help you react physically (as in *Bear! Run!*), but it unfortunately also does this when you recognize a threat that doesn't put you in bodily harm (as in *Kids! Teasing my kid!*). When that happens, it's crucial that you pause and take a moment to calm your physical symptoms before trying to use your brain.

Here are some ways to placate your raging stress response so that you can tiptoe past it to access your wise and thoughtful brain:

- Concentrate on your breathing. I know you know this. But people rarely remember to do it when it counts. Get in the habit of noticing your breathing when you are simply irritated and not in crisis mode, then start practicing calm, slow breaths. It's helpful to count in and out on those breaths, too. Breathe in for two, out for two. Increase the count as you're able.

- Move your body in a different way. Jump up and down, take a fast walk, do push-ups, or clench tight fists and then release. Your body's physical response needs to be disrupted, and when your brain can't do the job, you have to fight fire with fire, or in this case physicality with physicality.
- Focus on what your five senses can take in. Try this trick of observing your surroundings and listing one thing you can smell, taste, see, hear, and feel. Repeat until you feel more present.
- Change locations. Find a new spot to sit, stand, or lie down where you feel more peaceful. Feeling physical support like a chair, floor, or wall to help brace you can be a comfort and pull your brain back from any catastrophizing you may be feeling.

Start practicing these coping techniques in response to small-scale issues. Did you forget to set a timer when you put the chicken on the grill and hey, kids, now it's pizza night? Did your expensive linen shirt get shrunk in the dryer down to doll size? Did someone cut you off in traffic? Every day you're given plenty of opportunities to practice coping techniques. Do it. When the big things happen, far worse than a burned dinner, you can call on them without much effort or concentration because you're accustomed to leaning on them already.

Getting in the Right Headspace

Once you've tended to your physical reactions, it's helpful to sweep out your brain so you have some space to work. Here are some things that can help you mentally prepare to face the challenge ahead:

- Wallow in misery, anger, or confusion for a little while. It's too hard to march forward before you've had a chance to feel what's come over you. Don't deny yourself the opportunity to be human first. Pull those covers up over your head for a day (or two, it usually takes me two). The world will wait.

- Keep some perspective. No one likes to be told "It's not that bad" or "At least you still have a roof over your head, the dog, your health, whatever" when they feel rotten. But after you've marinated in rotten for a while, it's probably helpful to remember that this is not the end of the world.

- Put your gloves on and get ready to do hard work. Now that your body and brain are synced up to work together, the next steps are to decide what to do and then do it. The kinds of gloves you choose are entirely metaphorical and up to you. Maybe you need your well-worn leather yard-work gloves so you can handle this tough job. It might be a good occasion for boxing gloves so you can fight through this challenge. You might need some hospital-grade medical gloves to clean up all the excrement on this one. Or maybe you need some soft, cashmere, elbow-length beauties to make the task at hand a little easier on you. Choose the right tool for the job and the right tool for your personality.

Try to Be Observant

This can often be a matter of keeping things in perspective. *Oh well, could be worse* is a helpful mantra for this. You notice your kid's room is insanely cluttered. *Oh well, could be worse.* Your teen has one or two friends but no big group to go to the football games with. *Oh well, could be worse.* Your teen doesn't like studying but loves working with their hands. *More than oh well. Great!* Don't confuse your worries with their problems. Observe how your child is *actually* doing, not what you suppose could be a problem.

Importantly, observing is not snooping. You will either die of boredom or create useless anxiety for yourself if you turn over every rock looking for more problems, real or potential. You don't need to expose yourself to the daily dramas of teen life by reading all their texts, checking their online grade portal daily, or touching base regularly with teachers, coaches, and friends to make *sure* everything is okay. Think of observing like visiting an art museum. Walk through and look closely at everything on display, but don't cross over the velvet ropes and look behind the paintings.

What Should You Be Looking For?

Sometimes, failure will announce itself loud and clear. A call from the police or principal can be an obvious tip-off! But more often, failure tiptoes in more subtly. Here are some things you can keep an eye out for:

- Are you hearing about a possible problem from more than one reliable source, or more than one time, from a trusted source? Have multiple teachers suggested your child is losing focus in class? Has a close friend of yours mentioned more than once that your child talks a lot about hating school? You should ignore fleeting rumors, jokes, or mischaracterizations from the masses, but follow leads that come from people who know your child.
- Do you notice your child's emotional reactions becoming overwhelming to them and unbearable to family and friends? Are sadness and anger taking over most aspects of their life and spilling into your happy family times, too, without much break? It's perfectly normal for teens to ride an emotional roller coaster with all its ups and down, slow climbs and high-velocity plunges, twists and turns and loop-de-loops. A full range of unpredictable, yet varied, emotionality is part of adolescence. But if your teen has gotten off the roller coaster and slid

themselves into a luge, don't wait to see where they're headed. It's straight downhill. They need you to pull the brakes.

- Is your child developing a knee-jerk response to hard situations that might make overcoming them even harder? Maybe you can share with them your analysis of whether you are a fight, flight, freeze, or fawn type and ask them to observe what their go-to reaction is for a while. Now might be a good time to expand their toolboxes through some good modeling and discussion, using yourself as the example.

- Are you hearing your child? Are they giving you clues to a bigger problem, but you're either not tuning in or asking them to stifle those feelings? Are you underestimating their struggle or writing it off as just how teens act?

Be as cautious and unemotional as possible during this observation phase. If you notice your child has been acting depressed for a couple weeks, there's no need to call an inpatient treatment center, force them to go out and do things, or plead with them each night to just act like themselves again. Watching and noticing allow you to become aware of impending crises you might be able to avoid. They shouldn't trigger an instant freak-out.

Should you trust your gut during this observation stage? Maybe. It depends on whether your gut is the trustworthy kind. Think back to your fight-or-flight response and keep in mind that your very particular gut, that part of your psyche that informs your instincts, intuition, understanding, and reaction type, has been forged in the fires of your very specific life experiences. This can be helpful. For example, if you were raised by a narcissist, you may be more tuned in to people in your child's life who are controlling or manipulative. This gut can also be harmful. If you have not taken the time (and to be frank, benefited from the unbiased guidance of a professional therapist) needed to fully process being raised by a narcissist, your gut might implore you to please a narcissist to stay on their good side. Guts aren't foolproof. Examine yours before you rely solely on it to captain your decisions.

A concluding disclaimer: Observation is helpful some of the time, but like your gut, it isn't foolproof either. Please don't spend any time beating yourself up when your child's circumstances completely surprise you. Humans are good at camouflage, and teens, especially, have a vested interest in keeping their lives private. It's a basic and universal part of growing up. Observe what you can, and don't feel guilty about the things you were unable to detect.

CHAPTER FIVE

Three Steps to Overcoming Failure

Step right up, ladies and gentlemen! This amazing tonic will cure your baldness, purify your humors, and bring you unlimited happiness! In just three easy steps you'll be on the path to physical salvation, financial profit, and spiritual reward!

No one likes a snake oil salesman. There is something intriguing about that spectacular pitch, though, isn't there?

So here I go. In just three steps, folks, you'll be on your way to shedding that failure and becoming the wise, respected, and successful person you were always meant to be!

I really mean it.

While I'm joking about the sideshow carnival barker, I'm serious about this process. It may appear that I'm oversimplifying this huge feat with three steps, and there's a reason for that too. It's because I am. No one in a crisis does well with complicated directions. You know what to do if you ever catch on fire, right? You stop, drop, and roll. If your Saturday morning cartoon PSAs or annual elementary school field trips to the local firehouse gave you fifteen steps to get out of a fire alive, you'd panic and, well, you know what would happen next.

If you need to escape a fire, there are endless things you can do beyond stop, drop, and roll. You could call 911. You could scream. You could open a door for your pets to escape through. You could put a wet cloth to your face, and so on. Those are all good things to do if you can, but keeping it simple is the key to surviving a crisis. I'll borrow this approach with a three-step process for getting through, and growing from, failure. I'm also going to give you lots of options and examples for many variations of things you can do *as you're able* to add them in, but to keep from getting overwhelmed, don't worry about remembering them. You can refer here and think them through carefully when you are ready. All you need to recall are these three steps:

Contain

Resolve

Evolve

Contain: Step one is to contain the problem. You may also need to contain your child, as in keep them safe at home, but the point is to control the spread of the crisis. This is when you will do whatever is needed to stop the metaphorical bleeding by applying an also metaphorical tourniquet. Quite literally: Go to the doctor if that's what the situation calls for. Shut off the Wi-Fi. Lock the front door. Take the day off work. Throw away the alcohol. Call the school. Do whatever it takes to limit further damage.

Resolve: Step two is to begin to resolve the damage. This is when you'll take action to fix the wound, not just stop it from bleeding. Unlike the first step, you don't have to act with urgency here. I'll give you lots of options to choose from when you're ready, just know that resolution takes careful thought, time, and action.

The best way to prepare for this step is to load up on patience and compassion.

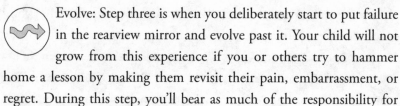 Evolve: Step three is when you deliberately start to put failure in the rearview mirror and evolve past it. Your child will not grow from this experience if you or others try to hammer home a lesson by making them revisit their pain, embarrassment, or regret. During this step, you'll bear as much of the responsibility for letting go as your child, if not more.

Now that you have a high-level view of these three simple steps for turning your child's failures into character-building moments, let's take a closer look at how exactly each one works in detail. And don't worry if this process feels foreign or overwhelming to you at first. In the next eight chapters, we'll go through specific scenarios using these steps so you can see how different parents used them successfully.

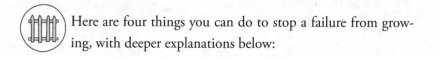 Here are four things you can do to stop a failure from growing, with deeper explanations below:

- Control the narrative.
- Affirm your child.
- Shrink your child's exposure.
- Gather the truth.

Control the Narrative

Okay, your child has failed in some way—broken a curfew, thrown a party in your house while you were out, cheated on a test. You've taken deep breaths and maybe even some time to consider how you will react and help your child through this crisis. Now you need to think about who needs to know about it and how you would like them to find out if they must. It's time to contain and communicate key messages.

People are drawn to crises. In part they want to help, and in part it soothes their fears to know *they* were spared a crisis. They'll want all the details. They'll call to check on you and sometimes to gather information to satisfy their own curiosity or pacify their fears. They'll talk among themselves from the edge of your bubble. This is human nature. I'm emphasizing this because you'll want to do what you can to control the narrative.

Before we discuss whom to tell and what to say, allow me to address the seeming contradiction in saying it's time to contain the message and the point I raised in the first pages of this book: that not being honest about our mistakes dooms us to repeat them sometimes. This is still true, but sharing and talking about failures with people you trust, with people you choose, is very different from a massive and uncontrolled broadcast.

First, decide who needs to know about what's happening. For your own sanity, you may want to confide in a close friend who can be trusted to keep your story close. You'll need a safe space to vent and process how you're feeling. You might also need to tell people your child regularly comes into contact with, especially if your child will be missing from events for a while. And of course, loop in any helpful experts as needed to keep your child safe. As your circle of communications broadens, you'll run the risk of your child's story becoming twisted. To minimize that risk, be prepared with a couple of sentences you can share when inquiring minds want to know. Keep it simple, short, grateful, and repetitive, if necessary. "Thanks for asking about how Claire is doing. We're staying close to home for a while, but I appreciate your concern. She's all right, but we had a [health concern, family matter, school issue, whatever high level of detail you're comfortable sharing] that we're working on, and I'm sure she'll be out and about soon. How's your kiddo doing? I saw her team had a big win last week!"

Keep in mind, your child might be sending their own messages out at the same time. You can only control what you can control. If your child is willing, you can brainstorm together what would be a satisfying enough response to friends without divulging too much. Or maybe your child wants to shout about this from the rooftops, particularly if they are angry and feel victimized by your response to the situation. Short of duct-taping their mouths shut, you can't do much to keep them from talking. If this is your situation, take a deep breath and carry on. Do what you can to affect messaging, but don't get hung up on what you can't control. Wasting time and energy trying to get your resentful child to comply with keeping their personal information quiet will drive you insane and pull you from your important work in the next stage of this process.

Affirm Your Child

If you have had to contain your child or your child's exposure to a problem, they are probably reeling. Take a moment after you've pressed pause to connect with your child and any immediate family members who may also be affected. Your primary message should be clearly rooted in love. I know, your kid might not be speaking to you right now. It's okay. You can write something short and sweet on a note and slide it under their door if necessary. Your message might sound something like this: "I know this is a really difficult time. Bottom line from me is: I love you, though I understand if you don't see it that way right now. I'm taking a day or two to gather my thoughts about what to do next, and I'll definitely be asking for your input on that soon. I'm here if you want to talk or just watch TV together. If not, just know that I'm on your side."

It's important to note that even if you are wildly angry with your child, you shouldn't punish them by denying them your attention or affection. If you normally kiss them at bedtime, keep doing that. If you send a nice note in their lunch every day, now is not the time to stop. Maintain the rituals of your affection despite the presence of this new failure in your lives.

Even if you are wildly angry with your child, you shouldn't punish them by denying them your attention or affection. Maintain the rituals of your affection despite the presence of this new failure in your lives.

Shrink Your Child's Exposure

When a failure shows up, you may need to quickly limit your kid's exposure to any number of things: friends, technology, the media, nosy neighbors, or whatever might cause further harm during a vulnerable time. When your child's world gets too big, it's your job to make it smaller. (I'm talking about their world suddenly opening up in a way that exposes them to imminent harm, not the natural expansion that's expected and needed for teens to grow.) Did your child get taken to the hospital with a potential overdose? That world needs to get smaller fast. Is your child being targeted online by someone who appears to have malicious intent? Shrink that world now.

A swift response can be difficult for some parents. It can draw public attention to a problem if people start questioning why your child isn't showing up for social events or hasn't been joining in regular online games. You might worry about overreacting and coming across as too harsh, but don't fret: You can always reverse your initial, swift action. When real danger creeps too close, you won't go wrong putting a tourniquet on the problem first to stop the bleeding and then assessing whether a bandage could have done the job once you have more time and information.

It can also be hard for parents who already have fraught relationships with their teens to do anything that might send them retreating further away. Fear of a kid's disconnecting for good—or even worse, hurting themselves—causes some parents to let failures fester longer than they should. And finally, sometimes it's just exhausting to think about making a big move. Parents are already tired and stretched too thin, so asking them to move quickly can be overwhelming and cause a total shutdown.

If any of these reasons resonated with you, consider that your child needs you to do this to keep them safe. Hedging on this can cause a breach in your containment, and your child might be exposed to opportunities or people that can make the situation worse. Your bold and swift action doesn't have to be overwhelming. This isn't *you're grounded for the rest of your life!* This is more like *we are going into a forty-eight-hour lockdown until I decide what to do next.*

Gather the Truth

The next step of containment is to make sure you have as much context as possible about the situation. You can't come up with a solution if you don't understand the problem. It's time to gather information from people whose assessment and opinion matter. Don't ask every person who knows your child to weigh in on what they think could be happening. Consult anyone with reliable, firsthand insight, as well as a doctor, therapist, specialist, or whoever might be able to provide relevant, expert insight about the reality of your child's situation.

 Here are three things you can do to resolve a failure, with deeper explanations below:

- Take action.
- Update communication.
- Engage your whisper network.

While the containment phase is about limiting your child's negative exposure, the resolution phase offers an opportunity to train your teen in the kind of positive response you hope for. Research shows that most adolescents respond better to offers of rewards than to threats of punishment. And in terms of motivation, Ayelet Fishbach, author of *Get It Done: Surprising Lessons from the Science of Motivation,* says that like puppies, humans learn best from positive reinforcement when you're trying to teach them new behaviors. If your new puppy pees on the floor and you yell, they get that peeing on the floor makes a scary sound come out of your mouth. But they don't know peeing outside makes you happy unless and until you immediately scoop them up and run them outside to the grass, then give them a treat. Yelling might relate to bad behavior, but it doesn't motivate good behavior.

Similarly, if your teen breaks curfew and you yell at them, they learn that the consequence for staying out late is your anger. If you ground them, they learn the consequence is anger plus restricted freedom. If you establish that coming home on time for six months merits a later curfew, they learn that following your rules has benefits.

In this way, training your teen requires opportunities to test the rules and to learn what elicits a negative response and what draws a reward.

Take Action

Below is a list of things you and your child can refer to when you're ready to figure out how to move past a failure experience. Don't worry, you don't need to memorize all of these, and you may think of more on your own. In the back of this book is an appendix you can cut out for easy reference.

Consider from the list below which action, or set of actions, will best help you resolve this experience of failure. For many of these menu items, you may be able to incentivize your child's compliance with rewards of affirmation, approval, and increased access to the things and people they desire.

Educate—Sample scenario: You found out your child's friend was busted for underage drinking. Now your child is freaking out because they like this person a lot and don't want you telling them they can't hang out together anymore. Your plan may include reading together about the effects of drinking on a developing brain, learning the signs of addiction, googling and then practicing ways your child can say no to substances without feeling dorky, or researching ways to support a friend through a tough time.

Define Consequences—Sample scenario: Your child has crashed the family car twice due to distracted driving. Your plan will likely include limiting access to car keys as well as a plan to repay some or all of the costs associated with your insurance deductible or rate increase.

Foster Connection—Sample scenario: Your child is increasingly withdrawing from family and friends, refusing to interact with peers in person or online. Your plan may involve helping them find opportunities to forge new connections where old ones have broken.

Rebuild Trust—Sample scenario: Your child has a 10:00 p.m. curfew on weekends, and they've been coming home on time, then sneaking out at night through their window to spend time with their friends in the park. Your plan will probably include a list of things they can do to rebuild your trust in their ability to make safe decisions.

Seek Perspective—Sample scenario: Same as above, different curfew. Your child has a 7:30 p.m. curfew on weekends, and they've been coming home on time, then sneaking out at night through their window to spend time with their friends in the park until 8:30 p.m. Your plan may include seeking new perspectives on what can reasonably keep a child safe, perhaps by engaging with other parents or experts on the topic, to provide insight into whether your rules might be driving their rebellious behavior.

Enable Interventions—Sample scenario: Your teen has been engaging in sex with her much older boyfriend without using protection and while under the influence. She refuses to protect herself from

STDs or pregnancy, and you fear her substance use may be an addiction. Your plan will likely need interventions with specialists in the mental health field who can assess what steps will best keep your child safe. You may need to explore residential therapy if recommended by professionals.

Reprioritize—Sample scenario: Your child tells you they don't feel like themselves in their assigned birth gender and they've had intrusive thoughts about hurting themselves. Reprioritizing may mean studying a topic you hadn't thought much about until now. It may mean spending more time and attention on this child for the time being. Education and connection with people who support and accept your child are going to show up here, too.

Apologize—Sample scenario: Your child took beer to a friend's house, where they drank when the parents were out of town and were busted by the neighbors. In addition to discipline and education, your plan should include one or more good apologies. I wrote about good and bad apologies in my book *Fourteen Talks by Age Fourteen* and have excerpted a brief highlight here for guidance:

A good apology does not

- blame other people for misinterpreting your actions
- blame others for feeling hurt or offended
- blame circumstances for clouding your judgment
- waste words convincing people you're a good person who just made a mistake

A good apology does

- explain what you did wrong
- acknowledge whom you've hurt and how
- say what you will do differently
- accept consequences

Make Amends—Sample scenario: Let's reuse the same one we did for Apologize, but this time make it more complicated. Your child took beer to a friend's house, where they drank when the parents were out of town and broke a picture frame in the process. Obviously, an apology is still in order, but it isn't quite enough, since the friend's parents will be out of money to replace the frame. Ideally, the kids who were drinking would all pitch in to have the frame fixed or replaced, and even for the house to be cleaned if needed.

Update Communication

During the contain stage, I advised you to keep your communication brief and tightly controlled. Now that you know your plan and are ready to move forward, you'll probably have to widen your circle of communication and be a bit more explicit.

That said, this failure that has arrived in your child's life is their story to tell. Yes, it affects you in monumental ways. Still, it's not yours. Include them in this process and give them ownership over whether, how, when, and even if messages get out about what happened.

Now that you know more specifics about what's happening and what the immediate future will hold, you'll be better prepared to answer inquiries from curious parents or nosy neighbors. Depending on how close you feel to the person, your answer might range from "All good! Nothing to see here" to a high-level explanation of what happened and what they can expect to happen next. Often, parents, teachers, and coaches are genuinely concerned and want to be able to support you *in the way you want them to.*

This might sound like a brief statement about what happened, such as "As you know, we discovered Jamie was engaging in some question-able behavior while gaming online." A boundary establishing what you're willing to share, such as "That's not my story to share, so I won't go into details out of respect to him." A little information about what you are willing to share, such as "I did think you should know he isn't allowed on his gaming system for one month. During that time, he will be allowed to use his phone daily for thirty minutes to communicate with friends but will not be seeing friends outside school or team practices until the month is over. As a parent of his friend/favorite coach/ dear friend of the family, we wanted you to know so you will understand why he isn't available, hanging around like usual, happy at practice, and so on." And maybe some insight into how you see this unfolding, such as "As he takes time to think about, and hopefully understand, the risks associated with what happened, we are also hopeful that we can gradually loosen the parameters around this and allow him back into gaming incrementally." And finally, some guidance for caring friends who want to be supportive, such as "If you happen to see him, please treat him as you always have. And if anyone asks, you can share what I've told you here. Thanks for your support."

Engage Your Whisper Network

You may be wrestling with feelings of parental shame or inadequacy as a result of your child's behavior or circumstances. I implore you not to let that stand in the way of figuring out what is best for your child. There are lots of reasons parents keep their children's failures private, and embarrassment and stigmatization are two of the biggest. This isolation creates a feeling that you are uniquely alone in your suffering. I assure you, you are not. There are plenty of people who would love to talk with you about their experiences, quietly and confidentially. I think of them as the parental whisper network. These parents may not talk openly about what their child has faced (again, not their story to broadcast), but they will lovingly empathize, point you in the right direction, or usher you to someone who knows more. Confide in one or two people you trust most if you need help making this kind of connection.

Chances are this may not be your best friend, though your best friend may help you find the right person to talk with. A friend of mine whose husband had gone through two bouts of cancer during the COVID pandemic said to me once about a personal crisis I was having, "Don't talk to the mere mortals out there. Find people who have been through *your* particular hell and talk with them." It is perfect advice.

In her book *Girls on the Brink,* Donna Jackson Nakazawa explains the scientific value of engaging with supportive social networks. We react to stress, whether physical, social, or emotional, through our immune and nervous systems, which are managed through the vagus nerve. Prolonged or repeated episodes of stress can trigger anxious, angry, or depressive moods as well as poor cognition. But, as Nakazawa explains, our bodies also come equipped with a built-in way to regulate these reactions: social connection. "When we turn to others for safe connection," Nakazawa writes, "our brain flips a switch and begins releasing protective signals throughout the body." Nakazawa calls this the Community Effect. The vagus nerve then begins sending signals of comfort and protection that positively affect mood, thinking, and behavior. Nakazawa's research clearly demonstrates that social support isn't just a fun thing to have when you feel good but an essential component of our success, safety, and health when we are in crisis.

Socially sequestering out of a sense of shame can have devastating effects on your body and brain. When you feel as if you're army-crawling through the trenches of your child's failure, confiding in others for support is key to being able to stand again.

 Here are six things you can do to stop a failure from growing, with deeper explanations below:

- Allow time and space for your child to process what happened.
- Triage your fears.
- Face one fear first.

- Uphold *Your Child's Bill of Rights.*
- Establish bonuses for good behavior.
- See new things.

Allow Time and Space to Process

Once you've tended to the more urgent matters of containing failure so it doesn't balloon, your child will likely need time to deal with the emotional aftermath. Give them extra space and time to process what happened. The rational, critical thinking portion of their brains, the prefrontal cortex, undergoes major construction during adolescence as it builds the pathways, synapses, and neurons adults use for complex thinking. As a result, the emotional center of the brain, the amygdala, steps in to assume many of the prefrontal cortex's duties. Whereas you would rely on your prefrontal cortex as you attempt to make sense of what's happening, your tween or teen can't. They'll draw on emotions as their primary processing tool. Allow time for them to process at their own speed, and expect a range of emotions to present themselves during this time.

Triage Your Fears

If you're not familiar with triage, it's a process by which medical professionals quickly assess and assign urgency to cases so they can treat the most critical issues first. I find it helpful to apply the triage technique to nonmedical problems when I feel overwhelmed.

At this point in the process, you might notice that your fears, which were initially muted by the necessity of taking quick action in response to the failure, have now begun to shout at you. You may be tempted to mute them again, or maybe now you start to really listen and ruminate on them. Neither is particularly helpful. Those fears will keep hollering louder and louder until you do something other than ignore or dwell on them without addressing them.

Start by listening to what the fears are telling you, and then make a list of what they're saying:

I'm afraid no one will want to be my son's friend after this.
I'm afraid people will think I'm a bad parent.
I'm afraid my daughter will keep wanting to date boys who treat her badly.
I'm afraid my child's bad behavior is going to get them arrested.

And so on.

Now, think of these fears as if they were simply trying to give you feedback. My family follows the ten-second feedback guideline when in public. If someone can fix something in the next ten seconds, you should tell them. If they have spinach in their teeth, or they missed a button on their shirt, speak up. But if your feedback is about something they can't quickly address, why say anything? You wouldn't tell someone walking into an event that they're underdressed. Or that their hair looked better shorter.

Similarly, you can triage your fears by using a timed guideline to address feedback from your fears. If you made a long list, take the top three or four fears to start. Ask yourself if there is anything you can do about them in the next twenty-four hours. If not, make a list of those fears to be shelved and not thought about again until next week, or even next month.

Face One Fear First

Once you've identified the fears you *can* do something about within twenty-four hours, make a list of what you can do for each. Taking even small action against big fears is a great way to regain a sense of agency when your world feels out of control. It's also a great way to move toward growth instead of becoming paralyzed by dread and uncertainty.

Uphold *Your Child's Bill of Rights*

Affirming your child's rights is an important step toward avoiding the helplessness—and sometimes even hopelessness—that can accompany a failure. Take a moment during this phase to identify which rights from *Your Child's Bill of Rights* in the appendix your tween or teen will need to move past this bad experience toward agency and self-reliance in the future. Hint: It's often the one that repels you most. For example, if the school calls because your child took a water bottle from someone's locker, you might think they don't deserve the right to gather with their friends because they don't show their peers respect. And it may be that temporarily they do need a serious social time-out. But, to practice the skills associated with being a good community member, they will need access to their peers again soon. Fall off the bike, get back on. That's how you learn to ride.

Establish Bonuses for Good Behavior

Your child has gone through a lot. You don't want them to become stagnant, wallowing in their own hell. There comes a time when you will need to help them make their way back to their so-called normal life (hat tip to Claire Danes) and create ways for their world to gradually open again. If you've had to limit their lifestyle for a while, I recommend you handle this expansion purposefully and under your supervision at first.

Let's take the example of the young man from earlier, who lost gaming privileges and time with friends for one month. I do not suggest waiting until day thirty and then releasing him back to his old ways. This will only teach him how to serve his time dutifully. Instead, set up bonuses along the way that give him reason to do more than lock himself in his room and sulk until he's served his sentence. Example bonuses could be the following: *After one week, if you are willing to have a meaningful discussion with me about what happened and how it affects you, we will increase your cell phone time to include an extra hour on the weekend. After two weeks, if you can present some ideas about how you can avoid this type of dangerous situation in the future, we can allow friends to visit you at our house for two hours on Saturdays. After three weeks, if you are maintaining a positive attitude toward the family and staying on top of your schoolwork, we will bring the gaming system to the living room and allow thirty minutes of play in the evenings while we are also in the room.* And so on.

See New Things

Setting yourself up to move forward means at some point you have to call "time." Game over. Lights up. Everyone go home.

Don't let this failure be the headline of your child's life for too long. See new things.

Make a real effort to stop focusing on near misses and crummy attitudes. Widen your gaze and start to notice the good moments, however small, your child is having. As you do, you'll inevitably see an increase in more happy moments together.

When enough time has passed, your child will send you signals that they are open to reflecting on what happened. This could take a few weeks or a couple years. I know, totally annoying to have to wait indefinitely, but important to allow your child to move on from this without having to meet your need of constantly checking in to be sure something like this won't happen again.

Contain, Resolve, Evolve: Let's put these into practice using real examples of families who've experienced eight types of failures with their children and come out the other side better for it.

PART II

Eight Archetypal Failures

CHAPTER SIX

Failure to Follow the Rules: The Rebel

The world's largest open-air graveyard is Mount Everest, the path to the peak strewn with more than two hundred bodies, many perfectly preserved in the frozen air. Low oxygen makes hauling oneself up or down the peak treacherous enough. Add to that the physical burden of transporting a frozen body back down the mountain, and the risk of death to the rescuer becomes too great; so the bodies remain where they took their last breaths for all to witness on their journey to the top.

But what's the rule for passing climbers who aren't dead yet but are clearly suffering? This became a hot topic in 2006 when more than forty climbers passed David Sharp, slumped over in a state of distress, without offering him aid. Sir Edmund Hillary dubbed this behavior "summit fever," a phenomenon that takes hold of climbers and blinds them to anything but their goal of reaching the pinnacle.

I would guess a majority of tween and teen failures are driven by a kind of "adolescent summit fever." The path to popularity is littered by kids on the wayside, sacrificed and climbed over by others with the top in sight, or struck down by their own hubris or misguided attempts to achieve popularity at all costs.

As your child grows up, their primary job is to become independent. That means from *you*. I imagine this feels like floating in space without a tether. Seeking acceptance from their peers is a way for teens to tether themselves to community and establish that even though they are becoming independent, they don't have to be alone. Adults should understand this drive toward peer acceptance, because it is often the catalyst toward breaking the rules. It's what drives kids to play the Rebel.

It's easy for adults to think of rebellious kids as careless, cruel, or superficial—people who break the rules just so their classmates will think they're cool. To be fair, all sorts of kids, even yours, even mine, are willing to take risks and break rules to be liked, including doing things that end up hurting themselves or others. Craving popularity isn't as shallow an ambition as it seems at first glance. It's often the first step a young person takes toward becoming independent. Older teens eventually develop a strong enough sense of self that they need less and less affirmation from their peers, and most adults become so sure-footed and set in their important relationships that they care very little if they aren't impressing everyone. Your tween will get there. It just takes years of practice and development first.

The Lure of Popularity

In researching this book, I not only interviewed parents across the country about their teens' experiences with failure but also asked adults to share their personal failure experiences with me with an interest in whether those failures led to their future success in any way. My friend Gina shared her story about the lure of popularity and how it led her to break an unwritten social rule and her best friend's heart.

Gina had been best friends with Melanie through grade school. She genuinely loved Melanie and treasured their friendship. Yet when seventh grade started and two popular girls invited Gina to start hanging out with them, the sun hit the snowcapped summit of Mount Popular just right, and in the dazzling glow of its promise, Gina got the fever.

There was only one obstacle to her ascension: This new group of girls wasn't interested in bringing along Melanie, too.

That weekend, Gina wrote Melanie a letter, which she passed to her in school on Monday. In short, it detailed the ways in which the other girls thought Melanie wasn't cool yet (the way she dressed, the way she talked, the way she looked much younger than them) and concluded by telling Melanie that now that they were in junior high, Gina didn't think they should be friends anymore.

Gina might have seemed as if she had the ice of Mount Everest in her veins, but right after she watched Melanie read the letter, she was unexpectedly overcome with shame. What had she done? This, I'm convinced, is the theme song of adolescent failure. *What have I done? What just happened? Whyyyy?*

In the weeks following, Gina tried to apologize to Melanie, but Gina was already embedded in her new friend group and Melanie was alone, in shock, sadness, and mourning. Gina's apologies fell flat. Even now in her fifties, Gina teared up telling me this story. She had reached out to Melanie in adulthood to tell her how wrong she had been to treat her that way, and how good and undeserving Melanie was of such treatment. Melanie did not respond.

It is a wound that remains raw for Gina. When I asked her if this failure helped her grow, she was emphatic. "It changed everything for me. I never wanted to feel the pain of hurting someone like that again, so I became determined to be a true friend. It changed all my relationships going forward." I can tell you, as one of Gina's closest friends, it is an honor to be loved by her. She is generous, thoughtful, and wise. Had she not had that experience in seventh grade, she might not be the super friend she is to so many women today.

One of the benefits of failure is that it can position a person to be a gifted teacher. The worst math teacher I ever had was a math whiz. He couldn't see where or why I wasn't making the connection and seemed baffled when I didn't understand. "You just need to solve it the way I showed you" was about as good as his instruction got. The best math teacher I ever had was horrible at math in high school. Just as I was getting stuck, he could anticipate why; he understood where the signals were getting crossed, and he knew how to explain the process to me in unexpected ways, because he had needed to develop those skills to be able to learn the math himself. Gina's experience mirrors this. She had failed miserably at friendship once, enough to teach her where the pitfalls were, only to grow into a model friend later in life.

Why Kids Fudge the Rules

Some rules are explicit. We have laws, codes of conduct, and house rules (implied, discussed, or written) that we know we must follow. We have social rules, too, that aren't hard and fast but that most people generally agree upon, such as don't ditch a loyal friend for a chance to hang out with the popular crowd. All of these rules, from the ones we codify to the ones we just kind of have a feeling about, come with gray areas.

Don't cheat on schoolwork, for example. Everyone knows this one will get you in trouble. Cheating is rule breaking. But . . . what is cheating? Looking at someone else's paper and copying down the answer? Yes. We all agree. Is asking Siri the answer to your math homework cheating, even if you can't solve it on your own? Is overhearing the civics essay question from kids who took the test in an early class period, then looking up the answer before your class, cheating? Is using your older sibling's book annotations to study cheating?

Gray everywhere. Especially in the adolescent brain where a shift from concrete to hypothetical thinking is under way. Little kids are great at knowing right from wrong. They think in black and white and absolutes. Teens, not so much. As they gain the ability to think hypothetically, concepts become more malleable. The good news is, this sets your child up to think about nuanced issues like social justice and equality. It allows them to advance to bigger brain work in school, past five times four and into solving for X when X is unknown in an algebra equation. To a little kid, a number can't be a letter. That's just wrong! To an adolescent, the world is less concrete, and the hypothetical becomes possible. This understanding of the adolescent brain may help parents approach conversations about rule breaking with a goal of helping kids *define the boundaries of a gray area.* Yes, X can be a number, but it can't be a song note. And yes, asking Siri for the answer may not be cheating, but you still don't know how to solve the problem for your next test. Problem not solved.

Even when it comes to social situations, teens find themselves in that hypothetical gray area often, as Gina did when the popular girls invited her over at Melanie's expense. What seems obvious to us with our fully developed and experienced adult brains is still murky territory to young people.

When to Worry

We can all expect our teens to rebel—to break rules, big and small. If your child never broke a rule, I'd worry about why they were so bent on pleasing people or what they were doing behind your back. If breaking rules is common and expected, though, you might wonder why I've devoted the first chapter in this section to the failure to follow the rules. Good question!

Rule breaking becomes a failure in a couple ways that concern me. First, when it's chronic and kids can't engage in meaningful discussion about *why* they're breaking the rules, it signals a possible disconnect from consequence, and that can feel like a call for help. A child who is a contrarian and debates all the rules will concern me far less than a child who says, "I don't care," and breaks rules for seemingly no reason. I'd want the parents of that child to do a deeper dive into what's motivating their behavior. Teen boys—more often than teen girls—who display a persistent need to be reckless and to break the rules, can be struggling with depression and should be evaluated by a therapist for ways to help.

The second way rule breaking edges toward failure has nothing to do with the child's motivation to break a rule and everything to do with how they internalize what happens next. Here, we can't predict what type of rule-breaking reaction would cause child A versus child B to feel like a failure, but we can know how best to respond to these situations to keep a child from believing this screwup says they are or aren't a good person.

For a deeper look at how a child can grow and learn from this kind of failure, let's see how using *Contain, Resolve, and Evolve* tactics worked for one family. Then, after the case study, I'll reply to some common questions about rule breaking.

MEET THE REBEL

Case Study: How Carin "Failed" to Follow the Rules

Bill and Tamara describe their daughter, Carin, as "pretty nerdy" in middle school. She didn't have a big group of friends, and she yearned for a group to belong to, like the ones she saw all around her at school and especially on her favorite shows.

When high school started, Carin tried out for the volleyball team and discovered she was good. A sudden star on the team, she was enjoying her newfound popularity a little too much. When some of her teammates started sharing videos of the latest social media challenge with each other, called "devious licks" on TikTok, Carin decided to impress them with her take.

The devious lick trend involved kids taking videos of themselves doing something dangerous or damaging on school property. Carin filmed herself removing rolls of toilet paper from the bathroom stalls and throwing them in the trash, then posted the video to TikTok.

In her case, Carin wanted the thrill of fame without hurting anyone, so immediately after recording her stunt, she returned the toilet paper to the stalls so no one would actually be caught in an embarrassing position. She even took pictures of herself doing the right thing. (This, I think, is an adorable look into Carin's character.) Unfortunately, she kept those photos for herself and uploaded the prank for everyone to see.

School administration had recently been overwhelmed with incidents of vandalism as kids returned to school post-pandemic with pent-up energy. When a student showed Carin's video to a teacher, the school decided to make an example of her. Carin was suspended for three days and kicked off the volleyball team for the rest of the year.

Bill and Tamara never thought their daughter would be so impulsive, especially since she had shown them devious licks videos on her phone before, called them stupid, and said she would never do something that dumb.

And then she did. Was this an indication that Carin wasn't who they thought she was? How would a suspension and being kicked off the team look on college applications down the road? Would Carin's newfound interest in popularity get her into increasingly worse trouble?

Gather the Truth

Tamara went directly to the school when they called about Carin's "vandalism." Those quotation marks are mine, not the school's or her parents', because Carin quickly reversed her prank and nothing was permanently damaged. Nonetheless, the school explained the chaos these incidents were taking on the environment and defended its need to send a strong message to the student body that this kind of behavior must stop. Carin happened to be the one who got caught, an important legal lesson for much later, I suppose, when she could process that it doesn't matter if you do the worst thing possible; it matters if you do anything that can make you complicit in a bigger crime. The person who drives the getaway car, for instance, still goes to jail even if he didn't rob the bank or brandish a weapon.

Speaking with the school administrators gave Tamara enough information to talk with Carin, who then shared her side of the experience. When Tamara asked Carin how another student saw the video so quickly and then told a teacher, Carin admitted she had not only posted the video to TikTok but shown several friends, too. Tamara thought this would be another important lesson down the road: Be careful who you trust.

Control the Narrative

Once Tamara and Bill had a chance to debrief, they decided not to share any additional information with parents and friends about Carin's suspension from school or the volleyball team. Even so, Tamara said parents started reaching out to her immediately. That gave her an opportunity to share the end of the story about Carin's returning the toilet paper to the stalls, which Tamara thought was key to Carin's reputation. Still, she didn't want to downplay Carin's decisions to post the prank on social media, to trust that her peers would keep her indiscretion a secret, or Tamara's belief that the school had every right to crack down on an epidemic of bad behavior. In a case like this, where the rule breaking wasn't dangerous or harmful, I think saying less probably helped the rumor mill die down more quickly. Had her parents raised a stink, poor Carin would have stayed in the spotlight a lot longer, and then parents would have found increasing opportunities to weigh in on *all* of it: the right thing to do, what they would have done, what *their* kid would never do (oh, okay), why social media is the root of all evil, what's wrong with teachers today, why the volleyball team has to suffer, why the school can't afford two-ply toilet paper, and so on.

Shrink Your Child's Exposure

The school took swift action when they suspended Carin and removed her from the team. As Tamara told the story to me, I wondered out loud if the punishment fit the crime. Tamara said they, too, were surprised by the severity of the discipline, but her focus was on Carin and how to help her process her loss so that she would learn the right lessons from it. For this reason, she and Bill felt hesitant to add more consequences to her at home, although they did shrink her exposure to social media by removing TikTok from her phone for one month and installing parental controls indefinitely so that they could talk more about what happened and the consequences that come from sharing content on social media. This, unsurprisingly, upset Carin, who already felt disconnected from friends, but her parents were more concerned about making certain Carin wouldn't repeat her mistake of impulsively posting on social media before she had time to digest what had happened.

Affirm Your Child

Bill and Tamara let Carin know they were upset that she'd made such an impulsive decision but that they also understood her true nature was demonstrated by putting the toilet paper back. After three days, Carin was allowed back in school and her parents spoke with her before her reentry about not beating herself up over this incident. They wanted her to know that even though she had to accept her punishment, it was a limited consequence. Carin was still the conscientious student, the strong athlete, the kind student teachers had paired in middle school with special needs kids on the playground or to walk to the office, and the daughter whom they enjoyed spending time with. They were direct and specific in explaining that this incident didn't change any of that.

 Resolve

Take Action

Educate

Carin's parents felt they needed to educate her about the distinction between intention and perception. Though her prank was not intended to hurt anyone, the perception was that she was taking part in a wider movement to vandalize the school that undoubtedly was causing damage, both to school property and to morale. As with breaking the law, Bill and Tamara explained that not having bad intentions won't shield you from consequences.

The distinction between intention and perception is one all kids need to better understand. A child swings a bat without looking around first and knocks someone in the back. "But I didn't mean to!" is not much consolation to the child who was hit. Parents can help kids build maturity in this area by acknowledging intention—"I know you didn't mean to"—and then redirecting to what could be done to avoid this in the future and what can be done now to make amends.

Seek Perspective

Because the school's response would have long-reaching social effects for Carin, her parents wanted to be sure that she didn't become depressed or detached from what gave her a sense of pride and identity. No longer being a member of the volleyball team stung. It helped to talk about the time left in the season and to put that into perspective. She was missing four weeks, not a year. They encouraged her to talk to her coach, who assured her that next season she would be welcomed back and that they would miss having her on the court for the remaining practices and games. In the meantime, her parents encouraged her to practice and stay in shape for the next opportunity to play, which could include joining a rec league outside school so she could stay sharp.

Update Communication

When your child flops famously like Carin, they can quickly become celebrity gossip. You may find it helpful, if rumors start to swirl, to update your communication to other parents, coaches, teachers, and close friends and family about your child's situation so that you may continue to keep their story contained and accurate.

This isn't your opportunity to rewrite the truth, convincing everyone your child was set up, unfairly accused, or victimized. Even if they were, you wouldn't have to work hard for people to know this. Reasonable adults will understand this from the facts about what happened and draw that conclusion themselves. If you campaign for people to side with you and your child against someone else, it will make other parents uncomfortable and nudge them toward doubting whether you are a reliable narrator. Consider yourself Joe Friday from the old *Drag-net* television series. Just the facts. That's all we need to know.

Engage Your Whisper Network

While you don't need to crusade for people to side with your child, or to affirm that you are still a good parent despite your child blindsiding you by getting suspended, it will put you at ease if you can speak candidly with a couple of people who have experienced a similar situation. Perhaps you reach out to another parent whose child was suspended to ask how they coped. Or it doesn't have to be such a one-to-one correlation. Just talking with another parent who has been caught off guard by their teen's behavior will reassure you that these situations, though jarring, are normal. Unburden yourself of the stress this may evoke by engaging with a small whisper network for advice on processing the experience and moving on. You'll likely be reassured to hear ways other rule-breaking kids have course corrected with time and guidance.

 Evolve

Allow Time and Space to Process

It feels cool to be a rebel in front of classmates or friends, but it's embarrassing to be caught breaking the rules by an adult. Acknowledge this with compassion then allow time for your child to process their reaction. When embarrassment is at the root of how someone feels, it could manifest itself either as a shy retreat or as an angry outburst. Anxiety can spike after an embarrassing incident. Though you may be upset with your child for what they've done, recognize that they can't move forward until they have time to process any emotions caused by this new self-consciousness. Time will help, as always, but some anxiety coping skills will be useful here, too. Breathing techniques, meditation apps, journaling, grounding, and movement are all excellent ways to process these emotions.

Triage Your Fears

Rule breaking elicits all kinds of parental fears, some about our children's character and some about our own reputations as parents. Take a moment to think through and list the fears this brings up for you. If this exercise produces some anxiety for you, you might also consider why. Did you grow up in a house that felt unpredictable or volatile or where you needed to keep the peace? Were you expected to be perfect to compensate for stressful family dynamics? You might have reacted to that by being a strident people pleaser at home and secret rebel on the side. Or maybe rule breaking of any kind made you extremely nervous. How you react to your current fears is rooted in how you were treated as a young person. It helps to borrow this lens and weed out your own childhood traumas from legitimate worries about your teen's circumstances, which are presumably quite different from what yours were at the same age.

From the vast world of worrisome things this rule-breaking failure might bring up, here are some possibilities:

> I'm worried my child will get a bad reputation with the teachers and administrators.
> I'm worried other parents will tell their kids to stay away from my child.
> I'm worried a suspension will cause my child to fall behind in schoolwork.
> I'm worried being kicked off the team will cause my child to lose confidence and maybe end their sports career.
> I'm worried people will think I'm a bad parent because my child got in trouble so publicly.

I'm worried my child won't learn from this and will keep breaking rules to impress their friends.

I'm worried my child thinks being popular is more important than having integrity.

After you've listed your concerns and shelved any that can't be addressed in the next twenty-four hours, it's time to get to work doing simply what you can to mitigate any immediate worries. Of the fears listed above, many are, as usual, out of your control. The one I think is the best candidate for handling in the first twenty-four-hour period is the concern over falling behind on schoolwork. As hard as it feels, I'd shelve the others because they aren't time sensitive and, instead, focus on coaching my child through sending emails to each of their teachers about missing school and trying hard not to fall behind on work.

Face One Fear First

Starting with the small action of emailing teachers together (the email coming from your child with your guidance on wording and formatting) might produce more than one good result. First, your child will get the information they need to stay up to date on schoolwork. Second, showing a proactive, can-do attitude should impress teachers and soften that fear you have about how teachers perceive your child because they broke school rules. And third, focusing on just one task can help a child move from feeling helpless to feeling in command of their fate, which will have a boosting effect on their self-esteem.

Uphold *Your Child's Bill of Rights*

When your child fails to follow the rules, you may be tempted to shrink their world drastically so they have fewer opportunities to break rules again. In some cases, this may be entirely warranted to keep your child safe. But where safety isn't of primary concern, as in Carin's case, being overly restrictive will backfire. Your child still needs access to some rights from *Your Child's Bill of Rights* to move forward and grow. For Carin, who failed to follow the rules, I think the following rights are most important.

Right: Negotiate and Self-Advocate

When your child breaks the rules, it's tempting to think they've forfeited the right to advocate for themselves or to negotiate for their best interests. We sometimes adopt a prison-style mentality toward our kid's mess-ups—*you did the crime; you can do the time.* True, kids need to be held accountable for breaking rules and consequences are important, but suffering in silence is not the best way to learn. Kids who feel heard by their parents during times of stress, and who are invited to collaborate on the best way to move forward after failure, build respectful negotiation and critical thinking skills that will serve them well once they leave home. When you find yourself saying to your college freshman, "Talk with your professor about whether you can have an extension on that project" or "Let your manager know you have some ideas for improving the project flow," you want them to feel confident in their ability to speak up for themselves, and they will, if you've respectfully engaged them in this process long before they leave the nest.

Right: Choose Their Own Friends and Gather with Peers

Breaking a rule just to look cool in front of kids at school can be a hard thing for parents to accept. Recall the biological drive tweens and teens feel to connect with their peers, and remind yourself it's that very drive that will lead them to become independent, live outside your home, and support themselves someday. Even kids who break the rules need to know when and how they can reconnect with peers. Maybe they won't be allowed right away, but do let them know when it will happen, whether that's based on a calendar date or when they meet specific criteria. Keeping this a mystery is a power play, and your child will be easier to live with if they know when they can reconnect with their friends.

Right: Receive the Benefit of the Doubt

You may have a strong hunch as to why your child failed to follow the rules. Chances are, with your experience and insight, you know what triggered their failure better than they do. Still, when your child explains what led to their breaking a rule, give them the benefit of the doubt. Teens are entrenched in a narrow view of their confusing lives, and they lack the advantage of your broader, adult perspective. It's okay to take them at their word. Fighting over the why of it all or trying to get them to see it from your perspective isn't helpful. With experience, they'll see things differently, but for now this is their truth.

See New Things

At the end of the Evolve phase of failure management, it is every parent's responsibility to say, "This situation has reached its conclusion and we are moving on." Don't be afraid to say this out loud to your child. How liberating it would be for them to hear from you that you can see what they've learned from this failure, just as you can see how they'll grow from it. Be explicit because we all benefit from a succinct summary of what we've learned to help it stick. "I can tell you've learned a lot from this experience, like to be more careful about who you trust to share private information with, not to share things on social media that you don't want everyone to see, and that you understand even if your intentions aren't bad you can still get in serious trouble. I think you'll move forward with a better understanding of the risks involved in breaking rules, especially when you do it so you will fit in. I'm so sorry you had to go through this, but ultimately I think it's made you smarter and stronger and no one can deny that's a good thing!" Then promise you don't intend to keep bringing it up, but if at any point your child wants to revisit this incident to talk about some aspect of it again, you're there for it.

Quick Answers to Common Questions About Ways Kids Fail to Follow the Rules

Q: I asked my fifteen-year-old son to stay home and watch his ten-year-old sister while my husband and I went out to have dinner. When I came home, I found my daughter alone, watching a movie, with her brother nowhere in sight! She told me he went out with some friends to get food but would be back in an hour. When I immediately called my son and told him to get home, he was defensive, saying, "You never said I couldn't leave the house at all. I just left to pick up some food. You've left her alone for an hour before!" I think he should have known exactly what I meant when I asked him to watch his sister. How do I get across to him that this behavior is unacceptable and manipulative?

A: Yes, I would be livid, too. Yes, the behavior is unacceptable. Where we may run into a gray area is whether it was also manipulative. Your son probably used his newly acquired hypothetical thinking skills to justify breaking the rules and leaving his sister unattended. Here's how I imagine his thought process going: First, he'd seen you had left his sister home alone before (though I know that was at your discretion, different circumstances, and so on, but he's not thinking that way). Second, he prioritized his FOMO (fear of missing out) over the need to stay home while his sister was just watching a movie anyway. And third,

he guessed he could get away with it, and that—in and of itself—
probably meant to him it wasn't such a bad infraction.

Adolescents can do a lot of mental gymnastics to make rule breaking seem okay.

You won't always see it when your child is bending the rules to meet
their needs and desires, but when you do, in the case of your son being
a bad babysitter, here are a few different ways you could respond.

You could opt for *natural* consequences, letting nature take its
course, and whatever fallout comes from your teenage son's bad decision he will have to endure, but natural consequences can take a long
time to surface. Plus, natural consequences would cause collateral damage to his sister. Maybe their relationship becomes fraught because he
blames her for his parents' anger, or she blames him for making her feel
scared or neglected. I wouldn't be willing to wait this one out at her
expense.

Lots of parents opt for an unrelated, high-impact punishment in
hopes of causing the child enough agony that they'll recall the punishment next time they're tempted to make a similar bad decision. The
most popular punishment in this category is *take away his phone to hit
him where it hurts.* This approach is built on a premise that we can train
teens to behave how we want by inspiring fear of a contrived consequence. Sometimes this works, but it's more likely a teen will become
enraged by this type of punishment, and they'll lose sight of what they
did wrong as they ruminate on how mean and unfair you are. This type
of punishment doesn't prompt the child to reflect on what they did
wrong.

You can also employ *logical* consequences, which are outcomes you
determine (as opposed to ones that are naturally occurring) that relate
directly to what your child did wrong. In this case, you could point out
to your son that you trusted him to watch his sister, which he could not
do when she was out of his sight; therefore, this erosion of trust means

he will need to stay in this weekend instead of going out with friends, because you don't trust him to make good decisions right now. Perhaps, you explain to him that after you talk about how he took advantage of the gray area, and when he can show both you and his sister that he understands what he did, you will find that trust again.

You're going to run into lots of this gray area thinking with your adolescent, so give some thought as to which approach you prefer for the long run, and be prepared to respond with the best choice, instead of the one that's most emotionally satisfying to you in the moment.

Q: When I point out that my child has broken a family rule, they act completely blindsided. "You never told me I wasn't supposed to do that!" How am I supposed to react?

A: Try this: "I assumed this was something you would know without being told explicitly, but you're right. I never spelled this one out. So, no hard feelings today and we'll call it a freebie. In the future, now that you know, the consequence for breaking this rule will be [insert logical and reasonable consequence]. But even though you didn't realize you broke a rule, it still creates a bit of work for me. I have to [clean up from the mess the dog made when you didn't walk him, catch up on chores I couldn't do when I was calling around trying to figure out where you were, and so on]. I know this was an honest mistake on your part, and I would love your help fixing it. How can we both handle the unintended aftermath together?"

Q: We have a reasonable curfew for our teen, but they continue to ignore it. I need my sleep so I'm often in bed well before they are due home, and sometimes I fall asleep waiting. How can I get my child to stop breaking curfew and respect that I need sleep to be a happy parent and a productive person the next day?

A: Here's one thing you could consider: Ditch the curfew. Hear me out.

If a person continues breaking a rule despite all your best efforts to keep them in line, ask yourself if it's both reasonable and valuable to maintain that rule. If curfew is the main area where your teen deviates but otherwise they're responsive to rules, boundaries, and expectations, they may have a valid reason for wanting to come home when an event ends or when others disperse, instead of according to a time that feels arbitrary. This is not a solution for every teen, but some do quite well with sending texts to update parents on where they are and when they'll be home, instead of needing to be home by a set time each night.

If this isn't an option for you, you can continue setting expectations they won't meet, and then you will need to respond with the appropriate consequence. For instance, "Since you didn't come home before your curfew, I lost sleep worrying, and now I'm too tired to buy groceries and make dinner. I have to shift that responsibility to you for tonight so I can catch up on sleep." This will probably cause an argument. Get ready. But if you are willing to stick by what you said and ignore the negative feedback you get from your teen, you might inspire them to realize that being home on time is easier than having to make up for it the next day. Both approaches are totally fine, so pick whichever feels right to you.

Q: My teen pushes back on what is considered appropriate dress and behavior in public. For example, they often violate school dress code. They dye their hair strange colors, which wouldn't be a big deal, but it's not allowed at their place of work, and they end up losing shifts and income when they're sent home. I'm fairly tolerant, but they dress in ways even I consider inappropriate when visiting my parents or other older relatives (for example, shirts with lewd or offensive messages). How can I allow my child to express who they are without feeling stifled while still respecting the rules and decorum of certain situations?

A: Here we get into some nuanced territory between hard-and-fast rules and social expectations. When it comes to rules about dress that are required by an institution, the choices are to follow them, break them and deal with the consequences, or more formally protest them. If your child feels strongly against the dress code at school, I'd encourage them to take that fight out of their head and into the court of public opinion. They can write an op-ed for the school paper or organize a petition to present to the administration. Make yourself clear that without evidence to support their position, they're probably just tilting at windmills. If they can support their claim with real data and not just feelings, they stand a chance at effecting real change.

As for hair color and work, I doubt there is much you or your child can do when the rules are at the discretion of an employer. So, in this case, natural consequences will probably handle the situation for you while you sit back to see what happens as your teen learns to navigate managers and workplace rules. Losing income is no fun, so if you want them to learn from this, don't subsidize them, unless you think the rule is bogus and want to!

Finally, dressing appropriately for people you care about feels like the most important issue here to me. Make a case for not upsetting other people by choosing clothes that can still be edgy but not insulting. In the event of a standoff over this, you have a couple choices here, too. Either you tell your child they can't go if they insist on wearing something offensive, or you can alert your family that this has become a thing and you're enlisting their support. "Junior is coming in a T-shirt that I hate. You will probably hate it, too. I apologize in advance. We've discussed it, but he is holding his ground that the shirt is fine. Please don't make any comments about his appearance—including the terrible T-shirt. I think if we ignore it, he'll pass through this phase more quickly. If we insist that he's wrong and make him change, he's going to dig in his heels and not come. At this point, it's more important to us that he spend time with family than prove a point in isolation."

The Silver Lining About Failing to Follow the Rules

It can be shocking and emotionally draining the first time you catch your child breaking an important rule. For kids like Carin, they'll feel self-conscious, guilty, or embarrassed enough to learn quickly when it's not worth crossing that line.

It can also be exhausting to deal with a contrarian teen who pushes back against little rules all the time. The silver lining to being the Rebel is that there are lots of rules in our world that need changing. A young person who looks at certain conventions, expectations, and even laws with enough of a rebellious eye will work hard to create change in their little corner of society. The key to helping rule breakers use their energy for good, not evil, is teaching them to direct it toward worthwhile causes backed by serious thought and research. Point your young revolutionary in that direction to satisfy their need for dissent.

CHAPTER SEVEN

Failure to Take Care of Their Body: The Daredevil

Salamanders can regenerate their limbs, did you know? Lose an arm, and they grow another. Starfish, too. Lizards can grow new tails if theirs are torn off. And the African spiny mouse is the only mammal on record that can lose an actual *chunk* of its body to a predator bite and grow new skin—not scar tissue—with brand-new sweat glands, hair follicles, and cartilage. Nature is mind-blowing, and . . . wouldn't it be amazing to be the mom of an African spiny mouse?

I suppose it's a trade-off. Mouse life expectancy is only four to seven years and I'd probably shriek and jump on a chair every time my child entered the room, but still. Imagine the comfort you'd take in knowing that if your Daredevil did something utterly reckless, like jumping from the top of a slide on the playground, or touching a metal pole with their tongue during a snowstorm, or skateboarding into the street without looking, they could regenerate their leg, their tongue, or a portion of their scalp.

Humans don't get this kind of anatomical safety net, though, and that means as parents we're very often on the verge of having a heart attack. And while there are measures we can take to protect our kids from hurting themselves—for example, making them watch *A Christmas Story* so they don't try sticking their tongue to a metal pole this winter—more often we have to hold our breath and hope for the best.

In this chapter, we'll look at some ways kids play the Daredevil by putting themselves in physical danger, but to do that, we'll need to acknowledge that not all threats to our bodies are equal. For one thing, we're human. We're fragile. We can't avoid getting hurt. I can't so much as wear clogs without twisting my ankle on an uneven sidewalk, so the prospect of keeping a teen in a bubble of safety when they're walking around in lanky, unbalanced bodies, with sleep-deprived and impulse-driven brains, is just not remotely possible. We need to agree from the outset of this chapter that we can't stop kids from putting themselves into situations where they could get hurt. They're going to play sports and take dares and learn to drive or ride mass transit, after all. Our focus needs to be on learning how we can help our Daredevils cultivate the skill of pausing before taking a risk and then teaching them how to minimize the damage when they don't.

Let's see how using *Contain, Resolve, and Evolve* tactics worked for one family when their son hurt himself quite seriously. Then, after the case study, I'll reply to some common questions about kids taking care of themselves.

MEET THE DAREDEVIL

Case Study: How Noah "Failed" to Take Care of His Body

Sandra and her husband, Terrance, were celebrating a friend's birthday when they got the call from another parent that almost stopped their hearts: Their son Noah had been taken to the hospital a few minutes earlier by ambulance. He'd gotten into some alcohol at a friend's house. A lot of alcohol. They should head to the hospital right away.

When Sandra and Terrance arrived at the ER, they were led to a room where Noah was hooked up to monitors with an oxygen tube in his nose. He would occasionally stop breathing, and the nurse would shake him to force an inhale. His internal organs were undamaged, a fact that seemed to surprise the medical staff. He had been throwing up for hours on end. After multiple police interviews, a clean CAT scan, and his body rehydrated, Noah was released. It had been only five hours since he had been admitted, and he was going home with his parents. They were grateful but in shock. They felt as nervous that night as when the hospital let them take their newborn baby home only fourteen years earlier. Could they be trusted to keep this child safe and alive? What would happen now?

It was the middle of the night when they arrived back home, so Sandra and Terrance brought their six-foot-tall, fourteen-year-old baby to sleep in bed between them, where they stared at him until sunrise, watching his chest rise and fall to be sure he was still breathing, as they did when he was a newborn in his crib.

The next day, their phones blew up with calls and texts from friends: theirs, his, and friends of friends who'd heard the news. Noah was suddenly the tabloid star of his high school. It was time for containment.

 Contain

Control the Narrative

The buzz was all about "what happened last night," and Noah's story was getting twisted. Rumors circulated that he had died. Sandra and Terrance quickly assured their closest friends that Noah was, in fact, home and safe. They would be figuring out their next steps and be able to share more details later, but for now that was the only important news they had to share.

Gather the Truth

Because Noah had blacked out, his parents couldn't rely on his account of what happened at the party. As texts and calls poured in, they leaned on the people who seemed closest to the events for details, even to questions that Noah claimed he *could* answer. Questions they asked included these: Where did the kids get the alcohol? Was anyone supervising the party? What was the timeline of events? Who called 911?

These logistical questions were the easiest to answer. The boys took the booze from a parent's liquor cabinet. The adult on site was in a different part of the home, there if they needed anything, but the kids were essentially unsupervised. One child called an older sibling who immediately called 911. Each of these answers provided points of education for these parents that they would address and I'll highlight in the Resolve phase of this study.

The question of motivation was hardest to answer and the one Sandra and Terrance wanted to crack open most of all. *Why?* Why had Noah been drinking at all? With teens, the cause of shocking behavior is hardly ever cut and dried. Questions tormenting parents in a situation like this range from *Is my child an addict?* to *Is my child an idiot?* and unfortunately the only way to get to those answers is to let enough time and experience accumulate that you can make an assessment as to the why of it all. Still, in this phase of truth gathering, though you may not get to the heart of the problem quickly, you'll be able to ascertain some of the factors that contributed to the situation at hand. The parents talked to many sources, including Noah, who could explain his behavior only by saying he didn't realize how bad it would be. He had a water bottle filled with a mix of hard liquors and he just chugged it. Terrance and Sandra felt this incident was the result of thoughtlessness, impulsivity, and probably an effort to show off and fit in, not a desire to hurt himself or an extension of an established partying habit. This early assessment would guide their next moves.

Shrink Your Child's Exposure

Sandra and Terrance were shocked by Noah's decision to drink (so young! so much!), so they decided grounding him was their best recourse in addressing the situation, as much to give them all time to process and learn from the experience as to punctuate the severity of what he'd done.

Because Noah's case was near death, containment meant not only wrangling a problem back down to size but actually keeping Noah inside the home to protect him from his own vulnerability and impulses. Sandra worked from home and Terrance took a few days off so they could all gather their bearings. Until they could work through the initial shock enough to make a rational plan to move forward, all three of them hunkered down.

Affirm Your Child

It was important to both Terrance and Sandra that they balance their own anger and fear from the incident with their overwhelming love for Noah. They both recall hugging him too much, sniffing his hair, and a wave of relief that would come over them every time they reminded themselves that he was still alive.

Though the consequences he faced at home were the most severe he'd ever experienced, and his parents stuck to them without exceptions, they also made it clear to Noah that he was loved and valued. While he was a captive audience, they did what they could to reassure him of this, by telling him he was loved and nonverbally as well, like making his favorite foods or watching his choice of movies together.

Take Action

Define Consequences

Noah's safety was so clearly at risk after such a devastatingly close call with death. His parents felt that shrinking his world, the initial action they took during the Contain phase, was key to his ongoing safety. Now that they had time to think more purposefully, their plan was to keep Noah home with them for two months, except for going to school. The terms of his grounding were as follows: He would be allowed to talk to as many friends as needed briefly at the outset to let them know he was out of circuit; then he could have access to his phone for only a short time each evening to touch base via text. Sandra and Terrance knew their priorities were to put the brakes on Noah's boundary-pushing momentum and to send a clear message that he needed to follow their rules to stay safe. At the same time, they recognized that completely limiting his social interactions could endanger him more, because his (age appropriate) drive to maintain new friendships and manage his damaged reputation could force him to break rules and go behind their backs to repair his social connections.

Often, parents throw the kitchen sink at scary situations because big failures deserve all the punishments. Be mindful, though, that your consequences meet your goals and aren't arbitrarily harsh. You should maintain strict boundaries and hold tight to your consequences while still allowing that your child needs to feel supported.

After you decide on the appropriate consequences, be sure to include bonuses during time served, like those I mentioned in chapter 5. Sandra and Terrance increased Noah's phone time incrementally, eventually allowed friends to visit for family dinners, then added unsupervised visits in the family playroom, and, finally, gave him early release by one week for good behavior. (Having those bonuses built into the plan, by the way, is one way to make sticking to the plan easier.) Sandra created a contract outlining the terms of the arrangement, and all three of them signed it.

Noah's parents' unwavering commitment to the terms of the contract was crucial. It can be tempting to start bending rules and making exceptions for your child when they are hurting. Don't confuse conveying empathy or compassion, both kind and appropriate feelings toward your child, with softening your boundaries, which is a disservice; because this was a potentially life-ending event, it was important that Sandra and Terrance remain faithful to their plan. This would convey to Noah two things, one a comfort and the other a warning. First, Noah would understand from this that when his world gets out of control, his parents can be relied on to bring it back into balance. This is a relief to all teens for whom the experiences of growing up can often be overwhelming. And second, should he ever be presented with the opportunity to do something this foolish again, he should remember that his parents didn't walk back his consequences before, and think twice.

Educate

Because Noah was taken to the hospital by ambulance, police were called to the scene, and he was given a citation and ordered to participate in a county-mandated substance abuse program for one month. Twice a week, for two hours at a time, he and Sandra attended together.

"Maybe that seems like overkill for a first-time offense," Sandra explained, "especially because the program seemed mostly geared at kids who had multiple arrests and were in gangs and at risk of being sent to juvie. I'm not saying I wanted him scared straight but . . . okay maybe a little. I was happy to have someone else hammering home the message. I wanted the danger he put himself in to sink into his head, and I needed it to come from every direction, because I was scared."

Rebuild Trust

Noah's parents' fear for his safety and doubts about his decision making didn't just go away when the terms of his grounding were complete. When Noah was allowed to hang out with friends again, he still needed to provide them with convincing reassurance that he wouldn't be drinking.

Noah came up with the solution for rebuilding trust on his own: He would FaceTime them from hangouts as much as they needed so they could see and hear for themselves that he was okay. This is not the kind of close monitoring I'd recommend parents insist on normally, but for Sandra and Terrance, whose son almost died the last time he went to hang out with friends, it seemed a reasonable bridge toward rebuilding trust.

Apologize

Noah's experience, though deeply personal, affected many members of his community. His parents took him the day after he came home from the hospital to apologize to the parents who owned the house where the drinking occurred, and to a neighbor who rode with him in the ambulance, to apologize for the fear and anguish he must have caused them all. Sandra felt it was important that the neighbor who rode with him, praying by his side while he was unconscious, have the opportunity to see Noah upright and to hug him, which she did with much relief.

Update Communication

When a story gets this kind of traction, it often gets spun in different directions. People like to know what happened, how it happened, and what's being done so it doesn't happen again.

In Noah's case, the parents in his community banded together quickly. Concern spiked that the boys in ninth grade were moving too fast and were in over their heads, so parents of that group met for an hour in person to talk about how they could support each other and their kids. During a crisis of safety, a communal meeting is a great way to get the message straight, plan for the future, and raise awareness and accountability. Here, in person, Sandra and Terrance shared the parts of their experience they felt comfortable talking about, including the plan to keep Noah home for the next couple months, except for going to school. The response from the other parents was empathetic and pro-tective. "It could have been any of these kids," they reassured Sandra and Terrance, and they vowed as a group to keep a closer eye on them all and stay in close touch with each other regarding safety. Parents bought locks for their liquor cabinets. They resolved to keep a closer eye on each other's kids when they were over. And since most of these friends had met recently at the start of high school, one parent offered to make a spreadsheet with all family member names and cell phones to ensure they could communicate easily with each other about where the boys were hanging out and share updates to any last-minute changing plans, which any parent of a ninth grader knows are almost constant. "The guys are gathering up their things and want to head to Stuart's to play video games. Is there a parent at Stuart's?" "I'm here! Send them my way!" They didn't keep up this close monitoring for the rest of high school, but for the rest of freshman year these parents felt they'd escaped a tragedy and agreed that for a while it was important to slow the group's momentum and create an environment where the boys knew the adults were watching while not taking away their need to spend time with each other.

 Evolve

Allow Time and Space to Process

Sandra describes Noah's evolution through his containment period exactly as if he were going through the stages of grief. His first response to being grounded was denial, in a sort of "this can't be happening to me" shock. Next came anger. Noah agonized over the unfairness that he should be kept away from his friends for so long! What if, when he finally went back to his friend group, they were all mad at him for getting them caught? His biggest concern was that since they'd just met at the start of the year, they'd drop him and move on. Then came bargaining, the anger subsiding into begging, pleading for the chance to make things better with his friends. Then a sort of mini depression as Noah resigned himself to his room and a deep sadness over his condition took over. And finally, acceptance as he rejoined the family to watch TV and talk more openly with his parents about his sadness and confusion and—at long last—to acknowledge and apologize for scaring his parents so badly.

Sandra, for her part, felt hurt that initially Noah seemed most worried about the effect this would have on his friends while she was suffering, and Terrance agreed that upset him, too; but both said that, in hindsight, allowing Noah to process the event in his own way worked out better than trying to force him to see their perspective too soon. Because they did not fight how he progressed through theses stages, he ultimately arrived where they wanted.

Triage Your Fears

Part of not getting stuck in moments of failure is allowing for closure. When safety is concerned, this is always harder to do for parents than kids. Sandra and Terrance might have been left with some looming questions that would make it hard for them to give Noah the freedom he needs to return to his regularly scheduled life.

Questions like:

Did their parenting make him do this?

Would he KEEP doing this?

Would other parents tell their kids to stay away from him?

Would teachers presume bad things about him?

Was Noah setting foot onto the path of addiction, and would the worst night of their lives keep repeating itself down the road?

Most of these questions will only be answered with time. Rather than chew on them constantly, notice when your fears multiply instead of becoming more manageable; then revisit the step of triaging your fears to determine what you can act on in the next twenty-four hours. As a reminder, if you can do something to lighten that fear within a day, make a list of those fears only and address them. If you can't, make another list and promise yourself you will shelve that list for a set number of days or weeks. You don't have to give those fears away, because they're still valid and meaningful to you, just put them on hold.

Face One Fear First

Let's consider fears around safety first. When discussing *Your Child's Bill of Rights,* I wrote there should be no double jeopardy—no using this event as a means of punishment more than once. Fear wants you to keep harping on this failure because it tells you if you don't, you'll stop paying attention and it will happen again. Fear wants all your vigilance. But it's wrong.

While Noah's kind of failure ranks high on the list of worst-case scenarios for parents, the scenario that ranks one higher is that this wasn't a one-off and could happen over and over again. Any parent's brain might wander there, fearing a *Groundhog Day* movie of living the same bad experience again and again. Still, this doesn't mean parents should condemn their child over and over for the same crime because they are scared of that possible outcome. Ironically, you'd be casting your kid in a *Groundhog Day* of his own in order to avoid being in one yourself. And let's face it, locking your child in the house and telling them you don't trust them will end in the exact opposite way than you hope.

Yes, it's terrifying to let your kid have another chance when their last one ended in an emergency room. This is why it's so important to structure their return incrementally, so you can observe and make decisions based on what you see, not what you fear.

The other big parental fear here is one of perception. Will this child's scandal brand him in a way that negatively affects his social and academic life, and what will this do to his self-esteem? Will he ever recover? It's understandable that this is where a parent's brain automatically takes them, but it never helps to catastrophize a situation by predicting the worst-case scenario. Some of the things we discussed in this chapter, like keeping communication succinct and positive, will lend themselves to protecting the child's reputation. After that, the next best thing a parent can do is let their child show people who they really are; keeping them away from the public eye for too long will only allow people to draw the wrong conclusions.

Uphold *Your Child's Bill of Rights*

Your child has hurt themselves. They have gone through containment and resolution of their issue with you. What's next? What rights come into play here, and how can you negotiate those safely moving forward?

In Noah's case, these three rights from *Your Child's Bill of Rights* seem most relevant to his ability to move past, and grow from, this incident.

Right: Choose Their Own Friends and Gather with Peers

Oh, hell no, you're thinking.

I get it. But parents don't get to just stop their kids from being social because they were bad at it initially. These things take *practice*. And you can't be in the room with him everywhere from here on out, so some of that practice must be independent. Your rights come into play here too, though. You deserve to have some peace of mind as you work through your child's return to their social life. Noah's offer to allow his parents to see him on FaceTime, for example, was a good stepping-stone to expanded independence for him while still respecting his parents' right to feel less terrified.

Right: Receive the Benefit of the Doubt

No one should be asked to keep paying for the same crime. Parents need to remember that their child wants to do the best they can and, if they're having trouble with that, they may need more serious interventions. Be careful, though, not to lump normal teen behaviors in with a bigger offense. Your child got caught drinking to the point of throwing up (scary and illegal) and they sleep late every weekend (annoying) and they leave empty granola bar boxes in the pantry (eh). Beware the danger of collecting their faults. Noah's parents should draw clear lines in their minds about what matters here and not add extra weight to each future mistake he makes by dangling his drinking incident off the arm of the scale. This is only going to send that child into hiding. And that's where kids are least likely to be safe.

Right: Make Mistakes and Have Opportunities to Fix Them

"But I can't relax and let my child out there, because he might hurt himself again."

Not might. He will. Not in the same way, hopefully, but in some way. He is a human being who, like all of us, will make bad choices or face bad luck and get hurt from time to time. When Noah makes his next mistake, whatever it may be, his parents can invite him into the process of making amends. Apologizing, coming up with a plan to do better, and reflecting, all can be helpful here.

How Community Can Help

One reason we might have difficulty learning from failure is our very human inability to ignore bad feelings (shame, embarrassment, pain) and redirect our attention to what the experience might teach us for next time. In other words, failure feels bad, and we often dwell there in the muck instead of compartmentalizing the pain and focusing our attention on what serves us better.

We all know, firsthand, how terribly hard it is to get over ourselves. We clean, bury, and ignore evidence so we don't have to think about what we've done. The more energy we spend on those things, the less energy we have to put toward growth. Which leads me to the question: But *how* do we stop ruminating on our bad feelings?

Noah's story might provide an answer. Compassion, support, and acceptance are key to moving on. All people, but especially children, deserve to know we love them and that our love and acceptance are not rooted in their accomplishments. When we do this for a child who has failed, they can stop putting their energy into concealing their failure and instead begin to move on and learn from it. Keep in mind the science behind Donna Jackson Nakazawa's Community Effect (which I first referred to in chapter 5) that explains the powerful physical and mental effects of communal support and acceptance, without which we all suffer in serious ways.

I interviewed another parent whose child's story was similar to Noah's in two important ways: It involves a child who got into trouble with underage substance abuse, and it was thanks to a supportive community that they got back on track. An important distinction, though, is that the child in the next story had a different motivation for using. While Noah's failure was one of impulse, this next child was struggling with an undiagnosed mental health issue that led to using drugs. As I mentioned in the introduction to this book, *mental health struggles aren't failures*. I share this anecdote to highlight the lifesaving and life-changing effect a community of caring adults can have when they intervene on behalf of kids who have done something to create distance between them and the adults who take care of them.

Kami is a single mom whose bright, loving daughter, Marisa, was offered a debate scholarship to a prestigious university. Her first year there, she became overwhelmed with depression and began self-medicating with marijuana. It was her debate coach who initially noticed the changes in her behavior. At first, she noticed Marisa texting in the debate group at all hours of the night, often with grandiose plans for tournaments, sometimes slamming certain team members for their lack of commitment, effort, knowledge, or skill, and then she'd sleep through practices.

Her coach saw that something unusual was happening. As Marisa started to withdraw more from the team, her coach could have let her fade out or quit. It would have been easy to write off her strange behavior and stay focused on the team and the students who showed up at practice and needed help. Instead, she made it a point to find Marisa in her dorm and talk with her. When she did, Marisa denied anything was wrong at all. She became indignant at the implication that she needed help. So what if she was missing some of the practices? She was still one of the best members on the team, and she would make it count at tournaments.

Marisa's coach saw more than a student with too much confidence. She saw signs of possible mental illness, and she reached out to Kami so her family could figure out how to help Marisa. Because her coach thought to intervene, Kami was able to get her daughter the help she needed, including a diagnosis of depression as well as something called THC-induced psychosis, which better explained her manic behavior. The marijuana kids consume today is much stronger than what parents remember from their youth, and for those who are susceptible, THC-induced psychosis can happen even without extensive use.

Marisa also took a semester off to regroup and get well. When she returned to school after her semester off, she found she needed to repair her relationship with a few teammates she had angered, and she worked on that by being honest about what she was going through and taking responsibility for hurt she caused. Most of her teammates welcomed her with open arms. A few opened up about their own, or their family members', experiences with mental illness, and Marisa became the de facto support person for teammates who needed a safe, nonjudgmental person to confide in about their emotional lives. Again, Marisa having depression wasn't a failure, but a casual observer looking in from the outside might have seen her behavior as a failure, without understanding the bigger picture. Thanks to her coach's commitment to looking deeper, Marisa received the help she needed and is now thriving in college.

Quick Answers to Common Questions About How Kids Fail to Take Care of Their Bodies

Q: My son hurts himself all the time in astonishing feats of Jackass-*like daredevilry. Will I ever be able to relax?*
A: Yes, I think you will. Either he'll outgrow his impulse to jump with-

out looking or you'll get used to it. In the meantime, I'm sure you'd like a way to keep him out of body casts and yourself off tranquilizers.

Begin by observing when these types of injuries occur most often. Is it only when friends are watching? Does this happen after several late nights with little sleep? Or is this something you see when your child is acting more emotionally needy than usual? If you play detective, you might notice that these incidents spike in relationship to what else is happening in your child's day, week, or life. If you can tie the behavior to other conditions, that will give you a head start on how to address it. A neuropsychological evaluation may indicate if medicine or therapeutic coping skills would help control impulsivity. If it's more of a showing-off instinct, some thoughtful conversations and potentially some reasonable consequences (guess who's going to start paying some urgent care copays, kiddo?) could be enough to help redirect your child. Maybe, and I'd bet on this one no matter what, he needs an outlet for his energy that creates opportunity to take big risks but in a safer way. Bottom line, pay attention to when this happens and what else is going on before you make a diagnosis and act on it.

Q: Why isn't cutting in this chapter?
A: Great question. If you're looking for information on self-harm, I have included it in chapter 11, "Failure to Handle Their Feelings."

Q: My tween sneaks junk food at every opportunity and balks at the healthy meals I prepare. How can I persuade them to take better care of their body by eating more nutritious foods and exercising regularly?
A: You can't. This is a huge topic and an emotionally loaded one, so I'll refer you to some great resources on body acceptance, nutrition, and movement. For expert advice I trust on our developing bodies, seek out Rebecca Scritchfield's work in *Body Kindness,* read Ellyn Satter's books explaining the division of responsibilities in feeding and eating, follow Maya Feller's Instagram examination of nutrition and wellness in

BIPOC communities, subscribe to Virginia Sole-Smith's well-researched *Burnt Toast* newsletter, and listen to the funny and data-driven podcast *Maintenance Phase.*

That's a huge assignment, so in the meantime know this: Between ages twelve and sixteen, boys gain an average of fifty to sixty pounds, and between ages eleven and fourteen, girls gain an average of forty to fifty pounds. Adolescence is when kids start to gain weight so they can build adult bodies. It's hard to gain sixty pounds on spinach alone, not to mention carbs and dairy and sugar taste great. It's okay if these foods increase during adolescence. Choosing what goes into their bodies feels liberating and grown up. When you try to control this, tweens and teens fight it, either outright or behind your back. Most of us don't eat the way we did in middle school anyway. Our palates, social interests around food, and understanding of how food makes us feel evolve over time, within our social circles, and not because Mom or Dad or Coach told us we were doing it wrong. Bottom line, not eating or moving the way parents would prefer is not a failure, and if you spotlight these, even gently, as areas needing improvement, your efforts may backfire into disordered eating, poor self-esteem, or damaged relationships. Yes, there are things you can do to steer your child in a direction that teaches them to feed themselves well and move with joy, but consult the experts listed above before you begin.

Q: My tween pierced his own ear, then hid it under a hoodie for weeks. Now he has a raging infection. What's worse, failing to take care of his body or lying about it? Do I dole out two punishments, one for the ear and one for the cover-up?

A: I have a feeling most parents think lying is the bigger crime, but for me it's the piercing. That's not because I think ear piercing is a crime, but because lying is just so common in adolescence it doesn't really freak me out. I don't love it, but I get it. Kids lie for lots of reasons, and it ramps up during the tween and teen years. It's not an indication, by itself, that your child lacks integrity, and most teens outgrow this bad habit. You should certainly address the lying so your child knows you see it. Sometimes being called out is enough to put a stop to this kind of thing. You can also tie some natural consequences to lying, if the deceit is persistent enough that it affects your ability to trust your child, especially with regard to their ability to stay safe. For example, "Because we've had several incidents of lying recently, my trust is eroding. We're going to lower your curfew/reduce your social life/enforce more home-work or chore checks until I have a better sense I can trust you at your word." Remain as calm and matter of fact about the lying as possible. When your child learns you can respond to their experiences—even their failures—without overblown emotions, they're less likely to lie. But when they think you can't handle the truth, well, you're facing down Jack Nicholson screaming at your face in *A Few Good Men*.

Back to the infected ear. The second reason this is a bigger issue to me than the lying is that an infection that gets into the bloodstream can be life threatening. There are some natural, lesser consequences here, too—for example, a gross-looking ear instead of a cool-looking pierc-ing. You will want to tailor your reactions to your child's disposition. A teen who is mortified won't need you to make the point crystal clear. But for a teen who doesn't seem to get it, punch up those consequences by making your child call the doctor to schedule an appointment for antibiotics, purchase the medicine with their own money, and talk with you about how infections work in the body.

Q: What if your child keeps failing to take care of their body? For example, what if they get caught smoking pot, get in trouble, but then keep doing it. What should parents do when this stuff happens repeatedly?
A: If you're seeing a pattern of behavior, your best action is to involve professional help. A pediatrician or therapist is a great place to start. Keep in mind, doctors, psychologists, and psychiatrists are people, too. They bring their own experiences and education to every patient's

situation. Being a professional doesn't make them perfect. Sometimes it doesn't even make them good. Rely on your whisper network to find a good recommendation, invest the time in multiple consultations to find the fit that's right for you and your child, and check what you're being told against high-quality medical research on the subject.

The Silver Lining About Failing to Take Care of Their Bodies

For kids like Noah who find themselves on the brink of irreparable physical harm, failing big can be an eye-opener that changes their current course. An important part of being a teenager is learning where your limits are: physical, mental, moral, sexual, and others. Noah was so focused on tending to his new high school social life, he lost sight of his limits. The silver lining to being the Daredevil is that you won't need to worry about subtlety: It teaches a lesson in a way that has an undeniable effect. Imagine walking through a dark house during a power outage with your arms outstretched trying to make sure you don't bump into a wall, and surprise! You slam your shin into the coffee table and tumble ass over teakettle. This is what it's like to be a teen. You can focus so hard on avoiding one bad outcome you leave yourself unprotected elsewhere. A hard stop, however painful in the moment, can be a blessing in disguise if it teaches you where your limits need to be. Just don't be the parent who points to the coffee table and shouts, "Watch it!" every time your child enters the room going forward. The light is on now and the bruise is reminder enough.

CHAPTER EIGHT

Failure to Perform Well in School: The Misfit

I remember the first time I felt dumb.

It was sixth-grade Parents' Night. I was a new student, but this was my fourth school since kindergarten, so I was used to change. I was also used to being one of the brightest in my class, and I lived for Parents' Night, where my teachers gushed about my work and I'd confidently lead my parents to my desk, through my folder of work, on a tour of my accomplishments. This night, however, my homeroom teacher had hung essays around the room so parents could read samples as they milled around.

Mine was . . . bad. Only I didn't know that until I saw everyone else's. This tour was not going as expected.

I hadn't read my new classmates' work until that night, when I realized they were all Doogie Howsers and I was definitely the academic Misfit among them. Our prompts came from photos cut from magazines. They used complex sentence structure and made compelling arguments supported by evidence on topics like heart transplants and racial injustice. I think I described a party on the beach where people "danced and stuff."

My dad,[*] after we left, cut right to the point. "So, it looks like you'll have a little catching up to do." I was crushed. But he said something next that I remember with perfect clarity. "This is good. You were used to being at the top of the class with nowhere left to go. Now you can go higher. You'll always rise to the level of the work being done around you."

For me, that became an operating principle when I felt I was struggling to keep up. If I surrounded myself with people who were high achievers, they'd lift me up, too. A rising tide, after all.

That was far from the last time I would feel dumb, but the way my dad framed that experience helped me put it into perspective. There are lots of topics I avoid because I can't string enough intelligent, or even relevant, words together without embarrassing myself, but I still love being around smart people who can. How we talk to kids about their intelligence has a huge effect on how they'll assess their abilities later in life.

Kids fail to perform in school for myriad reasons, and the variety of misfit students who come up against this is huge. Kids like me who are people pleasers and perform well until they are bumped up to a harder level of work. Kids who have learning differences and develop coping mechanisms to mask them, but then the work requirements start to outpace the ability to cover up their struggles. Kids whose lives outside school make it hard for them to learn in the classroom. Kids who lack resources to keep up academically, or socially, which distracts them from work. Kids with health challenges. Kids for whom the system itself wasn't designed. But even though so many kids are not set up for

---

*. This story is about my stepdad, but I refer to him as my dad. Noted here only so later stories about my childhood don't appear to conflict.

success, we still expect them to perform. And since school is such a huge part of our children's lives, and we depend on it for a vision of our children's happy future, it can freak parents out when a child does not fit into the academic template in the ways we, or their teachers, expect. Reframing the experience of learning, as my dad did for me, is key to success.

When a child fails to perform well at school, it's a notification to adults that they need something: a new perspective, more stimulation, less stimulation, specialized instruction, a different environment, medication, therapy, tutoring, time, attention, or belief, to name a short list of many possibilities. Sometimes kids have a bad week. Sometimes they have a bad year. Think of all the changes tweens and teens process in one year just within their own development: changing brains, bodies, and sense of self. Then add to that an increasingly demanding academic schedule within a complex social environment. Schools are designed to meet the broadest needs of the most general population, so naturally, traditional schooling can't be the right fit for all kids, all the time. Don't panic if your child takes two steps forward and one step back every so often in school. As with most challenges in this book, I'm concerned about trends and patterns in a child's school performance. When adults notice these, it's time to help a child through their perceived failure toward growth.

For a deeper look at how a child can grow and learn from this kind of failure, let's see how using *Contain, Resolve, and Evolve* tactics worked for one family. Then, after the case study, I'll reply to some common questions about poor school performance.

MEET THE MISFIT

Case Study: How Max "Failed" to Perform Well in School

Raina's son Max always had a strong sense of self. An avid music lover, he dressed up for the first day of sixth grade as his hero, Carlos Santana, in a T-shirt and blazer with the sleeves rolled up, jeans, a medallion, and a fedora—which his mom reminded him he'd have to remove before walking into school. "They might not know who you are," Raina said, trying to gently prepare him.

But Max replied to her confidently, "It's okay. I know who I am."

Doesn't it simultaneously warm and fracture your heart to read that? It holds as much potential for joy as for pain, all depending on how Max is received.

As it turns out, Max never felt ostracized or ridiculed by his peers for being different. It ended up being his teachers who did that later, and it had nothing to do with his choice in clothing.

In school, Max struggled to keep up with his peers academically, though he was bright and self-assured. Max's teachers thought they had a good sense of who Max was, a boy with potential who never tried. Described as unfocused, unprepared, even "lazy" by his teachers, Max struggled to get the grades his teachers insisted he was capable of if only he would apply himself the way he should. At the same time, Max started to feel increasingly frustrated with his classmates, who seemed to bond over things he just didn't understand or care about. He spent most of his time socializing with his mom and her friends.

Raina enjoyed having Max spend time with her, but she worried about the teachers' assessment of his character and felt helpless to unlock this hidden potential they all seemed to think Max was suppressing.

When Max brought home his ninth-grade first-semester report card, it contained two Cs, one D, and two Fs.

Raina sensed something wasn't right. She didn't agree with his teachers that he just needed to try harder. After all, she was there every evening to see the hours of effort he was putting in, followed by almost nightly fits of crying in frustration over homework.

 Contain

Gather the Truth

Raina knew she needed more information to solve this incomplete puzzle. The public school district Max attended tested for dyslexia in kindergarten, but Max hadn't triggered any concern at that age. In third grade, though, Max was diagnosed at school with dyscalculia, a condition that affects approximately 3 to 7 percent of people and can show up as difficulty with numbers such as counting forward and/or backward, assessing quantity or size, judging distance, remembering numbers without reading them, and solving basic grade-level math problems. So, while Raina, his teachers, and Max knew about this learning difference around numbers, they didn't understand why his work seemed affected in so many academic areas outside math.

Raina says in hindsight Max had gotten by on his intelligence and charm through elementary and middle schools, though even in seventh and eighth grades his teachers were starting to lose patience. And by high school, his teachers' frustration led Raina to look into testing outside school, something she would have done sooner if the cost hadn't been prohibitive. During his ninth-grade year, she brought Max to an educational psychologist for a full neuropsychological evaluation and discovered he had both dyscalculia *and* dyslexia, a learning disorder that affects approximately 20 percent of the population in their ability to process written and sometimes spoken words. So, in addition to his struggle with all things number related, Max's dyslexia affected his reading comprehension, writing, spelling, and even some social skills, like confidently expressing his ideas or being able to understand subtle jokes. Neither of these learning differences, however, is a reflection of Max's intelligence or determination.

While it was nice to finally have answers, Raina felt angry at the school for labeling Max lazy for so many years, and she worried what damage that caused, even for a kid with his confidence. She also worried what this would mean for Max's future. He had recently stopped putting in effort at school because he failed to get the results he expected. Would he remain unmotivated, and how would this affect his future?

Affirm Your Child

Raina felt that a big part of helping Max move on rather than get stuck in his failure was affirming his strengths. She credits "really listening to my son" as the reason they established a strong bond. Raina made it clear to Max that he wasn't lazy but that his teachers misunderstood him, and from here on that would change. In fact, Raina made sure her son knew that she saw how hard he worked before his diagnosis and that his grades weren't a reflection of his effort. Raina says, "He really trusts me, and he trusts himself, too, now."

Control the Narrative

Sharing a diagnosis is a personal decision and one that the child should be involved in making. In my private parenting group on Facebook, Less Stressed Middle School Parents, this topic comes up a lot. Parents wonder not only about sharing personal health information with schools, insurance, and family or friends but also whether they should tell their own child about their diagnosis. Will knowing you have a learning difference, or autism, or ADHD, or a mental health diagnosis such as depression or anxiety, particularly at a young age, create feelings of inability or "otherness"?

Would recording a child's diagnosis on an IEP (an Individualized Education Program for which a child must have a diagnosed disability that requires special educational support) affect their class options going forward or their reputation with peers and teachers? If therapy is part of a treatment plan, would filing insurance with a diagnosis affect options for a child's future employment, say, if they wanted to work for a government agency? These kinds of questions parents ask themselves are ongoing, and each one breeds more uncertainty.

By and large, the parents in my group have a lot of experience in this area, and the vast majority with experience said that talking openly about their child's diagnosis with their child had positive results. Some warned that hiding a diagnosis that would later be revealed can indicate a sense of "wrongness" about that condition, which can evolve into feelings of shame. Many parents said their child felt relieved, liberated, and empowered to understand how their brain worked. It took away feelings of confusion and self-doubt, replacing them with a sense of purpose and a functional approach to moving forward based on their unique qualities.

Parents felt that having an IEP to document learning differences could be helpful, particularly for things like small group testing, extended test times, more breaks, and access to counselors, but all agreed an IEP is only as helpful as the school's ability to keep up with accommodations. Parents said the IEP was most effective when they made a big effort to stay connected to each teacher about their child's plan, since teachers have so many students with different needs.

On this note, it would be best to ask your child's teachers how they prefer you communicate about the IEP so as not to overwhelm teachers receiving multiple messages every day, even every hour, about students in their classes. One perceived downside to the IEP is the possibility for a child to be embarrassed at being set apart to receive accommodations, but experienced parents thought explaining to a child that failing their class assignments because they didn't receive accommodations would set them apart, too, in a more negative way.

And from my perspective, young people have always led the way in socializing acceptance of differences faster than adults (regarding, for example, gender, gender identity, sexuality, and race), and here again I think young people are generally more accepting of their peers' diagnoses than adults may realize. Specifically in terms of the IEP, armed with the knowledge to explain how and why accommodations aren't unfair, and that they don't provide extra benefits but simply level the playing field, I believe classmates will be both understanding and nonjudgmental of the various ways their classmates learn best and succeed.

Disclosing to insurance seemed to raise the biggest debate among the group. Of course, most families can't afford therapy without insurance, so this debate does exist within a bubble of financial privilege. But many parents in the group decided not to file for insurance because of the mandate for a diagnosis. They worried about their future adult being barred from joining the military or working for the government, or how a diagnosis could affect life insurance premiums. Guidelines for maintenance of mental health records by therapist vary by state, but any mental health treatment filed under insurance goes on your health record as a preexisting condition. While this sounds scary, I wholeheartedly argue that *not* receiving treatment is much scarier. So, if you can afford to pay out of pocket and leave this off the records of insurance, more power to you. If not, please take advantage of the mental health options provided by your insurance or community welfare programs. Thank goodness, mental health challenges are becoming increasingly normalized, and seeking out therapists to support one's mental health is becoming as socially acceptable as seeing a doctor for physical health.

Raina knew immediately that she needed to contain the damage done to Max's self-perception. Now that she had a diagnosis, she had a lot of research to do so she could understand how to support him and explain that he isn't alone, but it would take time. Meanwhile, she did two things to help Max resolve his feelings of failure.

Take Action

Seek Perspective

While she immersed herself in learning about his dual diagnoses, Raina still needed a stopgap to put in place that would halt the influx of failing grades. His public school was overcrowded and the support staff stretched thin, so Raina felt that keeping him there would only result in more frustration for everyone. In Raina's case, she found her whisper network online in forums for parents of children with learning differences. There, she discovered an option where he could continue at his high school part time and do homeschool part time. Raina works full time, but her mother lives nearby, so she brings a book to their house and is on standby to help Max as needed with his homeschooling or even just to keep him company sometimes so he isn't lonely while his mom works. This new hybrid schedule will allow Max to graduate on schedule with combined credits from both school programs.

Had she not had this option or been able to work out the logistics with her mother's help, Raina would have had to explore other approaches, including possibly switching to a private school for students with learning differences (not an option for Raina because of the tuition cost) or getting Max a more robust IEP and then following up regularly to make sure his accommodations are met, as well as encouraging and teaching Max how to advocate for himself at school.

Educate

Plans to accommodate Max's learning differences are still a work in progress. Raina says, "It took so much going with my intuition, because for years we were told he is so smart but just needs to try harder." In fact, Max is smart, but he needed to work differently, not harder. The system wanted Max to fit a mold that he couldn't, and he was slowly being labeled a failure because of it. Trusting her gut was the first crucial step to setting Max up for success. Raina's ongoing education involves transferring her new knowledge to Max so he can understand that his past results were not a reflection of his intelligence.

 Evolve

Triage Your Fears

Max's experience with school brought up a steady flow of fears for Raina, related mostly to his ability to function in an educational system that wasn't designed to support him and then in a world that relied on doing well in that system to succeed. Raina's fears sounded like this:

Is Max going to be able to graduate from high school and go to college?

Can we afford the kind of educational support Max needs?

If he doesn't graduate from high school, or go to college, will he be able to make enough money to live a happy life?

Since Max is still attending his public school part time, will his teachers take his diagnosis seriously? Will they know how to help him?

Will he be able to make friends his own age, or does he feel so different from his peers he won't try?

Face One Fear First

Raina knew that she'd be trying to calm her fears by continuing to search for answers long into the future. But for now, she decided that the one fear she could grapple with immediately was the fear that his teachers wouldn't be able to support him and would still see him as lazy.

It's not that Raina doesn't appreciate, trust, or respect teachers. But she does feel the system let her son down, and she feels a need both to protect him from this happening again and to protect students who would come after Max with similar differences. Raina's plan is to immerse herself in research and be a resource for his district so that other parents, teachers, and administrators can better understand how to serve kids like Max. It's as if Raina, who was both polite and soft-spoken during my interview, were heading up her own whisper network, but instead of whispering, she's pulling out a megaphone for those who need help.

Of course, most parents can't take this on as a second job, and most teachers can't find time within their over-scheduled days to take on extra learning, either. Raina says her tiny first step will be to explain in the simplest terms the dual diagnosis to Max's teachers and to ask them to rethink how they think of him when he's in their class. She wants them to understand he was never lazy, just at a huge disadvantage.

Uphold *Your Child's Bill of Rights*

Max, armed with new information about how he fits into his social and academic worlds, will need support to continue exploring his rights within those spaces. Below are a few ways Raina can support that by upholding specific rights.

Right: Determine Their Own Values

When Max was little, Raina imagined his future matching up nicely with her value system. For instance, there was no doubt he'd attend college. Now he may or may not. Maybe he'll search for a college that can support his learning style, or maybe he'll go part time so he can work at his own pace, or maybe he won't go at all. But he should make this decision based on what aligns with his values for himself, not on what Raina once envisioned or what his teachers once thought he was capable of. Having the right to define his own values will be key to Max's feeling that he's choosing what is right for him, instead of performing for others as a frustrated hamster trying to keep up on a spinning wheel.

Right: Practice Making Informed Decisions About Their Bodies

Max's brain works differently from the majority, but not so differently that he can't find other people similar to him from whom he can learn. There are lots of people with his dual diagnosis, and lots of research he can study to better understand what will help him be successful. He can and should learn as much as possible from the experiences of others to help him make informed decisions about what might work best for him. Once he does this, having the power to advocate for himself and armed with knowledge, he'll become empowered where he would otherwise have resolved to be an outsider.

See New Things

One great thing about part-time homeschooling, Raina says, is that it freed up a lot of time Max would have spent feeling frustrated with class work and homework. With extra hours in his week, he joined a band. He plays guitar and keyboards and composes his own music on his iPad. I don't know Max personally, but thinking of Raina's description of him walking into the first day of sixth grade dressed as an ode to Santana, I can't imagine a better outcome to his story.

I asked Raina if Max thinks about going to college someday, and she says she thinks he wants to go, but he's not totally sure. Now that he knows what's going on with his learning differences, he feels he has more of a possibility. Raina, for her part, thinks he would make a great lawyer and not for the jokey reason most parents say when they have argumentative kids. "He's a very calm, thoughtful, and analytic person," Raina explains.

Having a child who fails to perform well at school can be scary at first, but once you identify the cause, it can open doors to new and better ways of learning. For kids like Max who have dyslexia, for example, there can be many positive outcomes. Kids with dyslexia are often great at memorizing, solving problems creatively and using their imaginations, and holding engaging and entertaining conversations. They develop these compensatory skills and end up being messengers in ways beyond the scope of our "normal" vision. Take Albert Einstein, Steven Spielberg, Muhammad Ali, Richard Branson, Octavia Spencer, or Agatha Christie. If you have a child with a learning difference, google celebrities who share their diagnosis to give the examples that their difference can be a gift.

Questions About Some of the Many Ways Kids Fail to Perform Well in School

Q: *My daughter is in eighth grade and more concerned with her social life than her recently plummeting grades. How can I convince her that these people won't matter to her years from now, but getting bad grades is something she'll regret once she starts applying to college?*

A: While the people she is friends with now may not matter to her in the future, the experience of learning from these relationships is still valuable to her development. For that reason, I'd be cautious about saying anything that downplays all she's feeling and learning from her friend group now.

Still, we don't want her to fail her classes in exchange for having a strong social life. The two don't need to be mutually exclusive. My guess is, one of two things is happening. First, she's finding it hard to balance spending time on her schoolwork with her overwhelming need to not miss out on texting or seeing friends. Many kids her age feel their social status is precariously positioned at the edge of every new opportunity that presents itself, so even an unanswered text can have the power to knock them off the social radar. Or, second, she's discovering that as schoolwork becomes harder, it requires much more effort than she's used to giving, or she doesn't understand concepts quickly the way she used to, and either way this discomfort drives her to avoid the work.

Whether it's the first or second scenario, or some blend of the two, you can explain that you think her schoolwork *and* her social life are necessary for her to be a successful person. By acknowledging her time with peers as valuable, you'll prime her to be more receptive to your message. Next, explain that doing poorly in her classes puts her at risk to be separated from her peers—by new class placement, mandatory tutoring or enforced study times, or even failing and losing a grade level. Once you've presented the problem, *work with her* to establish ways she can maintain her social connection without sacrificing her education. One thing I've seen work well for other families is hiring a local high school or college student to help set goals and follow up on assignments, which can be cost-effective; your daughter will probably also prefer working with someone young and cool as opposed to her parent, who is so obviously ancient and "doesn't get it!"

Q: My son was in the gifted program at his elementary school. Now that he's in middle school, he is getting bad grades. I don't know if it's because he's not sure how to study at this level, or if he's bored because he's not challenged enough in his new classes. How do I figure this out?
A: It's common for parents to see the wheels come off the cart in middle school as kids start to juggle multiple classes and teachers who have different expectations and styles of teaching, the organization of materials and content becomes more complex, and social distractions become more powerful. With so many variables, it's not simple to root out the cause or causes of a drop in performance. You're wondering if your son's situation is caused by a lack of skills or a lack of interest. To determine if it's a lack of study skills, you can engage him in studying with you or with a friend, trying different techniques: some auditory, some visual, some active, and so on.

If it's boredom, you could benefit from a professional assessment. A psychologist can test your son for his learning style and let you know if he's a divergent learner. The psychologist J. P. Guilford pioneered this term in the 1950s and helps us understand ways divergent thinkers differ, such as being creative, hands-on problem solvers, whereas convergent learners prefer following a set of instructions to a conclusion. It could be that your child's learning style isn't a match for his current instruction. If that's the case, you can look into whether your school offers special programs for this or consider switching schools, with your son's input. Finally, if you don't have the option to change his school experience, you can educate him to better understand how his brain works best and create scenarios at home that allow him to work in the way that suits him.

Q: My tenth-grade son is smart, but he only applies himself in classes where he likes the teacher. If he doesn't like the teacher, he won't talk in class and he does the bare minimum on assignments to get by without failing. How can I convince him he's only punishing himself with this attitude?

A: Trying to convince a teen that something they don't care about today will suddenly matter to them in the future can make a parent feel like Sisyphus, who was forced by the Greek god Zeus to push a boulder up a hill for all of time. Every time Sisyphus thought he had made it to the top, the boulder would roll down and he'd have to start again.

There may be moments when your son nods and agrees with you, in theory, but the next time a teacher does something to irritate him, here comes your boulder down the hill again. Teens learn from experience, not from platitudes. Or Greek myths.

But while you may not be able to say much to convince him about the future, you might be able to influence him through examining the past. Quick, hop in my DeLorean and calibrate the date to the day your son hit his first home run! Sadly, I don't have a DeLorean or a time machine, but my hope is that you can bail us out of this one. You have a lot of memories of your son growing up. Search for one when your son did well, despite having an uninspiring coach, teacher, leader, captain, or teammates. Tell your son the story of how he overcame a tough situation before and what he has to show for it. Imagine if he had decided not to try back then, for that awful coach or annoying scout leader or boring sensei? If you can provide your son with at least one example of why it paid off for him to do his best even when he didn't like the person teaching him, or the kids he was working with, or the activity itself, you'll be armed with "proof" instead of speculation.

If this approach doesn't resonate with you or your son, here is another angle: Incentivize doing well. Have a conversation about his outside-school goals, something he wants to work toward, and run an experiment. You can phrase it that way, too. "Let's experiment with this and see what happens if you try hard in this class despite not liking the teacher. If you're able to [insert metric like improve by one letter grade, or get above an 80 on all homework, or spend thirty minutes every weekday studying], I'll pay you as if this were a job with either cold hard cash or a later bedtime or more screen time or whatever we agree on." Maybe he's only working for the payout, but at this point does it matter? By treating this as an experiment, you can show him what he's capable of, and hopefully the satisfaction of success will motivate him in other classes next semester.

The Silver Lining About Failing to Perform Well in School

School is a highly imperfect construct. Days are long, classes may not be engaging, students are exhausted because the school schedule is at odds with their sleep needs, grading portals make everyone crazy, teachers are underappreciated, underpaid, and human. Some are better than others. Part of the experience of going to school, I think, is to be gracious and accepting, that everyone is (mostly) trying hard, to put up with the kids and teachers who drive them insane, to work through boredom, to prioritize. There are many positive things to learn from the foibles of everyone else! The silver lining to being the Misfit is that kids who struggle with this system learn how to pull out and see larger systems with perspective. Once they understand that not every person will succeed under the same circumstances, they find uncharted paths to follow, leading the way in innovation and breaking the mold.

CHAPTER NINE

Failure to Show Concern for Others: The Ego

You're exhausted from work and are cooking dinner with a tearstained face from a bad meeting, when your son walks right past you and says, "Oh. Can I get Taco Bell instead?" Or you're going on a special family vacation that you've been planning for months, and your daughter says at the last minute she doesn't want to go because she'll miss a party. This lack of concern can make you feel as though you were raising an ego-maniac who cares only about themselves. But are you really?

A friend of mine told me that when she was twelve, her father came into her room at 10:00 a.m. on a Saturday, gently woke her up, and told her he'd fallen off a ladder and needed to go to the emergency room to have his ankle looked at. My friend, who is one of the nicest women I know, was so mad at having been woken before noon that she screamed at him and pulled the covers over her head.

She is now an accomplished business owner and mother of two thoughtful young women, and she baked me a loaf of chocolate chip banana bread when I had surgery. She is the opposite of a self-obsessed, ego-driven narcissist. But her dad probably had some doubts after the ladder incident. He definitely didn't speak to her for the rest of that weekend.

Almost everyone will tell you that it's normal for adolescents to be self-centered. They're right. As tweens and teens pass through the developmental phase the psychologist Erik Erikson termed identity versus role confusion, young people struggle with the conflict of defining who they are as individuals versus who they are as members of a family or community. This work usually begins at around age eleven and lasts through the early twenties. Anyone raising a tween bears witness to this conflict daily. As I wrote in my first book, *Middle School Makeover: Improving the Way You and Your Child Experience the Middle School Years,* "It is incredibly hard for kids to learn who they are and where they fit outside of 'parent world.' It will take some trial and error, many mistakes, and a dash of rebellion to leave your safe haven and strike out on their own."

But try they must, and that means spending what to you will seem like an inordinate amount of time marinating in their own egos, where they see things only from their own perspective, instead of continuing to happily function as a smaller version of you. Painful and annoying as this phase can be, kids who don't get this opportunity to play the role of the Ego and be fully submerged in their own self-interests can have difficulty moving on to what Erikson dubbed the next phase of human development, intimacy versus isolation, where we grapple with our newly earned sense of independence and our desire to be in relationship with others. It's nearly impossible to be successful at each new stage of human development if you haven't mastered the earlier phases. Young people who don't have years of individualization under their belts might be more likely to find themselves in toxic or codependent relationships, because it's hard to be in a healthy relationship with someone else when you haven't figured out who you are first.

I remind parents often that these years of identity development may be hard on us, but without them the future will be hard on our kids, not to mention on us if we need to support them emotionally or financially through their quest to find themselves. We all know people who can't seem to find happiness in their relationships. They seek to be loved and want someone else to make them feel whole, but they haven't figured out how to love and satisfy themselves first, and so these relationships end reliably and predictably. Keep this in mind the next time your teen is acting selfishly. Spending a little time as the Ego now will set them up for success later.

Get on the Same Team

Parents of adolescents must accept a certain amount of isolation from their kids. For example, a thirteen-year-old might spend all their free time in their room for weeks on end, and one day when they emerge for dinner, they're more open to talking with you. Kids "cocoon" in their rooms to explore the world of possible changes available to them as they set on the path to becoming young adults, and rooms are a safe place to try things out before debuting them for the world. Perhaps when your little butterfly emerges from their cocoon, they'll look like the same old caterpillar, but seem just a bit more self-assured, or maybe they'll have black hair, not blond, heavy eyeliner, and a slight Australian accent. Unlike butterflies, your child can't transform with a one-and-done isolation. They will cocoon and emerge repeatedly until they find the version of themselves that makes them most comfortable. Rather than seeing this as neglectful, you should know that you're giving your child the opportunity to build a strong sense of self, and the more you encourage this, the more likely your child will successfully pass through the identity development phase of growing up and be better prepared for the next phase of finding healthy relationships with peers and then with family again.

However, when a child's egocentric behavior turns negligent or cruel, it's time for parents to rein in that behavior. Yes, kids can and should begin to figure out who they are separate from their family members. "Yes, and" while they're doing this work, concern for others and responsibilities toward the family do not disappear. Here is an example brought up in my online parenting group.

A mom asked if her eleven-year-old was old enough to understand the necessary give-and-take of their relationship. She felt her daughter was reaching a selfish place where she required more and more things from her mom, like rides to friends' houses or oversight at a pet-sitting job, but her daughter wasn't willing to reciprocate that effort when she asked her to join on a Costco run or to go with her while walking the dog. "Is she old enough to get the concept 'I have given to you, so you can give to me'?" this mom wondered. "Am I asking her to be more emotionally mature than she is at eleven?"

The short answer to the second question is yes, if you're asking her to *want* to spend time with you in recognition of what you do for her. What she wants to do isn't driven by what's fair and reasonable; it's driven by her developmental need to figure out who she is. Note, too, the difference in the examples the mom cited. The daughter's age prohibits her from being as independent as she'd like, so her mom has to give her rides and double-check that the neighbor's pet stays alive while they're out of town. If the mom agrees to letting her daughter take the job or play at friends' houses, she also agrees to some level of support and oversight. The mom, on the other hand, can go buy groceries on her own without her daughter's support. She can walk the dog alone. It may not be as fun as with company, but it's a regular part of her routine that she can do without support and oversight. A direct quid pro quo wouldn't make sense or be appropriate in such a fundamentally lopsided relationship.

Now, it is often the case that when your child asks you to drive them somewhere or help them with a personal issue, you pull from the limited allotment of time you could have spent on yourself, and you spend it on them. Many girls are raised to be martyrs, and I've seen many mothers do this to the exclusion of their own well-being. Please don't be of service to your children to the extent that you deprive yourself of time to recharge your own batteries, but as a parent you can't avoid being of service altogether. So, while you shouldn't expect your child to look for ways to pay you back for your investment in them, and you definitely don't want to use language that makes them feel they owe you for parenting them, you *can* explain that there are times when you need help and ask for what you need.

One way to talk about this is to use a team metaphor. You might say, "We're a team and that means sometimes we'll do things for each other, even when it's not our first choice of fun." A parent in my Facebook group said she puts it this way to her son: *I know going to the bank with me isn't fun, but going now will save me a separate trip later. I appreciate you saving me that hassle. Let's use that extra time to go by the skate park on the way home. That should be fun.* This approach minimizes making a child feel indebted and instead establishes an environment of collaboration.

Taking It Too Far

So yes, it's perfectly normal for your teen to think mostly about themselves. In that case, though, how do you know when regular self-centered teenage behavior has crossed over into failure territory?

For me, the answer rests on this tenet: Teens can, and should, be completely interested and invested in exploring who they are becoming, and they should be able to do this *without intentionally and repeatedly hurting anyone else.*

I wanted this tenet to be simple, a teenage version of the Hippocratic oath: First, do no harm. But teens hurt themselves, us, and each other all the time. The writer in me needed to clarify the muddiness of the word "hurting" with a bit more specificity, which is why I added the lawyerly language of "intentionally" and "repeatedly" to give that word more heft.

It's impossible to avoid hurting people altogether, all the time, especially because pain is subjective and what hurts one person bounces off another. It does help to notice when and why the people you live with hurt so you can be sensitive to their needs. I don't expect kids to be able to do this right away, although older teens do seem to have a good read on what makes their parents happy, disappointed, or hurt by the time they're ready to leave home.

In my house, my husband can receive negative feedback without an ounce of insecurity, while I cry at the slightest whiff of disapproval. On the other hand, I can tackle hard conversations that make him wince. He can lift weights through exhaustion that would cripple me, but I can hold a yoga pose long after he's cursed and crumbled. He can wake fully and rise to action if the phone rings at 3:00 a.m. if a teen needs a ride, or a co-worker in another country has a work crisis. Whereas I feel an ache deep in my bones if I don't get an uninterrupted nine hours of sleep; I'm of zero use to you if I haven't. We feel and react to the discomfort or pain in our lives in totally opposite ways, so it's no surprise that when we felt hurt by our kids, it was never at the same time. What wounded him didn't even hit my radar, and vice versa.

It would be totally unrealistic, and a cruel expectation, to believe our kids will never hurt us. Every relationship brings with it the possibility for pain, and parenting is no exception. What matters is if your child can adjust *after* causing you pain, and if not, then you might be headed into the territory of failure to show concern for others.

For a deeper look at how a child can grow and learn from this kind of failure, let's see how using *Contain, Resolve, and Evolve* tactics worked for one family. Then, after the case study, I'll reply to some common questions about failing to show concern.

MEET THE EGO

Case Study: How Jacob "Failed" to Show Concern for Others

Alan's son Jacob is sixteen and starting his junior year of high school. While most families in their social circle are beginning to talk about life after high school, Alan is having a hard time imagining how Jacob will function outside in the "real world." The past couple of years with Jacob have been draining as Alan has watched his son become increasingly self-centered, sometimes defiant, and nearly always "looking out for number one," as Alan puts it, with little regard for how his behavior affects the rest of the family.

Though Alan says there isn't one situation or circumstance that feels like Jacob's big failure moment, he can point to a string of events that have added up to his total frustration with Jacob's failure to show concern for others.

The night before his stepmom's birthday, for instance, Alan asked Jacob if he had gotten her a card yet, since he'd told him several times that he needed to do this. Jacob kept saying he'd do it, but the night before his stepmom's birthday he still hadn't. Alan gave him five dollars and allowed him to borrow the car to go to the drugstore that evening. A couple hours later, Jacob returned, and when Alan asked to see the card, Jacob said, "Oh, it must be in the car." He searched the car and couldn't come up with it. "I really did get it!" Jacob said. "But I also got some snacks with my own money, and I must have left it at Chris's house when I stopped over there after the drugstore."

Alan was fuming at Jacob's procrastination, his lack of focus, his selfishness, and his audacity to take his car to a friend's and hang out. But Alan would be out five dollars and his wife would be out a birthday card if Alan didn't stop what he was doing and drive Jacob back to Chris's house to get the card. Luckily, it was actually there, but Jacob didn't seem to realize what a huge inconvenience this was for Alan, not to mention the lack of effort and caring all this showed toward his stepmom, Tracy, who'd helped raise Jacob since he was five. Alan feels Jacob does the least amount possible for his family, without realizing how much they do for him.

Another incident that got Alan fired up was when the entire family had gone to Jacob's younger sister's soccer game one Saturday afternoon. When they pulled into the driveway after the game, they saw two of Jacob's friends leaving the house. Alan recognized the boys but wasn't even sure of their names. He reeled around in his seat to ask what Jacob knew about this, and Jacob immediately got defensive. His friend had left his hoodie there the last time he was over, and so Jacob left him a key under the planter to come pick it up. Alan was furious that Jacob had shared the house key without permission, which led to a huge fight because Jacob couldn't see why this was a big deal at all.

These kinds of selfish and thoughtless moments punctuated their lives periodically, and in between were a steady stream of small arguments over what Alan perceives as Jacob being unnecessarily defiant. If Alan asks Jacob to take his dirty shoes off at the front door, Jacob argues over how dirty the shoes *really* are instead of just taking them off. If he comes home past curfew, there is another argument over what caused the delay and why his dad needs to be more open-minded. Each time Alan tried to address a problem by either talking, yelling, or punishing, it seemed to have no effect.

Alan said Jacob's behavior makes him worry they will either have a huge fight or stop speaking to each other one day. He says he loves Jacob and doesn't want that to happen; he just doesn't see how this relationship suddenly becomes one where Jacob treats him with respect and consideration. "I want, just once, to be doing something, like carrying in groceries or changing a lightbulb, and for him to think, 'Oh, maybe Dad needs help.' But all he ever thinks about is what's fun or easiest for him."

Family, friends, and teachers report that Jacob is a pleasure to be around, so Alan knows the problem is centered on their home; in a way this makes him feel better knowing Jacob behaves well in public, but in another it makes him feel unfairly targeted.

Before middle school, Jacob was much closer with Alan. They shared a love of sports, food, and sci-fi shows. Alan doesn't feel confident that their connection can be upheld by these common interests anymore, because Jacob only wants to spend time with Alan on his terms and when there is some obvious benefit to him. Can Alan find a way to make Jacob see that his behavior is alienating him and hurting their relationship, or should he just ignore Jacob, give up on a happy home life for the moment, and stop trying so hard to teach Jacob to think about others, hoping that maybe it'll get better when Jacob gets a few more years and maturity on him?

Alan needs to find a way to contain the problem, which is Jacob's apparent inability to think about the needs of others before his own. To begin with, it will benefit Alan and Jacob both if they can talk in a way that feels nonthreatening and collaborative.

 Contain

Control the Narrative

Normally, the purpose of communication during this early phase of containment is to try to stop the rumor mill or to enlist support from a close group in keeping a child safe after a failure. In this case, there was no moment of crisis, more of a trend that needs addressing, so Alan doesn't need to reach out to anyone beyond his son at this point.

Alan's initial key message to Jacob would include setting the stage that Jacob should expect some changes to come, as well as explaining to him why this is happening. Alan can use "I" statements here to keep Jacob from becoming too defensive. Rather than starting with "you," which makes teens feel defensive, as in "you need to start changing your attitude around here," Alan can start with "I," as in "I think there are things we can do to have better communication so I don't get so upset about things happening at the last minute."

Also, timing and tone are key. Alan should schedule a talk with Jacob so he doesn't catch him off guard. He should also present it as an opportunity to solve a problem, not as an attack on Jacob's character.

For example, Alan could say, "Hey, I have something I want to talk with you about. It's not urgent, but also not something I want to push off for too long. We can do it tomorrow night after dinner if you'll go with me while I take Buck for a walk, or we can do it Saturday afternoon and I'll take you to lunch. You pick."

Jacob might feel nervous and press Alan for more information immediately, but Alan can buy time by saying he hasn't thought through exactly what he wants to say yet, but he wants to pin down a time now. If Jacob asks, "Am I in trouble?" Alan can say no, he's not in trouble, but that Alan has just noticed some things that need tweaking, and he wants to see how they can make improvements on both of their ends.

Leaving Jacob wondering, but not worrying, can be a good way to get him in the right frame of mind to talk seriously but not defensively. On the flip side, if the pending talk feels like a threat, leaving Jacob worrying is cruel.

Affirm Your Child

A nervous person is not a good listener. If Alan can affirm Jacob before they talk, even if he isn't feeling particularly complimentary toward his son in the moment, he can set the stage for a better conversation in the Resolve phase, which is coming up next. Wherever he finds small moments to praise him in the hours or days leading to the talk ("thanks for feeding the dog when I asked," or "I noticed you've been watching your sister's cartoon with her and I think she appreciates that"), he can plant a seed for more fertile conversation. The sentiment he leaves Jacob with should be affirming, not fearful. Something like this would work: "I really appreciate you setting aside Saturday lunch to talk with me. I'm excited to spend time with you. Think about where you want to eat and let me know."

Take Action

Foster Connection

Alan's concern is that Jacob has been a jerk and will continue to be a jerk. But treating him as if he were a jerk isn't going to inspire Jacob to behave better.

One of the hardest things we can do as parents is abandon our worry and simply hope for the best. It sounds almost reckless to treat someone with more grace than they've earned, because what if they then presume they're being rewarded for bad behavior? But it doesn't work that way. People, generally, do rise to the level of our expectations.

In an interview on *The Today Show* about the influence of his career, Ted Walch, a beloved Los Angeles teacher of theater, cinema studies, and philosophy of fifty years, said, "If I do only one thing with my students, it's treat them as a fellow adult, even though they're not. I treat their ideas with great respect, even though it's kind of ordinary. And I let them know they're safe."

Walch said, "A student put it better than I will. He said, 'You allowed me to find out who I am. You had the decency to treat me as the person you HOPED I would become.'"

I'm with Alan in that Jacob's behavior has become unacceptable and that he needs to make some changes, but I am also hoping Alan makes some changes, too, and pushes "reset" on how he reacts to Jacob in general, following Walch's lead. The key for parents and teachers alike is to offer feedback and correction when needed, but to draw a firm distinction between a person and their actions. Jacob is failing to show concern for others, but he's not a failure. Certain of his behaviors are unacceptable, but Jacob is lovable. If Alan can clearly explain this to Jacob when they talk, he can begin to resolve this issue before it gets further out of hand.

The problem with yelling or punishing alone is that it pushes a teen's defensive walls higher. Alan will need to put aside bad feelings, be the bigger person, and let Jacob know he wants more out of their relationship. The problem doesn't need to be defined as "Jacob is a jerk." The problem is that Alan and Jacob aren't connecting in a way that feels mutually respectful and supportive. Jacob may be failing to show concern for others, but if Alan can't find a way to reconnect despite that failure, they may move into a deeper failure territory where Jacob feels rejected by, and consequently rejects, his family.

Define Consequences

After Alan establishes the problem and how he wants to resolve it, he can bring up consequences. Jacob needs reassurance to recalibrate, but not an open door to treat others poorly. First, Alan will need to set reasonable expectations and then explain to Jacob what will happen if he fails to meet those expectations.

Measured against van Gennep's steps in a rite of passage from chapter 2, Jacob seems to be stuck in stage one: separation from their group. He hasn't entered phase two yet: a time of being tested. Jacob needs a test so he can learn from it and then rejoin his community—in this case his family—as a better version of himself.

Being yelled at isn't a test for a teen boy. They're pretty good at tuning out adult anger or weaponizing it back toward us. Being grounded can be useful when you need to put a quick stop to dangerous behavior, but it's not much of a thought provoker. And taking away privileges is appropriate when the privilege is tied to the problem, like taking away a cell phone for cell phone misuse, for instance. But none of these punishments creates a meaningful test that will usher Jacob into thinking more about others.

Most often parents won't need to fabricate tests to help usher their child into adulthood. Life does this reliably enough on its own. However, in this case, I think Alan can take things into his own hands a bit here since this failure revolves around the dynamic at home.

A real test could be set up this way:

1. Alan explains the issue he sees with Jacob's selfish behavior using "I" statements. "I feel taken advantage of when ___." "I would feel more willing to compromise if you ___."
2. Alan invites Jacob to do the same. He opens a discussion to ways each of them can improve their

demeanor at home and their relationship. Maybe Jacob
wants Alan to explain things before getting angry.
Maybe Jacob asks permission before assuming his
actions are acceptable.

3. Alan offers Jacob a way to earn more of what he wants
(probably freedom or independence). If he passes this
test, he earns privileges.

4. If he fails, he can try again later.

5. I hear you . . . So what's the test?! It really could be a
hundred different things, but since Alan expressly shared
his desire for Jacob to see him working and offer to help,
here's what comes to mind for me: Alan creates a list of
things he wants to get done around the house. Jacob
spends 11:00 a.m. until 2:00 p.m. with him the next
four Saturdays in a row. During that time, they knock
out everything on the list from changing lightbulbs to
fixing the broken back deck rail. If Jacob is a good
apprentice, he will graduate from Alan's school with two
extra hours added to his curfew. If not, curfew rolls back
by two hours. Note: Alan will need to define how a
good apprentice performs on the job: hustles when
needed, shows up on time, doesn't complain, stays past
2:00 p.m. if in the middle of a task, and so on.

The test can go in any number of creative directions, but you should
avoid anything that looks or sounds like emotional manipulation. Trying to shock a teen into being more thoughtful by, say, removing all
their belongings from their room doesn't make a teen grateful as much
as it makes them compliant for long enough to get their stuff back. This
kind of punishment is akin to spanking but for an older kid. It releases
your own pent-up tension and maybe it motivates compliance through
fear or defeat but won't do much in terms of fostering mutual respect.

Emotional manipulation can also be a guilt trip or a demonstrative threat. Parent: *You're gonna look back one day and regret this. We won't be close. You'll need me one day and I won't be there.* When parents say this kind of thing, they hope it will shock a child into having an epiphany. Hoped-for Child Response: *Oh! My mom is right! I can picture a day when I will look back on this behavior and feel so lonely and full of regret that I didn't show more respect and earn my parents' lifelong love and support.*

Ouch. Keep your focus on the present moment and what needs to happen to improve your current situation.

Can you be firm? Sure! Can you be direct? You must. Can you be serious? Of course. But you also need to be fair, remembering you are dealing with someone who, though they have presented themselves lately as a self-centered dolt, is still a child, is someone you love more than life itself (remember?), and is going through a fragile time of life. If it helps, pretend you are giving an employee a performance review. Adopt the tone of a corporate HR director to convey all the critical information without the sense of shame or disappointment.

One final thought on what not to do here. Resist the urge to take your child to a homeless shelter or hospital to make them feel more appreciative. Volunteering is a great thing to do, especially as a family. Research shows that teens who volunteer regularly have nicer attitudes toward others, although I wonder if that's a reflection on the nature of kids who choose to volunteer and not necessarily how volunteering changed kids with poor attitudes toward others. Nonetheless, the desire to volunteer should be driven from the goodness of your heart, not as a tour of other people's hardship so you can teach your teen a lesson.

Update Communication

At this point in the process, Alan can expand his circle of communication if he wants to enlist some help from his wife or other family members and friends. When kids start pulling away from their parents, they make it look as if they know everything and don't want any guidance from anyone, but they still appreciate, and need, help from trusted adults. By letting key people know that Jacob is putting up barriers at home, and that Alan would appreciate a trusted coach or close friend occasionally giving advice around being a considerate teammate, friend, or family member, he can make sure Jacob is getting the feedback he needs to grow into a more thoughtful young man. Most teens find it a sign of respect when another adult speaks to them in a mature way about grown-up things, when, ironically, they find the same message from a parent to be overstepping.

Engage Your Whisper Network

A whisper network is where Alan can finally say whatever he needs to get off his chest. Alan needs to be restrained when he talks to Jacob so that Jacob is open to hearing him, but with a few trusted friends, Alan can relieve that pressure valve with humor, complaints, and f-bombs as needed.

Triage Your Fears

What holds most people back from growth is fear, and we parents stifle our own children's growth because we're afraid of what could go wrong. In Alan's case, his fears might sound like these:

> Will Jacob fail his at-home apprentice test, and if he does, are we at a dead end?
> Will Jacob decline the challenge and not even try?
> Is Jacob's lack of concern for others a fixed part of his personality?

Did I create Jacob's inability to show concern by not being a better father?

Will the tension between us grow so much that someone says or does something that ultimately causes permanent damage to our relationship?

A lot of these fears center on big what-ifs. They represent the great unknown, which is a frightening space. To triage these, Alan will need to focus on what he can address most immediately, giving himself twenty-four hours to act on just one thing so he doesn't become stuck in the mud. That small action will prevent him from spinning out into bigger fears that are ultimately out of his control. From this list, the fear that I would address first is the second, because it is the most immediate thing he can plan for: Will Jacob decline the challenge and not even try?

Face One Fear First

The best way for Alan to act against the fear that Jacob won't engage with him is to plan his approach and think about how his own reaction to this possibility will steer what happens next. The hope is that by offering a big enough reward for passing the challenge, Alan can get Jacob to agree to a month's worth of Saturdays contributing around the house and that Jacob will walk away with more than a later curfew. He may also develop a new appreciation for all Alan does for the family, some new home improvement knowledge, and a harder work ethic at home. That would bring Jacob through his rite of passage to being a better member of the community. But, if Jacob gets angry or sulks at the proposition, Alan needs to know his next move.

Teens are impulsive thinkers. They rely on the amygdala, the emotional center of the brain, to make quick decisions. If we give them time to mull things over on their own terms, they are more likely to draw on the prefrontal cortex, where reasoning and critical thinking function, to solve their problems. My advice to Alan would be to plan for a negative response and to offer Jacob more time to think before he commits. He can even set that up when he proposes his idea by saying, "I want you to take three days to think about this before you decide either way. Think it through from every angle, and in three days we'll talk again." Then Alan should bite his tongue every time he wants to add something or bring up a new point over the next three days! Alan could also invite Jacob to come back with his own ideas he'd like folded into the plan. The more invested Jacob feels in solving the problem with Alan, the less chance he feels that he's the embodiment of their problems.

Uphold *Your Child's Bill of Rights*

When a child shows lack of concern for others, it's hard to think about doing nice things for them. But upholding their rights is less about being a nice parent and more about making sure your child doesn't get stuck in this state of failure and has ample opportunity to grow. Let's look at what rights Alan will be upholding for Jacob with this approach.

Right: Receive the Benefit of the Doubt

Alan may find it difficult to give Jacob the benefit of the doubt that he won't continue being increasingly difficult, but it's worth revisiting what Ted Walch's student told him: "You had the decency to treat me as the person you HOPED I would become." This gets to the heart of giving benefit of the doubt. It's about hope for the future, not about rewarding bad behavior. Teens grapple with the concept of becoming an individual versus being part of a community. It's hard work. It's confusing work. It's essential work. The benefit of the doubt is a key right to helping them do this work without judgment.

Right: Negotiate and Self-Advocate

Why bother allowing a selfish teen to have a say in how you react to their insolence? Why not just bring down the hammer and insist on better behavior? There is nothing wrong with insisting on better behavior. How you insist will make a world of difference in whether your child complies, and whether they comply out of obedience to get you off their back or to earn back privileges, or whether they comply because they want to treat you better. Allowing Jacob to advocate for his own interests may seem like an allowance for selfishness, but it's actually an invitation toward adulthood. Jacob is keen to be there, but he's still figuring out how. A negotiation of terms will give him practice finding balance, which he needs.

See New Things

To be happy in a relationship, you should focus on what's going well. Even when that's hard to do. I'll share an example from my very recent experience. Last night, my husband and I got take-out Thai food. He likes adding a little soy sauce to his dish, and I prefer ponzu. This morning, as I was tidying up the kitchen after breakfast, I noticed the soy sauce bottle was still on the counter. As I reached for it to put it back in the fridge where it belongs, I caught my inner voice grumbling, "Why can't he just put stuff back?"

I wiped the counter and cleaned up after the breakfast I'd made, and just as I was about to leave, I saw the ponzu bottle sitting by the sink on the kitchen island. Judging me.

In other words: It's so easy to notice the annoying things our family members do, as easy as it is to overlook our own bad habits. It takes a real effort to break our gaze from what's going wrong and shift our focus to what's going right.

It's so easy to notice the annoying things our family members do, as easy as it is to overlook our own bad habits. It takes a real effort to break our gaze from what's going wrong and shift our focus to what's going right.

In Alan's case, it's time for him to stop reminding himself of all the occasions when Jacob was inconsiderate, especially if it's become a reflex to think of those first. Then, if all goes well, Alan might start relishing those Saturdays together to connect with Jacob, and eventually he'll have to let Jacob evolve into his next phase of adolescence, later curfew and all. That will bring new issues, but now that the two have established a way to tackle issues collaboratively, each one should be treated as its own unique challenge, not as though it were piggybacking on past problems. For Jacob to grow past this failure, he can't be continually reminded of it.

Questions About Other Ways Kids Fail to Show Concern for Others

Q: My fifteen-year-old daughter "borrows" my things without asking, and I find myself having to ransack her room to find a shirt, hairbrush, or book she's taken without my knowledge. Usually, when something is missing, it's deep in the abyss of her room. She seems apologetic-ish when I'm put out by this, but she keeps doing it. How can I teach her to treat my things with the same respect she'd treat hers?

A: If it's true that her room really is a junk-pile lost and found, maybe your question is moot. I mean, do you really want her to treat your things with the same level of respect she treats hers, or is she already doing that when her things are tossed haphazardly right alongside yours into the chaotic abyss? You'll need to be more explicit about your rules and expectations around borrowing items and caring for them to sharpen up these blurred lines. First ask yourself, do I ever take her things without asking? Many parents assume their children's belongings are also theirs because they paid for them. If you find yourself in this camp, you may be sending mixed signals about communal property. Next, decide if there are any items she can borrow without asking. Perhaps there are some things you've always shared and will continue to share without tightening up the rules. Books may be fair game, but not clothing, for example. Totally up to you. For the rest of your stuff, you'll need to do more than say, "Hey, please treat this [sweater] with the same respect you would your own," knowing she would leave her own sweater at a friend's house for weeks or under a damp pile of workout clothes in her bathroom. Determine what matters to you when lending your things and communicate those expectations to her. Then—this is important—before this goes any further, let her also know the consequences for not following your rules. If she borrows a sweater, she should do so knowing that if she damages it, she will need to pay for you to dry-clean it—or whatever you think is fair. It sounds to me as if your daughter has just gotten thoughtless with boundaries around the house and needs the lines drawn again clearly for her so she can meet your expectations.

Q: My son and his friends are in seventh grade, and the level of trash talk that goes on among them is astonishing. I hear it when they play video games and see it in group texts and on their social media. I think it's mostly done to be funny, but sometimes I can't tell if my son is starting to believe this is how people should talk to each other and that putting people down is not only okay but expected. Should I step in to explain that this is not okay or let him figure it out, which I'm imagining will only happen after he is on the receiving end of the trash talk that goes too far?

A: Whether playing a game online or on the blacktop at recess, young boys and grown men are always going to incorporate trash talk into their competitive strategy. As an observer, and an emotionally sensitive one at that, I am continually astonished at the mean things athletes and gamers can say to each other while they play. The key in being able to do this without developing a reputation for being either a full-time jerk or a brat is to learn how to dish out and receive trash talk in a light-hearted way. For seventh graders, this concept can be nuanced and hard to grasp, so this is where you come in. Without banning the way your son and his friends prefer to communicate, you can ask some questions to get him thinking, maybe even about professional athletes or older kids at school, so he doesn't get defensive if you start asking explicitly about his friend group. Here are three questions that can guide a good conversation on this subject:

- What kind of guy takes trash talk too far?
- What kind of guy is usually the type who gets upset during trash talk?
- Who is the celebrity or person you know in real life who is the most natural and effective at trash talk?

In the introduction to this book, I mentioned the work of Erving Goffman and his theory of impression management. People who posture for a crowd, especially young adolescents, do so because they need to see something positive reflected back at them. It may help you to frame this bravado and negging as a way teens can urge their audience to reflect back the image they want others to see: a winner, an achiever, a top dog. In my experience, trash talk is most rampant in fifth through eighth grade, and by high school it slows way down, though, as I said earlier, many grown-ups still engage during games. To help your son grow into the kind of man who does this appropriately, remember that while he is at home, you are the referee, and you can call "foul" anytime the trash talk goes too far. Save your son from social and professional repercussions by defining what does and doesn't belong in trash talk. Jokes or attacks on things a person cannot change about themselves (race, identity, and physical differences) are off limits and will not be tolerated.

The Silver Lining About Failing to Show Concern for Others

Most people grow out of this failure to show concern for others, or it can be coached through purposeful parenting. Kids like Jacob have a stronger need to feel independent, and if you have a child like this, this phase of life may be rockier than you expected. It's not, however, an indictment of your relationship, your parenting, or their personality. The silver lining to being the Ego is that these kids are strong and often make great leaders because they have confidence and resolve. Remain flexible in your approach and firm in your goals. By doing so, you can allow your child the benefits of independence balanced with the responsibility that brings. Kids who get to strengthen their muscles as they find this balance between contributing and receiving are much more prepared to launch into adulthood.

CHAPTER TEN

Failure to Connect with Peers: The Loner

I started seventh grade with a best friend I carried over from elementary school. Heather was funny, outgoing, and crafty in a way I thought of as worldly, but my parents described as sneaky.

Heather, in addition to being the person who introduced me to a *boynton* in chapter 2, taught me how I could write a letter that would still reach her at summer camp *without* putting a stamp on the envelope. All I had to do was put her name and camp address in the return address position and my name and home address as the addressee. In this way, we could save twenty cents on postage while also experiencing the deviant joy of outwitting the system, and all for the small inconvenience of receiving news a mere two weeks later once the envelope was returned to sender for lack of postage. If you'd asked me and Heather, adults who paid for stamps were suckers.

We explored the world together, making discoveries that ranged from Silly Putty art to the *Days of Our Lives* soap opera, in the breezy and confident way that twelve- and thirteen-year-olds can oscillate between being children and being teenagers. Shortly after seventh grade, Heather and I befriended a new girl to our school, Rachel, and the three of us became a trio . . . until Rachel and Heather started doing more and more without me.

A tale as old as time. I found myself alone.

As a kid, being ousted from the group had me questioning everything about my self-worth. As an adult, and in particular an adult who specializes in helping kids and parents through early adolescence, I understand not only that being ousted from my friend group wasn't a reflection on my value as a friend but also that my experience was not unique—even if at the time I felt like the only seventh grader stranded on exile island.

Most tweens and teens experience feeling like the Loner sometimes; even the ones who seem to be surrounded by others can feel alone in a crowd if they don't feel completely understood. And the vast majority of adolescents experience at least one major friendship closure where one person wants to stay the course but the other needs to move on. This is a normal and necessary part of growing up. In fact, research suggests that only 1 percent of friendships formed in seventh grade last through high school. Early adolescence is a time of social ebb and flow between potential new friends. I had some loose ties with girls in my grade that filled the gaps between friendship soulmates, including a couple girls who tried bringing me into their fold, and in hindsight I regret not being warmer to their kindness, but I was still hurting from being dumped and afraid of getting burned again. It took until spring of freshman year in high school for me to make a meaningful new friendship bond that filled that void.

Watching your child's friendship end is difficult, especially if you're attached to the friend or their family, but it's no reason to panic or get involved. When we give kids space to figure out who they are becoming, and whom they want to share their emerging self with, these things tend to work themselves out, as they did in my situation.

I share this because I don't want you going into this chapter worrying if your child has been through a friendship breakup. It would be highly unusual if your child *didn't* experience being the Loner for some period of their adolescence.

Parents *should* be concerned, however, when patterns emerge showing an inability, or a disinterest, in making connections. If your child finds themselves in a series of failed friendships where they felt victimized, or on the edge of their peers' social relationships for years in a row (as opposed to one hard year), or without one friend they can call on when they are lonely, this is when an intervention will help. These may come in the form of social mentorship or joining a social skills group, one-on-one counseling, testing for neurodivergence, or changing the environment by switching schools, teams, or camps to offer the child a fresh start.

For a deeper look at how a child can grow and learn from this kind of failure, let's see how using *Contain, Resolve, and Evolve* tactics worked for one family. Then, after the case study, I'll reply to some common questions about being disconnected from peers.

MEET THE LONER

Case Study: How Ava "Failed" to Connect with Her Peers

Edwin and Barbara's daughter Ava was part of a close group of friends throughout elementary school. They played hockey on the same team Edwin coached in a small Massachusetts town, and their parents often threw parties together where the kids ran around outside while the parents had drinks and socialized. Ava, always the life of the party, used to organize treasure hunts or games for her friends during these get-togethers.

The summer before sixth grade, Ava flat-out refused to go to the Fourth of July celebration her family always hosted with their friend group. Making the situation even more delicate, the party was at Ava's house. After negotiation, bribing, and pleading failed, Barbara told the guests Ava was sick while Ava hid out in her room for the entire afternoon.

Did something happen? Had someone hurt her? Ava's parents wanted answers, but Ava could only say that nothing had happened, she didn't want to hang out with those girls anymore, and she wanted to go to a different middle school. In addition to being shocked and stumped by Ava's declaration, Edwin and Barbara were put out, because this meant they'd have to learn about new middle school options, as opposed to funneling Ava into the same school her older sibling attended, a place that already felt like home to her parents. Ava couldn't, or wouldn't, articulate to her parents why, despite their attempts to understand, but she insisted on going somewhere else.

Her parents could have insisted she stay put, but seeing how determined and sad she was, they agreed to follow her lead. That fall, Ava enrolled in a private school one town over. Because the school drew from different suburbs, as opposed to a more traditional neighborhood public school, it was also more diverse in many ways. Barbara and Edwin hoped this would be a fresh start and that with so many new options for friends, Ava would be revived into her former gregarious self. Unfortunately, though she sometimes talked to her parents about kids at school, Ava never hung out with anyone outside school hours. She became increasingly less happy, less herself, according to her parents. She seemed to trudge through middle school without much connection to her peers and by eighth grade had declared she wanted to go to a different high school altogether where she didn't know anyone.

Barbara would sometimes look at old photos of Ava and wonder where her fun-loving, vivacious daughter had gone. Would high school, with its sea of new faces, be a chance to start over or would it be more of the same? Was Ava simply a changed person, doomed to a life of loneliness?

 Contain

Gather the Truth

I encourage parents to gather information in this first phase of post-failure containment so that they can better understand the scope of the problem and maybe gain insight into why this happened or if it's happened before, and then use that information to inform their response.

This situation is different. Tread carefully when the circumstances involve a child's removal from a friend group, no matter whether the child pulled themselves out, as Ava did, or if they were rejected. If your child is disconnected from peers, you may feel a strong impulse to ask other parents for their take. Here are some ways that can play out:

Your child thought they were close to a friend or group of friends, but the feelings weren't reciprocal. No one wants to give feedback as to why their child doesn't connect with yours. Someone in the equation has qualities the other finds annoying or just doesn't vibe with. We expect little kids to keep enjoying the people they've always enjoyed as they grow up, but that's not realistic. Hunting for feedback puts other people in the awkward position of having to tell you why their child is pulling away. "To be honest, Ann, it's just that Roger finds Ethan's bad sportsmanship incredibly annoying." What will you do with that information? Just . . . make Ethan a better sport? Wouldn't you already have done that if you could? Or, far more likely, the other parent will deflect with some vague nicety. "Gee, yeah, I guess they haven't been spending as much time together, but I know Roger thinks Ethan's a great guy. He's probably just busy with baseball or something . . . Roger really loves baseball these days. Anyway, gotta get to practice!"

There are rare adult friendships where, of course, you can ask if your friend has any insight into why your kids no longer connect, when the adults involved accept that friendships change during adolescence and can talk about it happening without judgment. But honestly, what will that information get you? If you report what you've gathered to your child, what will it get them? "Don't worry, sweetie, I found out what's happened: Apparently, you're just irritating. I know that's sad to hear, but if you work on that, you can find friends who are a much better fit."

If your child's friendship dissolves, it's usually best to treat it the way you would if your friend were going through a romantic breakup. Don't get involved other than to be a kind and supportive distraction from their heartache. Don't say anything bad about the ex in case they get back together. Listen more than you talk.

Now that I've cautioned you against gathering the truth when friendships dissolve, the one time I would consider it is in one just like Ava's, and even then I'd do it with an ever so gentle touch. Because Ava pulled away from her friend group and appeared depressed, it may be that her friends' parents know something about her mental health heard only through their children. So rather than investigating to find out what caused the breakup, in this case you could ask if anyone has any insight into why Ava seems different lately. You're not assigning any blame or asking about anyone else's child, just asking if any close parent friends might have heard something that would be a red flag about her frame of mind.

Shrink Your Child's Exposure

Some situations require swift action to contain the problem. Others require observation and agility to respond to emerging issues as they reveal themselves. Ava's parents felt concern about their daughter's change in personality and spirit, but they couldn't point to any one behavior that raised alarm bells for a safety intervention. Instead, they felt stuck in a sort of malaise, longing for her old personality to re-emerge as if it had just been on a long vacation. Their swift action came in the form of trusting Ava to advocate for herself and agreeing that she could switch schools.

Ava continued to get good grades, though she did drop hockey in addition to cutting way back on socializing. She was simply different and distant in a way that made her parents sad. Ava's parents did their best to increase her exposure to new people and experiences in hopes that this would improve her overall sense of happiness. So, in this case, because Ava was the one shrinking her exposure, they tried to gently let in more of the world when they could.

Affirm Your Child

In addition to letting Ava switch schools, Barbara says that one of the most important ways they affirmed Ava was by never forcing her to see a therapist. When I asked during our interview if they ever thought a counselor or therapist might help, Barbara said that Edwin had, in fact, suggested it a couple times but Ava vehemently refused.

An important piece of Ava's story is that her older sister has had lifelong mental health challenges that, Barbara says, sucked a lot of energy away from the other kids in the family. Her parents chalked up Ava's refusal to see a counselor to years of watching her older sister struggle in and out of therapy all the while serving as her older sister's "punching bag" (Barbara's words). A desire to distance herself from her sister had always been a driving force in Ava's life. So, though they are big believers in the healing power of therapy, Ava's parents let her make this decision for herself, and they credit that regard for Ava's autonomy with their ability to maintain a healthy relationship with their daughter.

In general, I am a huge believer in therapy, but I know that forcing a child into therapy can be counterproductive, unless the child is in danger of hurting themselves or someone else, or is experiencing a neurological condition known as anosognosia, in which a person isn't able to be reasonably aware of their mental condition. When these exceptions don't apply, parents can use these tips to gently encourage a child to try therapy:

- Give your child a central role in choosing a therapist.
- Make a list of what kind of person they'd feel most comfortable talking with (must be funny, must not be corny, must not condescend, must be smart, and so on).
- Unless your child is eighteen, their therapy isn't legally confidential from you, but you can encourage them to go by agreeing up front that anything they discuss with a therapist will be confidential—meaning you won't ask them or the therapist about what happens in session.
- Let your child know they are the "hiring" person here so they can interview several candidates to find the right fit. Most therapists offer a fifteen-minute meet and greet, which means very little time commitment from the child up front but certainly enough to get a sense of the therapist's personality.
- If your child would be more comfortable, they can email therapists questions before the first session to get a sense of fit or what would happen in a session.
- Equate a therapist to a pediatrician or dentist or physical therapist. This is a normal and necessary part of staying healthy.

- Normalize therapy by asking someone your child respects to share their positive experiences with therapy.
- If your child is on social media, share some accounts to follow that promote taking care of your mental health. Google "Instagram accounts that normalize therapy" for plenty of broad results; then you can customize the search to narrow it for your child by adding their identifiers or interests (athletes, black girls, teen boys, anxious kids . . . get as specific as you can).

Control the Narrative

Since Ava's friend group assumed they'd all move up to the neighborhood middle school together, initial communication involved telling close friends (both Ava's and her parents' friends) that Ava had decided to try something new. They focused on her interest in the music program at the new school, rather than disclosing that Ava had a change of heart about her friend group. One friend questioned whether the public school wasn't "good enough" for Ava, but overall most gushed about how they would miss her. Again, since Ava's experience didn't flame up the way some failures do, there wasn't a huge need to expand on why she was switching schools beyond "trying something new."

Ava's parents did all they could in the moment to support and affirm and protect their child. It's frustrating not to know the answer to what's bothering a young person, especially if it's bothering them to the point of interfering with their friendships. But beyond offering support and creating a nonjudgmental environment at home, sometimes parents must simply wait on a child to share.

 **Resolve**

Take Action

Barbara and Edwin knew this wasn't a situation that needed a structured approach to resolution. Ava hadn't done anything wrong. Forcing her to engage with her old friends or to continue playing hockey would only spawn more discontent; their goal was to find where their happy, gregarious daughter had gone, or at the very least, why she'd left so suddenly. Resolution, for their family, involved *fostering connection* and *reprioritizing*.

Foster Connection

Since connection was exactly what they craved and exactly what Ava rejected, Barbara and Edwin needed to be flexible and lower their expectations. Edwin learned that asking Ava to join him at the ice rink was a nonstarter, a development that initially caused him a lot of pain since this used to be their special activity together. Instead of trying to convince Ava that she could learn to love hockey again, he settled for asking if he could watch old episodes of *The Office* with her when she was in the living room. It wasn't how Edwin would have chosen to spend his free time, but he chose being near Ava over forcing her to have fun his way.

Reprioritize

Ava's parents also made a choice to reprioritize family matters during her middle school years. While her older sister still needed extra care and energy, they realized they needed more boundaries around how the girls interacted with each other. Barbara said she stopped thinking of her family as a unit of four, where she was always trying to keep peace against the turmoil, and instead began focusing on her one-on-one relationship with each daughter.

As Ava began to feel more like her own person, out from her sister's shadow and able to explore her thoughts and feelings without influence from her peers, she started to confide in her mom about what was really going on. Ava had come to realize she identified as bisexual. Both her retreat from her friends and the need to see herself in a new setting were helpful tools in getting to know who she was becoming.

Important: If you opened to this page and started reading here, please check chapter 1 for a definition of failure and explanation of the stories you'll read in this book. In no way is Ava's, or anyone's, sexual identity a failure. The only failure I see regarding development of sexuality or gender is when adults fail to affirm a child's identity. The reason I included Ava's story in a book about failures is to illustrate that sometimes a moment in life can feel like a failure to thrive, when it's really a successful exploration of oneself.

Sometimes a moment in life can feel like a failure to thrive, when it's really a successful exploration of oneself.

Most adolescents go through periods of isolation and exploration. These are two primary ways kids figure out who they are in the world: by cocooning in their rooms as they get to know their emerging selves by focusing on their own thoughts, and by venturing into the world to figure out how to become more independent outside the family unit.

Ava spent several years isolating herself from others as she figured out the many changes that come during early adolescence, which I often refer to as the Middle School Construction Project. This is the period of life when kids begin to build the three fundamental things they need in order to become adults: an adult body, an adult brain, and an adult identity. For all tweens, this time is chaotic in the sense that it's full of constant change. For children who identify as LGBTQ+, some grapple with the added complexity that a part of their project includes changes they fear will make them unpopular, misunderstood, unsafe, or unacceptable. Thankfully, we've made huge strides as a society, and without a doubt young people are more accepting than adults when it comes to understanding a range of sexual and gender identities. Nonetheless, we know that kids still face discrimination and hatred from some peers, adults, lawmakers, and authority figures, so grappling with feeling even more different at an age when everything is already uncertain can weigh heavily on a child.

Ava came out to her mom in eighth grade. Barbara says she was surprised, but she hugged Ava and let her know nothing would change. Ava waited a year longer to tell her father, whom she'd been extremely close to in elementary school. Edwin also reassured Ava that he loved her and accepted her. He later expressed confusion to Barbara, not Ava, in understanding how people experience bisexual attraction. Barbara thinks it would have been easier for him to understand Ava saying she's a lesbian because he's more of a black-and-white thinker. Sensing this about her dad might have caused Ava to hold back longer in coming out to him, but I don't know for certain. It's worth noting, too, that a 2013 Pew Research Center survey found that bisexuals are "much less likely than gay men or lesbians to have 'come out' to the important people in their life."

After Ava came out to her parents, her personality seemed to brighten again. She started working a part-time job and spending more time with friends outside school. Her parents were overjoyed.

Update Communication

After Ava came out to both her parents, that didn't mean she was ready for them to tell the rest of their family and friends. Experts in gender and sexuality agree that outing a person before they are ready can have disastrous health and safety implications. So, while Barbara and Edwin might have wanted to tell their friends—either as an outward expression of support for their daughter or as a token of explanation for why their daughter had pulled away—this, as I often say, was not their story to tell.

Though no updated communication outside the family was necessary, Barbara did offer to help Ava, when she's ready, in talking to extended family members. It can be exhausting for a young person to field questions from relatives about whether they have a boyfriend/girlfriend yet or if they're excited about an upcoming dance. When the time comes, Barbara says Ava knows she's prepared to help her with any line of questioning from less sensitive family members.

Engage Your Whisper Network

The beauty of a good whisper network is that it's discreet. Without outing her, Ava's parents could find solidarity and support through any number of online or community resources for parents of LGBTQ+ children. In fact, I think it behooves all parents, even if their child identifies as heterosexual, to have a full and modern understanding of the gender and sexuality spectrum. There are many great groups, books, and websites available for educating oneself, including PFLAG.org and Identiversity.org.

 Evolve

Allow Time and Space to Process

Adolescents experience failure to connect with their peers for lots of reasons, and there are plenty to consider that I'll address toward the end of this chapter. Regardless of the reason, remember that losing a friend or friends can create feelings of loss and even grief. You may assume that once your child appears to have moved on, either by making connections with potential new friends or by just seeming happier and less distant, the problem is in the past. And it may mostly be, but feelings of grief, embarrassment, or vulnerability can still pop up unexpectedly.

In Ava's case, she processed her changing sense of self privately, before talking with her parents about her sexuality and then coming out to more family and friends. Coming out doesn't mean the processing is over. Parents of LGBTQ+ children shouldn't be surprised if their child goes through many iterations of coming out to different people along the way and if they still need time and space to reflect on how this affects their social connections.

Triage Your Fears

Whether your child rejects others, or gets rejected, not connecting with peers can breed a long list of fears. Here are some of the fears that clouded Barbara's mind as Ava pulled away:

Is Ava lonely and hurting?
Could loneliness grow into despondence, and how will I know if Ava is really suffering?
Is my child a bad friend?
How have I contributed to Ava's failure to connect?
Am I going to lose parent friends because Ava is pulling away from their kids?
Has something scary happened that no one is telling me about?

A tween or teen's social life is shrouded in mystery most of the time, but especially when they are working through a social conflict.

Barbara probably won't get much useful information about what happened to make Ava pull away so quickly, so it makes sense that her fears would grow around the great unknowns, leaving her to speculate about how this disconnection will affect Ava's mental health and future happiness.

As she waits to see how this situation evolves, she should consider if any of her fears can be addressed, or begin to be addressed, within twenty-four hours. If they all seem overwhelming, as this list does at first, take just a tiny piece of one of these bigger fears as a starting point.

Face One Fear First

The one thing I'd want Barbara to tackle right away is this worry that her child's loneliness will outgrow her ability to handle it and that Barbara won't know how badly she's suffering. She can't fix this fear in twenty-four hours, but she can do two specific things to start.

First, knowing that Ava confided in her about her sexuality, she can presume Ava thinks of her mom as someone she can trust. With that confidence, she can ask for a heart-to-heart talk to see the degree to which Ava is lonely. It may be much worse in Barbara's mind than in reality. If Ava is lonely, Barbara can thank her for confiding and ask if they can compile a list together of what might help Ava cope. If she isn't particularly lonely and is okay with fewer close friends at that point, Barbara can know to keep an eye on whether she's projecting more pain onto the situation than necessary.

Second, Barbara can tell Ava that anytime she wants to talk about how she's feeling, she'll be available. For Ava to trust that her mom continues to be a safe place to unload her emotions, Ava will want to know her mom (a) will *mostly* listen, (b) won't try to fix anything unless Ava asks, and (c) won't judge Ava or anyone else involved.

Uphold *Your Child's Bill of Rights*

Right: Choose Their Own Friends and Gather with Peers

Barbara and Edwin may feel anxious about Ava's finding a new group, but Ava deserves the right to go at her own pace and to trust friends at her own discretion. If her parents appear emotionally uninvested, they *might* be able to maneuver Ava's exposure to a few new people without being detected, but it takes subtlety and artfulness to play matchmaker without looking as though you were trying too hard on your child's behalf. Parents who openly play this role risk signaling to both their child and their child's peer group that the child is incapable of making friends without help. Ava has the right to choose her own friends and/ or to choose not to choose quite yet.

Right: Seek Independence and Not Be Relied On by Caregivers for Personal, Emotional, or Financial Gain

Parents are bound to worry when a child's friendship ends. Things become more complicated when the parents of both kids are friends and they don't know how to maintain their adult friendship around awkward and detached ex-friend kids. Crucial to everyone's happiness is for the parents to distance themselves and their friendship from what the kids are going through. Barring intentional trauma caused by one child to another, parents probably don't need to get involved in kids' friendships ending. They especially shouldn't puppeteer future interactions between the kids in order to make the adults, themselves included, feel less awkward. Parents shouldn't expect their children to solve this for them by making nice with kids they don't like or trying to salvage old friendships for parents' ease.

Ava has the right to stop being friends with her old social group, even if it makes things socially awkward for her parents. Her parents have the right to insist on some amount of tact and social decorum from Ava, including treating former friends politely in passing. Beyond that, it is up to them, not their child, to navigate any disrupted social connections.

A child does not owe an adult being friends with anyone to make the parent's life more fun or less tense.

Right: Access Accurate Information from Multiple Perspectives and Sources on All Topics

Your child is going to bring many discoveries about themselves and their world to you. Climate change is terrifying. So are school shootings. Pronouns are a thing now. So are openly gay rappers. That comedian you love is widely considered a misogynist. That comment was body shaming. It's weird to use punctuation when you text me. It's weird when you text me.

It may be all new to you, and some of it may seem too trivial to respond to, while some of it may seem too heavy to even know where to start. Need some relief? Encourage your child to teach you what they know and to show you how they know it. Read their articles, watch the TikTokers or YouTubers they learn from, and talk about why it's important to them as well as what makes a source reliable. Remind yourself of the things you thought were important that your parents blew off, and accept that you can't be the gateway to knowledge on all things for your child, because too much of it is new, so be willing to uphold your child's right to learn from others and make sure it's a wide variety of others so they aren't learning in a bubble (yours or that YouTuber's).

Ava has the right to learn as much information as she craves about her emerging sexual identity from reliable sources, both in real life and online. Barbara and Edwin can affirm this right by buying her books that are highly rated by readers who identify as bisexual, by encouraging her to join groups that advocate for her rights and educate her about the experiences of others who share her identity, and by reading those books and joining parent groups themselves to increase their collective knowledge.

See New Things

At a certain point, it's time to say this episode of failure has come to its conclusion and we're all moving on. If you continue to press for your child to identify and explain to you what went wrong, you may be "interviewing for pain," a phrase Dr. Michael Thompson popularized in his book *Best Friends, Worst Enemies.* If you don't want your child to wallow in unhappiness, you must avoid being the person who always brings up what could be going wrong and instead show interest in happier parts of their life, not just the worrisome ones.

As for Ava, she switched schools again after middle school, returning to her neighborhood public high school, and though she didn't reconnect with her childhood friends, she did find her place. Going to a new school is a great opportunity for kids to reinvent themselves. This can be a helpful way to mark closure on the past and a new beginning.

Quick Answers to Common Questions About Ways Kids Fail to Connect with Peers

Q: I'm seeing a pattern with my young teen. They seem only able to maintain a friendship with one person at a time. Unfortunately, they quickly tire of that friend, cut them off, and then move on to obsess over someone new until that friendship bores them and it happens all over again. Is there anything I can do to help them be better at managing multiple friendships?
A: I see the conundrum as clearly as you do. Instead of being the Henry VIII of friendships, your child would be so much happier as a Joseph Smith.

Friendship polygamy instead of friendship murder! (I have a twisted sense of humor.)

The point is, it would be good if your child could learn to juggle time and attention between friends instead of becoming completely engrossed with a friendship, then exhausted, and then executing, so to speak, said friendship. Your child would be less likely to grow weary of a friend because they'd have more variety, and the friends would get to avoid being blindsided and hurt. Win-win. But is it possible?

Maybe. I think you should bring this up as an observation but try to withhold any notes of judgment. You might begin this way: "I noticed last month you spent most of your time with Jonah. Now I'm hearing a lot about Eric but nothing about Jonah anymore." If you simply state what you observe and then get quiet, your child has the chance to fill in the blanks for you without trying to find the answer they hope will please you. Use this entry point to get to a place where you can offer some feedback.

This pattern you're noticing could indicate a short-term habit they'll outgrow, a lack of flexibility, or a trait of neurodivergence. Track whether you notice this tendency in other aspects of your child's life to better understand what this tells you about them. Regardless, some gentle conversations about how to juggle more than one friend at a time would be useful. Perhaps it doesn't occur to your child that this would be a good thing, or it does, but they can't figure out the mechanics of how to do this. With coaching or role-playing, they can get there.

Q: My daughter started at a new school this year, and even a couple of weeks in she's struggling to find friends. She says everyone already has their friend group and no one wants to take in a new person. She repeatedly asks people to do things with a low success rate. She's starting to feel defeated and resentful of always having to initiate things. Why can't other kids be nice?

A: When you say she repeatedly asks peers to do things, I wonder if she's asking a variety of people or focusing on the same kids who aren't receptive. Have a conversation about not just how she's approaching other kids but whom she's approaching. Also, approaching an existing group *is* hard, and as you mentioned, her success rate is low. Could she look for other lonely islands who aren't part of a bigger group and see if she can connect one-on-one that way?

This piece of advice may not apply if she doesn't have a device, but has she tried connecting online first before initiating a hangout? A lot of kids use technology to lay the foundation for a new friendship. Like it or not, communicating the way the vast majority of her peers communicate will help, whether that's through iMessenger, Discord, FaceTime, or whatever is popular for her age-group where you live.

Most important, I think shifting her target from making friends to finding an interest will be the most helpful thing she can do. Once she finds her activity, friends might be there waiting. Is she open to trying new things? If you can encourage her to sign up for activities that feed directly into what brings her joy, whether those activities are at school, outside school, or even online, she has a better chance of finding her people there.

Intellectualizing your child's loneliness this way can be helpful, albeit hard. It becomes even more difficult and dire, though, when you aren't seeing that come-and-go of sorta-kinda friends, and instead it feels as though you were watching your child slowly disappear inside themselves, isolating from friends and family. This kind of disconnection was the case with Ava, whose family I interviewed for this chapter, and so many other families I've worked with over the years.

The Silver Lining About Failing to Connect with Peers

While it is painful to watch a child struggle to find their fit in the social world, we do know that many very happy, successful adults went through this themselves during adolescence. I am one of them who wandered a bit aimlessly for a couple of long years during middle school before finding two lifelong best friends in high school. (Hi, Jenna! Hi, Sarah!) The silver lining to being the Loner is that kids who go through this are often the most blindingly beautiful adults you'll ever see. I'm kidding. Truthfully, they are usually resilient and funny adults. It may take longer for some people to find where they fit, but it can lead to a deep appreciation of, and loyalty to, others later in life.

CHAPTER ELEVEN

Failure to Handle Their Feelings: The Sensitive One

In a poll I took of 1,047 parents and grandparents, this is the failure that respondents said worried them most. Understandable, since failure to handle one's feelings *sounds as if* it were going to lead to a mental health crisis, and a mental health crisis *sounds like* scary and unknown territory, and *that sounds as if* it might even lead into a parent's worst nightmare: suicide. Nine percent of high schoolers reported a suicide attempt in 2019. Since the pandemic, in a study of suicide data in fourteen states, five states reported an increase in teen suicide.

Let's address this worst-case scenario immediately so you'll know what red flags to watch for if your child is walking a difficult path. If your child expresses feelings of being a burden or wondering what it would be like if they weren't here, connect them to a trained professional immediately for evaluation. If you discover texts or online searches for ways to end your life, or if your child says outright that they are thinking of suicide, take them to the emergency room immediately.

It's crucial every parent know what to look for in terms of suicidal ideation in children, but statistically speaking again, most children won't take things this far. In this chapter, we'll look at ways in which failure to cope with hard feelings more commonly manifests itself and what parents can do to encourage better self-care and self-awareness among tweens and teens.

First, we should acknowledge the difference between not feeling good and not being able to *cope* with difficult feelings. Every one of us, teens especially, have periodic days or even weeks where we find ourselves in a heightened state of overwhelm, sadness, boredom, irritation, fatigue, doubt, or sensitivity. Normal, normal, normal. It feels bad to feel bad, and feedback that tells us "this feels awful" is helpful because it can motivate us to make changes that can increase our chances of feeling better.

Henny Youngman, master of the comedic one-liner, nailed that feeling in probably the most famous dad joke of all time:

Doctor, it hurts when I do this.

Then don't do that!

We all receive feedback about how we're doing, nearly constantly, from our bodily systems, our friends, our bosses, even nosy strangers, and if certain feedback makes us feel consistently bad without a strong enough payoff to override or numb the feedback, we make a change. Feedback, no matter the source, can be painful, but pain isn't the same thing as a persistent inability to cope.

Whether circumstantial or biological, internal or external, sometimes people can't fight through the feedback, and they need an intervention to help them. Therapeutic and/or chemical interventions can help. Every child will go through phases of heightened vulnerability, but if they are stuck in the mode of the Sensitive One for long periods without any hints of getting over it, I recommend employing your whisper network to find out who the best professionals are in your area to intervene on their behalf.

Also note, there is a huge difference between your child not being able to handle their feelings and *you* not being able to handle your child's feelings. I experienced this myself, just this morning.

About two weeks ago, our two-and-a-half-year-old dog, Bert, who often reminds us that he is still a puppy, and the world's most consistently costly one at that, ate my daughter's new sneakers. My daughter is twenty-two and just home for a few weeks before heading to law school. That is to say, she is an adult in most ways, and a highly functioning one at that. The sneaker thing, though, I could tell, really stressed her out.

We have a lot going on at once in our family right now, including the recent and unexpected passing of my mother, and we're on edge. Anyway, the dog ate the sneakers, and when I saw my daughter's face fall as if she were about to cry, I blurted out, "I'll just buy you another pair!" I didn't even give her time to have her reaction. Frankly, it was the easiest thing for me in the moment. If you had been there watching, you might have thought I was spoiling my daughter. The truth is, it wasn't even about her. I needed to make myself feel better. I needed one less difficult emotion around *me* at that moment.

If that were the end of the story, I'd be okay. But this morning, this very morning, as I sat drinking my coffee and watching the news before heading off to write this chapter, I spotted my son's brand-new, half-eaten sneaker under the coffee table; Bert panted at me from the couch, nothing but pure love radiating from his expensive eyes.

"Did you leave your shoes down here last night?" I asked my son, extremely rhetorically. My stomach tensed, knowing I had just set a precedent with my daughter's shoes. If I didn't replace his sneakers, as I did so eagerly—and so recently—for his sister, this would go into the file every kid keeps of ways their parent favored their sibling. I couldn't deal with that, either.

You see how I'm the one who failed to handle her feelings here, right?

My efforts to keep everyone placated, most of all myself, came at a cost. Quite literally, hundreds of dollars in replacement sneakers that I would have much rather spent on, oh, anything else, but especially something nice for myself. But there's also a cost to the kids, of not letting them learn to work through disappointment, the sting it takes to learn better habits, or the compassion to help a mom who's maybe having a tiny meltdown of her own after a rough few months.

When you notice discord in your house, ask yourself who is filling the role of the Sensitive One here and if they need help coping with their emotional load. Try to guess what percentage of the issue bothers you versus what percentage bothers your kids; then focus your relief tactics on the person feeling most affected.

Most of the time, though, I would bet your teen feels things more intensely than you. Adolescents have less experience handling complicated emotions, and their emotions are often outsized thanks to the restructuring of their brains. While adults assess social situations, solve problems, and think critically with their prefrontal cortexes, teen brains undergo a remodeling in the prefrontal cortex, which drafts the amygdala, the emotional center of the brain, into a more prominent role. The emotional center of their brains is working overtime, and paired with an adolescent's natural inexperience, it makes handling emotions a tough job all around, which is why we recognize so many kids as the Sensitive One archetype . . . they're designed this way.

In this chapter, we'll explore ways adults can intervene when a child's emotions become too big to cope with on their own. How a parent reacts will signal whether hard emotions are bad and to be avoided at all costs or a normal part of being human that, with practice and support, can be managed in balance with other parts of life. As with all medical issues, please seek a qualified, professional opinion on the best approach to your child's mental health. This chapter will give insight into how you can respond, but not into your child's specific emotional needs.

For a deeper look at how a child can grow and learn from this kind of failure, let's see how using *Contain, Resolve, and Evolve* tactics worked for one family. Then, after the case study, I'll reply to some common questions about not being able to handle feelings.

MEET THE SENSITIVE ONE

Case Study: How Lizzie "Failed" to Handle Her Feelings

Lizzie was raised by her biological mom, Val, and Val's partner, Katrina, in a blended home with Katrina's son, Evan. Two moms, two siblings, one happy family, until several months ago, when Val and Katrina separated, to Lizzie's perception, out of the blue.

Val explained that Lizzie felt blindsided by the separation and has been grieving over Evan and Katrina moving to another home. Val and Katrina still live near each other and plan to regularly interact with and support both kids, but it's all new to Lizzie, and she's feeling uncertain about a lot of things right now.

Lizzie attends a school for academically gifted children in grades six through twelve, with a small student body and one building to house them. It's not uncommon for kids of different grades to hang out together at school, Val notes, and at the end of seventh grade, coinciding with her parents' separation, Val noticed Lizzie talking a lot about a tenth grader named Daphne whom Lizzie met rehearsing for the school drama club production of *Seussical*.

At first, Val was glad Lizzie had an interest in a new friend. It seemed to be a positive distraction from the changes happening at home. But as talk about Daphne ramped up, Val got annoyed and then concerned. Everything was about Daphne, from what Lizzie ate to what she wore. An unreturned text to Daphne could throw Lizzie into an emotional tailspin. Her mood, Val says, became entirely dependent on her interactions with Daphne. Lizzie even started speaking in Daphne-isms and commenting on how much they looked alike. *Yes,* Val thought but did not say aloud to Lizzie, *because you're modeling yourself in her exact image.*

Val hoped summer would pose a natural break from Daphne and assumed that a tenth grader wouldn't maintain a school friendship with a seventh grader over that break. But as Lizzie's obsession with Daphne continued to grow through the first several weeks of summer, Val realized that wasn't the case, and she became concerned enough that she sleuthed through Lizzie's phone to better understand this Daphne girl and her hold on Lizzie.

She saw the girls connected on social media sites new to Val, where Daphne was posting videos about taking laxatives to control her weight and smoking pot to control her mood. Through texts, she saw Lizzie asking Daphne more about these things: *How many laxatives was the right amount? How did she learn to smoke pot? Did she ever get caught?*

The laxative question jumped out at Val. She *had* noticed Lizzie was eating less these days. She would often say she was full from snacking earlier, even when they'd been together and there wasn't any snacking Val could see. At meals, Lizzie would push the food around her plate without eating. Was Lizzie restricting her food now due to Daphne's influence? Not to mention the curiosity about smoking pot. The red flags were really starting to fly.

Infatuation or Obsession?

Lizzie's story is not unique. I heard from three parents over the summer whose children were fixated on an older friend, so I reached out to my friend and colleague Dr. John Duffy, a clinical psychologist practicing in Chicago and author of *Parenting the New Teen in the Age of Anxiety,* to ask him if he was seeing an increase in kids acting obsessed with a friend among his clients.

In a word, he said, absolutely.

Dr. Duffy says this is different from having a crush or being infatuated with someone, both of which are short-term interests that most of us can relate to from our own teen years. "It's amplified now. A primary challenge of adolescence is developing a sense of self, and this takes time. Most of us, when we were younger, had the luxury of dipping our toes in the water [of self-discovery]—what if we look this way, or talk that way, or if we start swearing?" Dr. Duffy said. "We were allowed to gently experiment. Kids now have a kind of intensity [about figuring themselves out] at a much younger age."

According to Dr. Duffy, this obsession with becoming like someone else truncates a young person's own identity development. "Three or four years younger than when we started, [kids] hyper commit to the idea that they're going to be like this famous person or this cool person they know." Dr. Duffy explained that this kind of thinking arrests development because kids overcommit and sit in a space that doesn't suit them very well, and that tends to drive up symptoms of anxiety, depression, or obsession.

Dr. Duffy also says social media can play a big part in delayed identity development for kids having trouble finding their peer group. They have access to mental health information in droves, often on TikTok channels devoted to a mental health disorder. For example, a child who feels he doesn't fit in anywhere but relates to a TikToker who talks about his depression and how *he* doesn't fit in anywhere might start watching more and more videos about depression. Before long, depression videos account for the majority of this child's feed on TikTok. He becomes saturated in this content and starts to think of himself as a member of the online depression community. He may start to identify as depressed himself. After all, that is a big part of what an identity provides. It tells you who you are *and where you fit in.* Whether this boy's self-diagnosis is accurate or not, he now *believes* he's depressed, and that will make it harder and harder for him to imagine he's not.

Understanding mental illness at a young age can be key to learning how to cope and live with the challenges this presents. And yes, even TikToks about mental health can be affirming and lifesaving, but only if that discovery leads a person to interact with experts and professionals who can teach them how to manage their symptoms. Simply marinating in an online community and a self-diagnosis is dangerous.

I asked Dr. Duffy a few clinical questions parents may have if their child seems obsessed with a friend, celebrity, or online personality. Here are his answers:

Q: What are the red flags for when an obsession is unhealthy?
A: "There are two red flags, and they're in contrast to one another. One is, if your child is acting clandestine about it, kind of suddenly. They know on some level you wouldn't be okay with it. The other is being extremely steadfast about their obsession. Some kids will adopt this identity and test their parents with it. *This is who I am and you're going to have to accept that.* Parents can sense a quick and sudden change or a challenge that feels dark and maladaptive. They should trust their radar with either of these."

Q: How does a parent weigh whether they should wait and see if this fizzles on its own versus needing to step in?

A: "An obsession that doesn't fizzle on its own is probably being fed by the other person, right? They're giving enough attention to make the person want to chase or please them. They probably enjoy the feeling of adoration and mild fame, or they may even have a personality disorder that predisposes them to manipulate people to satisfy their unmet set of needs. Parents need to step in if a child is being manipulated."

Q: How should parents intervene? For example, if they notice an obsession isn't fizzling, how can they put up barriers, especially if they're afraid breaking contact with the other person could cause their child to react dangerously, like hurting themselves or running away?

A: "I like to differentiate between general parenting and parenting for health and safety. If the situation weren't so extreme, you'd ride this out and make observations. *I notice you seem unhappy when this person doesn't respond to your texts quickly. Talk to me about that.* But if safety is a real issue, be more assertive. Talk to them openly and directly. Because this is a personal safety issue, you want to convey *I'm in on this now.* Now this is our project, not just yours."

Back to Lizzie. In her case of following Daphne's every bad suggestion with worshipful devotion, Val knew quickly she needed to contain the problem. Let's look at how containment worked in this situation.

Control the Narrative

Val knew instinctively she had to jump right in and let Lizzie know she was getting involved. But how would she talk to Lizzie about this? Should she tell her ex, Katrina, with whom Lizzie still spent a lot of time? Should she contact Daphne's mom in hopes that she could tell Daphne to stop interacting with Lizzie?

Val started by limiting Lizzie's exposure to Daphne as much as she possibly could, and since it was summer, that meant taking away her iPad, which was her way of connecting to Daphne by text and social media. Her initial talk with Lizzie covered what she'd seen on her phone regarding laxatives and weed, and from there she bought herself time by telling Lizzie that until she could figure out what to do next, she was going to hold on to her device. Val told her she wasn't in trouble, a key point at this stage, but that for safety reasons Val needed to take this step.

Was Lizzie understanding and chill about this? Of course not. She fought back on every point and bargained nonstop, promising not to do any of the bad things Daphne was doing if they could only stay friends, vowing she'd help Daphne stop doing those things, and threatening she'd hate Val forever if she ruined her friendship. But since Val had already noticed some worrying changes in Lizzie's eating habits, she stuck to her guns and endured her daughter's anger while she thought of what to do next.

Val also decided to let Katrina know, since she had a vested interest in Lizzie's well-being and in many ways they were still co-parenting both Lizzie and Evan, though in separate homes. And finally, she opted *not* to call Daphne's mom after Katrina said that would only make things worse. From Katrina's perspective, Daphne's mother wasn't a stakeholder in Lizzie's health, and probably didn't have the power or interest to do much about making Daphne a better role model or keeping Daphne from talking to Lizzie. Instead, they would focus on helping Lizzie understand why this friendship obsession wasn't healthy.

Affirm Your Child

Because of the recent upheaval at home, Val made extra efforts to reinforce how much both she and Katrina love Lizzie. She explained that this change in their family shouldn't push Lizzie to grow up faster or change herself in any way.

And while Val thought Lizzie needed to hear that Daphne wasn't a good influence, she also knew speaking poorly of her friend would backfire. There was no need to Daphne bash, which Lizzie would only refute. Rather than dwelling on what was bad with Daphne, Val focused on what was good with Lizzie and how this relationship could be damaging to those parts of her: Her creativity, her enthusiasm, her sense of individuality, and her health were all at stake, but Val was there to help.

Shrink Your Child's Exposure

When she took away Lizzie's technology, it created a void of *nothing to do,* so Val had to actively seek ways for Lizzie to fill her time. Unplugging is always hard for the first few days, but kids usually sink into a new routine after they get past their anger and start exploring what to do next. Val signed Lizzie up for summer activities, pottery and painting classes, that she hoped would be good distractions and became more involved than usual in setting up time to hang out with old friends.

Take Action

Enable Interventions

The thing Val most wanted to know was whether Lizzie's change in eating habits was the beginning of an eating disorder, so she made her an appointment with a therapist who specializes in teen eating issues.

Early intervention is crucial with food issues, and waiting to see how a child's relationship with food plays out can be dangerous. It is much harder to stabilize a child once disordered eating has taken hold. Don't worry about intervening too soon. If you have any concerns about your child's relationship with food, don't delay in consulting with an expert on this topic.

Foster Connection

Second to intervening, a key step in helping a child through the forced breakup of a friendship is fostering connections with other people. Social support is helpful to all people after a loss, but especially to teens who thrive on social connection.

No child will be warm to the idea of their mom trying to replace a friend. Val should keep at it anyway. Even if Lizzie doesn't accept nine invitations to do something with her mom, she may accept the tenth. For her part, Val shouldn't take it personally when Lizzie declines. By continuing to suggest fun ideas, offering rides, hosting get-togethers in their home, and scheduling events with other families, she can show Lizzie that she isn't going anywhere, and eventually Lizzie will outgrow her resentment and take her up on something.

Update Communication

Resolving this situation will require open communication with the adults in Lizzie's life who love and support her. Even though Val and Katrina separated, Val chose to include Katrina in helping Lizzie, so it will be important to keep Katrina updated. For one thing, Katrina can support Val's rules about technology use and particularly communicating with Daphne when Lizzie visits her house. For another, Katrina can be another set of eyes to be sure Lizzie is eating in the way her doctor has suggested is best.

Triage Your Fears

Val's fears in a situation this intense may include any of the following:

Has Lizzie developed an eating disorder?

If yes, will Lizzie be able to recover?

Has Lizzie experimented with taking drugs?

Is Lizzie overly impressionable?

Will Lizzie be able to form healthy attachments with friends after this?

Will Lizzie trust her mom again, and will they be able to enjoy each other's company anytime soon?

Did Val somehow set Lizzie up for this by going through her separation from Katrina?

Could Val have done anything differently to better help Lizzie handle the separation?

It would be easy for Val to become overwhelmed. It's especially important that Val protect herself from that by choosing just one or two things from the list that she can focus on in the next twenty-four hours and put the others on hold.

Face One Fear First

Other than making the calls to find an expert who can help assess if Lizzie is in danger with her eating, which should definitely be the first practical step Val takes, the fear on this list that can be dealt with most quickly is Val's worry that Lizzie will lose trust in her. And while Val can't control how Lizzie reacts to being separated from her new friend, she also doesn't need to look away and wait for the storm to pass. A little planning can go a long way in managing how Val and Lizzie move through this storm together.

In the next twenty-four hours, Val can make a list of things she can say to, and do with, Lizzie to show her they're on the same team. Val can lean on her go-to phrases so she doesn't fumble around, and this will help her set the tone as positive and possibly even block any accusations from Lizzie about her mom not caring, not loving her, and so on. You know, the phrases kids call on when they're most vulnerable and hurt. It may feel silly, but having a little script to pull from can remove the doubt, tension, and anxiety from hard situations. Here are some phrases that can help:

- I see you're hurting, and I believe you when you tell me this.
- I want to help you feel better in a way that's safe.
- I'm on your team, even if you don't feel that way right now. I always am.
- This is hard and I'm sorry it hurts. I'm here to help.
- It's okay if you're mad at me and if you hate me. I'm not going to try to persuade you to change your mind. I love you and I'll give you some space.

Uphold *Your Child's Bill of Rights*

Because Lizzie's life was trending toward areas that could damage her health in long-term and serious ways—I'm thinking mostly of the food issue—many of the rights listed in *Your Child's Bill of Rights* won't be wholly available to her until her doctors feel she's on more steady ground. These two rights, in particular, give me pause in this situation:

- Maintain some privacy
- Choose their own friends and gather with peers

This doesn't mean she deserves no rights whatsoever, though. Here are a couple that can help Lizzie evolve through her situation.

Right: Take Risks

Because Lizzie needs to fill the void Daphne satisfied, Lizzie will benefit from being given the opportunity to take risks, just not the kind she was taking before. Because she loves acting and was active in her school's drama program, where she first met Daphne, a performing arts program could be a good fit for this since it inherently involves lots of risk taking. Her mom can also look into bigger risks beyond a drama class. Perhaps she could get headshots, audition for live theater outside the school setting, or find out how to get an agent so she could audition for commercials. Doing something that makes her nervous, but excitedly so, will take up some of that angsty space that was left when her friendship was terminated.

Right: Practice Making Informed Decisions About Their Bodies

It's unclear at this point whether Lizzie is going to be able to make her own decisions about feeding herself, but if she's not, she may benefit from more bodily autonomy in other areas so that she doesn't feel completely without agency over her body. This is an opportunity to discuss another piercing, a change of hair color, or clothing choices with more flexibility than she might have had before.

See New Things

Despite her anxiety around Lizzie's health, it will be important that food not become the only thing Val thinks about, and especially not the only thing she talks about with Lizzie. Dr. Melissa Miller, a therapist in Charlotte, North Carolina, who specializes in treating eating disorders, says, "When someone struggles with an ED [eating disorder], they think about food and their body *all* the time. Opportunities and encouragement from their parents to think about other things and to engage back in life as much as possible is crucial to recovery." Dr. Miller encourages the families she works with to limit food talk to mealtimes, and even then, to engage in social talk more than food talk. According to Dr. Miller, "We want thoughts on food to decrease in every way."

Once a supportive health team is in place, Val can relieve herself of the pressure of vigilance and shift some of her attention to what she and Lizzie enjoy, or what's perhaps more realistic at Lizzie's age, whatever Lizzie enjoys and will allow Val to be near her while she's doing. In this way, Val can feel sure their relationship isn't centered on what once went wrong in Lizzie's young life.

Similarly, as Lizzie inevitably makes new friends, it will be important that Val not regularly take the temperature on the health of those friendships. It's perfectly normal for kids to experience toxic friendships. This one might have hit Lizzie when she was particularly vulnerable, but Val needn't worry that Lizzie can't navigate other relationships with a balanced approach. Until there is a trend, there is no trend to worry about.

Quick Answers to Common Questions About How Kids Fail to Handle Their Feelings

Q: My son has always been girl crazy. Even as early as preschool he had crushes on girls and doted on them with handpicked dandelions at recess or homemade cards. He's thirteen now, and he is still very affectionate toward girls. We have coached him not to press his emotions on girls who don't reciprocate, but I'm worried if he keeps wearing his heart on his sleeve, he's setting himself up for heartbreak or worse if he doesn't learn to reel in his big emotions.

A: If your son has always been a romantic, and I assume not every object of his affection has reciprocated his interest, then you already have evidence he bounces back pretty easily. Thank U, Next. But even if he's more Taylor Swift than Ariana Grande post-breakup, no parent can shield their kids from the pain of heartbreak.

Whenever the first heartbreak hits, whether at fourteen or twenty-nine, it hits hardest because it's an unknown pain. Your son sounds resilient, adoring, and eager. If he listens and understands that only some people will want that kind of interaction with him, I think you can abandon this worry. If you think he doesn't understand this, then you need to up your attention to this matter. If he is not listening to you, or you can't think of a better way to explain consent to him (not just sexual consent, but also regarding space invasion, nonsexual touch, and time interference), you'll need to call on others to ensure he understands. A therapist, a guidance counselor, or even a smart family friend can do this for you.

Finally, since most parents will need to coach a child through heartbreak at some point, here are four talking points based on research around the intersection of physical and social pain:

    a. Emotional heartache hurts just the same as a physical injury. There is no need to feel embarrassed by your pain any more than you'd be embarrassed if you cried after breaking your arm.

    b. The same part of your brain that responds when you are physically hurt (the anterior cingulate cortex) also responds when you are emotionally hurt.

    c. Your brain's pain response is a way of keeping you safe. If you touch fire, ouch! You remember not to touch it again because pain lingers. Your brain uses pain to protect you from social danger, too. Humans thrive in healthy, mutually satisfying relationships. The physical feeling of your heart aching is your body's way of telling you to protect yourself because you're hurt.

d. Research shows us that having meaningful social ties is the most effective way to heal emotional pain, so when you feel grief, sorrow, or heartache, surround yourself with people who support you. Let them take care of you, just as you would if you had a broken arm. It's hard to imagine pain going away when you're in it so intensely, but over time the pain will become a memory, the same as with any other physical injury you've experienced.

Q: I have a daughter and a son. When my daughter is upset, she sulks. When my son is upset, he lashes out. I can handle the quiet, moody teen, but what am I supposed to do with a child who gets angry and mean? I can't just tell him he needs to calm down. That only makes him angrier.

A: We associate depression with quiet, withdrawn, checked-out behavior, and often that's how it manifests itself in girls, but it's not uncommon for depression to emerge as anger in boys. Unfortunately, this often leads to girls getting more grace and support for their emotional needs and boys getting in trouble. When your son lashes out, take a moment to step back. Wait a beat to allow some silence to take up space in the room. Sometimes the absence of your immediate reaction sends a strong enough signal, assuming the outburst is just a bad habit and not an emotional issue. After a pause, you can say something like this: "I'm not sure if you felt that was a strong reaction, but to me it felt hurtful. Maybe you've had a hard day, so let's take a break and talk later about what's going on." After an hour or so, check in on him and ask if you can talk in twenty minutes. I find that the more bread crumbs I lead up to a talk, the more peacefully they go—the kids and the talks.

If your son just can't regulate his outbursts and/or if he also can't acknowledge he's having them, suggest he talk with a therapist. A professional can provide him with the coping skills he needs.

Q: I know teen emotions are a roller coaster, but I can't tell when the mood swings are normal or a call for help. My daughter keeps a journal, and I want to read it and do a deep dive into her phone to make sure she's okay. How can I know more about what's going on if she won't tell me?

A: As far as diaries or journals go, I tell parents never to read them unless they believe their child is in imminent danger. Think of it as needing a warrant before you search a home. The police can't just *wonder* if something illegal is happening in someone's home, no matter how strange that person seems, or how suspicious their friends are, or how many neighbors complain about them. They need probable cause to search private property. Before you crack open the space where your child records their innermost thoughts, whether it's an old-fashioned, leather-bound journal with a lock on it, a ratty spiral-bound notebook, or a Google Doc on a laptop, make sure you have probable cause based on facts, not hunches. If not, you run the risk of (a) losing your child's trust completely, because I know adults who have still not gotten over this violation from their own adolescence, and (b) putting things in your brain that were never meant for your eyes that are alternately horrifying and harmless. Journals can be a safe space for teens to fantasize, so beware.

Phones, though, are a little bit different, depending on your child's age. Phones are much more complex tools than notebooks. With younger kids, I encourage parents to establish with new ownership that phones will be monitored occasionally for safety and etiquette reasons. Like any tool you give your child, you are responsible for teaching them how to use that tool safely and politely. What is polite tool use? Not mowing your lawn or installing a new deck at 2:00 a.m., for example. *The tool should be useful to you without being a burden, nuisance, or unreasonable interruption to others.*

And while diaries are premised on privacy, phones are not. That said, and broadly speaking, as kids age through middle school, parents should monitor less and less because being micromanaged on technology just sends kids into deeper hiding spaces. Even though phones aren't intended for privacy the way diaries are, *teens still use them that way.* This might make you want to scream, but picture this: You're at a coffee shop with your friend, talking about her recent separation from her husband. It's a deeply private conversation being held in a very public space. The man at the table next to you leans over and says, "I'm sorry, but I couldn't help myself. Maybe it's not entirely your husband's fault? It sounds to me like you've both done some things that are hard to come back from."

You would be horrified, and rightly so, at the intrusion. Imagine telling the man to F off or whatever you'd say in a situation that weird, and then him coming right back with "Listen, if you didn't want people to hear about this, you shouldn't have talked about it in such a public place. Maybe write it in your diary next time? You know whatever you say out here [*waves arms around the coffee shop*] can be heard by anyone and passed on forever."

This is how our teens feel when we read their phones. Yes, technically, private things they share on a device are subject to public consumption if someone screenshots their texts or takes a photo of their Snapchat. But for parents to lean in and read every message feels like the coffee shop invasion. Sure, it's not private by a certain definition, but is it *meant for you?*

Looking through a teen's phone is not nearly the same violation as reading a diary, but the decision to do so should be based on concern that is rooted in a little evidence, not just a desire to know more about your child or a generic concern.

In short, considering the "whether and when" of snooping versus safety checks, it comes down to this: How much evidence do you already have? If you have reason to believe that your child may be engaging, or about to engage, in danger that they cannot come back from (plans to meet up with a man they met online, buying drugs, thoughts of hurting themselves or someone else), you should check. If you just have a hunch that they aren't happy or in a fight with friends, talk with them but don't snoop.

The Silver Lining About Failing to Handle Their Feelings

Silver linings are all about what you learn about yourself. What has Lizzie learned? Stability—even when things seemed most disrupted in her life, her parents came together for her. In retrospect, she will be able to see this clearly. There is zero chance that twenty years from now Lizzie is sitting in a therapist's office bitterly trying to understand why her parents put boundaries on a few-months-long friendship. The silver lining to being the Sensitive One is being forced to learn which coping mechanisms don't work, which usually leads to learning which do.

CHAPTER TWELVE

Failure to Get Along with Their Family: The Black Sheep

The fairy-tale version of kids asserting independence looks like this: Your child sets personal development goals, makes a thoughtful plan to achieve those goals (get good grades, get a job, volunteer, surround self with good role models), checks in with you when they face a challenge in reaching those goals, and then, mere days after they've reached their goals, texts from their new apartment asking for your chicken salad recipe because home doesn't really feel like home without it.

The real version of asserting independence involves a lot more yelling, sulking, hiding, forgetting, and blaming. The path to independence is filled with kids who feel like the Black Sheep of their families. Angsty teen music, literature, and media make it very clear how misunderstood or undervalued the Black Sheep feel. Don't worry, most kids outgrow this as they mature.

In the meantime: Rolling eyes? Grunting short answers? Doing chores late? None of these are ideal in a housemate, but they are often just part of the growing pains parents run into when housemates are young teens. Imagine for a moment that your child is not a child but a puppy. (Stick with me as we briefly convert this metaphor from sheep to puppies. This book is a full-blown animal kingdom that would make David Attenborough proud.) Would you tolerate some nips from them? Sure, but not hard bites. Would you tolerate accidents in the house? Sure, for a while, but you'd be sure to praise them like crazy when they went outside. Would you tolerate barking? Sure, but you'd give them chew toys and pet them or take them on a walk when they were being too loud or unruly.

When a child enters adolescence, parents think "they should know better" than to behave antisocially at home. In fact, a young tween or teen is only learning how to become social at this age because "being social" takes on new meaning for adolescents. Prior to adolescence, they've followed your lead, seen you as both a companion and a protector, and thus mirrored your social habits. Now they're like puppies who must learn to adjust to a new pack order because their social world is newly focused on how they relate to peers rather than how they follow your lead.

Should your child know better than to be dismissive or rude to you? Yes. But do they? Nope. Don't beat yourself up over this new family dynamic. Remove the word "should" from your vocabulary just as you would if you were training a family pet. Take the time you could otherwise spend complaining about their behavior to train them anew to be reasonable members of your household.

Pop Quiz: How Do You *Really* Feel About Your Child Becoming More Independent?

> 1. My child and I have the perfect relationship. They trust me implicitly, tell me everything, never cause me worry because I know I've raised them to do the right thing, and they know I'm their biggest fan.

2. It's Saturday night and my child wants to watch a movie with me. Again. I wish they'd stop being so clingy because it feels as though they should be out there making friends, and I need some space.

3. My child has become a stranger to me. They are a pain to be around, and I hope they somehow turn out to be a nice, decent person, but I wouldn't bet on it quite yet.

Of these, the first scenario is the one that worries me. I suspect this child is having to suppress their own needs to please the parent. No relationship is perfect, and this characterization implies a lot of pressure to maintain perfection. Also, kids deserve to have private thoughts and feelings that they *don't* tell their parents, and parents shouldn't feel uncomfortable when kids pull away. This scenario doesn't indicate any moves toward independence by child *or parent,* and that feels like a developmental backfire.

Number two is less common, and probably not how we think of the typical teen. Still, some kids are late bloomers, perhaps with some anxiety sprinkled in, and the fact that this parent longs for some separation bodes well.

Number three is probably the most common. This stranger living in your home is behaving in a predictable, temporary way as they pass through the individuation phase on the way to becoming independent. If you identify with this scenario, please take comfort in knowing (a) most people do (which I mean less in a misery-loves-company way and more in a you're-totally-normal way) and (b) this chapter is for you! Here I will provide you with some tools for finding harmony. If you relate to scenario number two, you may not need this chapter—yet; but you'll still get insight into what to prepare for down the pike. And if you relate to scenario number one, you might take a pause. Maybe I've got this all wrong, in which case, by all means, carry on enjoying the beautiful relationship you've cultivated with your child. However, don't default to carrying on until you've really examined the dynamic.

Even with scenario three, though, how can you know when your child crosses the line from annoying teen behavior to a real failure in getting along? That line is different for everyone, but below is a list of where parents have told me they've drawn it:

- when the child becomes physically violent with a family member
- when the child intentionally and knowingly continues to cause hurt
- when disrespect is enduring and not occasional
- when the child's behavior consistently disrupts other family relationships (siblings, marriage, grandparents, and so on)
- when caregivers need to take time from other obligations to deal with bad behavior
- when the child makes false allegations against family members
- when communication grinds to a complete halt for an extended period
- when family members fear the child's reaction
- when the behavior creates legal consequences
- when the behavior puts family members in physical danger or at risk of reputational damage

If any of these ring true for you, you would benefit from an intervention with a neutral party who can help with family communication, especially if anyone's safety is at risk. In this chapter, we'll look at how parent reactions can inflame or soothe any negative, but not unsafe, interactions within a family.

Some Kids Don't Fit the Family Mold

Parents tend to freak out when their children act like, or think of themselves as, the Black Sheep of the family.

One of the biggest paradoxes in parenting is that we want our kids to be unique, and yet we also don't want them to stand out. They should be special only in ways that offer advantages, like having the best tennis serve or getting the perfect score on a standardized test. They should not be special in ways that might hurt them for being different. And we definitely don't want them to be different in ways that make them unpleasant to live with. We want them socially safe, sharing popular interests so they can easily make friends, or looking generally like other kids their age so that no one picks on them. And we want them to think and act like us. Is that too much to ask?

Be unique but not weird. Be different but not difficult. Be special but not mysterious.

We expect our sheep to fit neatly into our flock and our puppies to respect our pack and our little birds to tuck under our wings until they are safely ready to fly the nest. We have very specific requirements in our wild kingdoms.

When we talk about kids *breaking* the mold, we mean standing out in a good way. When we talk about kids not *fitting* the mold, we mean standing out in a bad way. One is thrilling; one is painful. But molds—do they really have that much value, especially during adolescence?

I've worked with middle schoolers for nineteen years, and the ones who struggled to fit in during adolescence usually found out, later in life, the mold was the wrong shape, not them.

Just as I tell everyone who turns against their own body as they try on clothes (friends, my kids, the kids I work with, *myself* when I am sane enough to remember my own advice), the problem is not with the shape of your body. The problem is with the shape of the clothes, and we can easily fix that with a trip to the tailor.

It's always easier to swap out the container than the thing you're trying to put into it. It also helps to shop around for different perspectives. A new store, a new school, a new job, a new neighborhood, a new news source, a new group of friends, a new doctor—there are lots of places to go looking for new ways to think about the mold you're trying to fit.

Now, I don't want to throw away all the conventions and boundaries and molds out there. This isn't the Wild, Wild West. I'm deeply comforted by the idea of a social contract, especially when it comes to polite behavior. I hate it when drivers don't zipper merge in traffic or when people have cell phone conversations on speaker in public. I wouldn't give them a thumbs-up and think, "I love seeing that person do their own thing!" Nor would I give them the middle finger because—social contract. What I'm saying is, when it comes to fitting in, what matters most are kindness, consideration, and cooperation. Beyond that, be who you need to be.

Easier said than done for teens who don't have the life experience or the autonomy to ditch their feelings about what everyone else is feeling, achieving, or wearing, and strike out in search of places where they better fit.

Not fitting into the norm can feel like failure, especially when it's the family you belong to that feels like a bad fit. In this case, as with my examples above, it's still easier to change the container than the thing you're trying to make fit into it. Family units need to be flexible enough to maintain reasonable expectations of each other while also making room for members of all shapes, sizes, abilities, identities, dispositions, and personalities.

Let's see how using *Contain, Resolve, and Evolve* tactics worked for one family in crisis. Then, after the case study, I'll reply to some common questions about not getting along with family members.

MEET THE BLACK SHEEP

Case Study: How Kayla "Failed" to Get Along with Her Family

James and Caroline have two daughters, seventeen-year-old Kayla and fifteen-year-old Abby.

Caroline describes her girls as good friends, fun loving and strong-willed. Caroline shared with me a story that started in the spring of 2021, while most families were still deep in pandemic lockdown and tensions were unusually high in homes that also served as schools and offices, and some would say mini prison complexes. One afternoon, as the girls were making food while listening to a playlist, a popular country song came on and Abby sang along. Kayla lunged for her younger sister's phone to turn the music off and shouted at Abby to stop singing. Their shouting escalated as they fought for the music controls. James, hearing the ruckus from his home office, raced in to tell them both to stop it, but they were in too deep to be silenced so easily.

After separating the girls and turning off the speaker, James tried to get to the bottom of the fight. Kayla, an outspoken advocate for others, told her dad the singer had been busted using the n-word on video, and they could not support him or his music in their house.

James countered with Abby's right to listen to whomever she liked, and the fight then jumped the tracks from Kayla and her sister to Kayla and her dad. Back and forth they argued about cancel culture, personal rights, whether the n-word meant different things in different circumstances, who could say it, who could not. James believed he was provoking critical thinking. Kayla felt simply provoked. At one point, it all came down to this. James brought up an example use of the n-word in pop culture, only instead of replacing the word with its abbreviated substitute, he quoted the full word.

Kayla stopped arguing as though she'd been hit. She looked squarely at her dad and demanded he apologize. He tried, instead, to explain that he wasn't using the word, he was quoting someone else, and that was when Kayla ended the fight for good. "You are a racist," she said, "and I will never look at you the same way again."

Kayla and James didn't speak a word to each other for a week. During those days, the house felt made of eggshells. Caroline tried to get them to reconcile, but their anger was too strong. After a week, she says, James's anger turned to hurt. He approached Kayla and asked her to rethink her accusation. "But you *know* me," he kept repeating. Kayla would not budge.

Over the next few months, Caroline says things slowly began to go back to normal. Kayla and James spoke to each other but less casually and still more strained than they ever had before. They ate meals, watched TV, and played with the dogs together, but every family moment was still edged in a stiffness they couldn't shake. James and Caroline wondered if they would ever go back to the easeful way they were, or if this was just the beginning of the end of their relationship with Kayla.

 Contain

Control the Narrative

Usually, controlling the narrative means attempting to manage how information gets out into the community. In this case, the audience isn't external; it's the family itself, mostly James and Kayla, though Abby and Caroline were affected as well.

As the adult in the situation, James needs to be careful about how he proceeds. If he insists on proving he isn't racist, Kayla can dig in her heels, and their relationship will teeter like a balance beam on a single point, with each on the opposing side trying to prove they're right.

Whether James is racist, or Kayla was wrong to accuse him, is not the messaging that requires their focus. Where this conversation derailed was the point at which Kayla demanded an apology for her dad's comment, which offended her, and James didn't comply.

James dug in his heels because he thought the central conflict was whether he was racist. He missed the point that instead of being right, he could have been attentive to Kayla's feelings.

Kayla thinks they're fighting over values. James thinks they're fighting over facts. In fact, they're fighting over feelings. Until they get clear on what they're talking about, they'll stay at an impasse. Repositioning tense discussions around feelings is helpful because feelings aren't right or wrong. They just are. It's much harder to fight at that level.

Affirm Your Child

Since James felt personally attacked, he might be inclined to skip over the chance to give his daughter a compliment as a means of making progress. You might, too, if your child has accused you of a moral failure, called you a name, or was just being downright rude.

Don't skip this step. The adolescent brain perceives criticism as a threat. In response, it shuts down neurons and synapses used to grow. When your child perceives feedback as criticism, they can't learn and grow from it in the way you hope. But, when the adolescent brain feels successful, it fires up synapses to learn. For this reason, beginning with telling your child what you see as one of their strengths is the best way to prepare a young person to receive feedback they can learn from. In Kayla's case, her dad could say something like "I want you to know I admire your passion for doing what's right. I hope you never lose that fire. I also think we need to talk about how we can disagree without shutting each other off."

Another way of affirming Kayla would be to acknowledge the power imbalance in their relationship. As the adult in the family, James has a lot more power than Kayla. Her heatedness around fighting with him could be cooled by his acknowledgment that it can be hard to feel strongly about certain things (what music family members should be allowed to listen to in common areas) and not be in any position to control them. At the same time, this can open a discussion about how families can meet each other's needs or remove themselves from upsetting situations.

Gather the Truth

As addressed in the section on controlling the narrative, it's nearly impossible to know the truth about someone's intentions unless you are willing to accept their word. James asserts he is not racist. Kayla asserts he is. How can either prove to the other they're not telling the truth? The only way forward to finding what's true is uncovering the truth about how they feel. We'll cover how to do that in the next section.

Take Action

Foster Connection

The biggest thing you can do when you experience a failure to get along with your child is foster connection, and to do this, you have to begin with the foundation of love and dignity for all. I know that sounds like rainbows and unicorns, but it really is important to work from a place where neither person feels condemned. The author and educator Rosalind Wiseman does terrific work in this area through her organization Cultures of Dignity, which teaches people how to resolve conflict by communicating openly and effectively. Her book *Courageous Discomfort: How to Have Important, Brave, Life-Changing Conversations About Race and Racism,* co-authored with Shanterra McBride, tackles how to have hard discussions about racism with family members. Wiseman and McBride suggest prompts that validate the other person's perspective as a way to prevent conversations from collapsing in on themselves. These two prompts specifically would be helpful starts for Kayla and James in resolving their conflict:

"Help me understand . . ."

and

"This must be really important to you, and I want to understand why . . ."

If James can approach his daughter from a position of wanting to learn from her, she'll feel validated, and then she'll be open to hearing his perspective, too.

At seventeen years old, we can expect Kayla, like any teen, to be emotional, withdrawn, confused, and even combative about the issues that matter to her most. Her parents will need to decide how to set the tone for living together in a home that encourages individualism, personal values, and healthy debate, without getting mired in unproductive fights.

But before they can evolve through this situation, there is another piece of Kayla's story her mom shared that makes evolving past this failure to get along harder for them. A few months ago, that same country singer who caused the big fight during quarantine announced tour dates. Kayla spent four hundred dollars on two tickets to the concert, one for her and one for her girlfriend. Are you stunned? I was! Then I thought about it. This is very typical teen behavior. It turns out the singer is her new girlfriend's favorite. When James learned about this, he practically went through the roof at Kayla's hypocrisy, and the whole fight got dragged out of the past. Kayla defended her choice to go to the concert because the singer had since apologized and the tickets were a gift for her girlfriend, not something she was doing for herself. (Apologies, you can see twice in this anecdote, are big for teens.)

At this point, James could have gone toe-to-toe with Kayla, poking holes all over again in her accusation against him as well as her recent decision to reverse her stance on the singer who started it all. But James decided he could keep trying to debate Kayla or he could have a relationship with her. Caroline says she believes that broken year finally got to him and he realized there was no way forward without listening more and convincing less.

 Evolve

Triage Your Fears

James and Caroline could worry about any of the following when it comes to Kayla's failure to get along:

Will Kayla ever feel close to us again?

For the remaining time she lives at home, will there be more and
more uncomfortable tension in the house?

Will this tension cause cracks in our marriage?

Since Kayla cut her dad off so quickly, will she do the same to one
of them again?

Is Kayla going to be this explosive with future friendships, romantic relationships, employers, or other authority figures?

Key to resolution is not feeling helpless or hopeless. By being honest
about their fears, then choosing one to address right away, James and
Caroline can evolve alongside Kayla into a time and space where they
can live together in, if not total peace and harmony, appreciation for
each other's company.

Face One Fear First

Most of the fears listed above fall into the "distant wondering" category
as most fears are apt to do, but the one that jumps out to me as first
priority may surprise you. It's the only fear on the list over which James
and Caroline have any immediate control as well as the only one that
doesn't even directly have to do with Kayla at all. It's the fear that their
daughter's behavior or personality will cause cracks in their marriage.
Right away, James and Caroline can begin to do things that will bolster
their relationship, regardless of how Kayla reacts to them. In fact, seeing
her parents focus on each other may put Kayla at ease during the tu-
multuous teen years. It's a real comfort for kids to see their parents enjoying each other. Taking Kayla out of the spotlight (or interrogation
light, depending on how you see this situation) will likely make her feel
less pressure to convince them she's right and they're wrong.

What will this look like for James and Caroline? It will look intentional. They should set time aside to enjoy each other through things

such as date nights, fun activities outside the house, scheduled walks, or scheduled intimacy. Taking it further, they might also seek coaching from a relationship therapist for ways to stay connected as their teens grow older and rattle the cage of domestic bliss. However they approach this, sharing the desire to stay close and prioritizing their relationship will serve all members of the household well through the often-draining years of raising (or being) an adolescent.

Uphold *Your Child's Bill of Rights*

This is where her parents can nudge Kayla through this failure to get along with them by reaffirming her rights even and especially when they don't get along. We often talk about unconditional love for our children, but sometimes teens want to feel *unconditional trust* more than anything, even after they've broken our hearts.

Right: Determine Their Own Values

You could have seen this one coming from a mile away. Ultimately, James and Caroline can only share their values with their daughter. They can't ask her to change hers . . . or stick to hers as the case was when Kayla reversed her stance on the singer.

Consider this: Having values is about aligning oneself with something positive. When Kayla contradicts her own values, it may look to her dad as if she were being a hypocrite. She may be! But arguing over this would be as fruitless as arguing over whether James was racist. Focus on whatever positive pull the child is responding to, and start your conversation there. Instead of saying, "This makes no sense! It totally goes against your values!" try "What do you value that's driving this decision?"

See New Things

Kayla's fight with her dad can't be the *only* newsworthy or interesting thing about who she is within her family. To help her evolve into a better relationship with them, James and Caroline will need to start noticing other things about her, beyond her ability to flip-flop on her ideals.

James and Caroline decided to do two things: first, to be patient and, second, to engage more on the future than the past. They recognize that part of what's driving Kayla's behavior is simply being young. With experience and age, they think she'll be less combative toward them. And since James has decided to drop his urge to debate, things are going well in that department. Kayla is starting to think about college and moving on to her next phase of independence, so that gives them an exciting new topic to focus on as well.

When "Failure to Get Along" Permanently Derails a Family

Do some kids pull away from their families during adolescence and make a break for it, never to return? Absolutely. Sometimes it happens, and sadly, this is beyond a parent's control. I've known many loving parents who fought hard to maintain a relationship with a child who was battling mental health or addiction challenges, for example, and despite colossal efforts, they still lost their relationship with a child who either would not or *could not* make the choices that would preserve a secure and mature relationship with them.

If they're dealing with a situation that evolves into a mental health or addiction challenge, parents need to know they can't, and shouldn't, try to fill all the caregiving roles in their child's life. Employing a team of experts is often key in maintaining the parent-child relationship. Note also that many parents have told me they misread warning signs of depression, particularly among teen boys. Rebellious behavior and not caring about consequences can be signs of depression. It may look like double-fisting life to drink it all in too quickly, which doesn't fit our image of sad, depressed, despondent. But in teen boys, it can show up this way, so if your child's failure to get along looks like wild behavior without fear of what might happen to them, it may mean they really don't care what happens to them. Seek out an evaluation from a therapist for depression.

Letting the therapists, doctors, and psychiatrists carry the burden of diagnosis and treatment can give parents the space to focus on the parent-child relationship, not being a "fixer." Some parents are so close to their child's pain that they fear allowing experts in will cause more damage ("it's not as bad as the doctor thinks"), or that addressing the problem head-on will hurt the child ("she's having a good week, and I don't want to disrupt that by bringing up treatment"), or that no else could know the child as well as the parent ("they only see the problems, not all the great things about my child"), or that following the expert's advice will damage the parent-child relationship ("they'll hate me forever if I make them do this"). These are understandable fears, but parents must accept that the path to healing travels through painful territory. Staving off today's hard decision in hopes that things will just clear up is rarely best for the child in the long run. Parents who ignore the repeated advice of a team of experts run a risk of long-term damage to the child, primarily, and to their relationship, secondarily.

Beyond these more extreme circumstances, sometimes kids fail to get along with their parents because they cannot meet the burden of their parents' expectations *for their relationship*. I'm not talking about responsibility-based expectations a parent has for their child such as doing chores or studying. I mean the expectations some parents have for their relationship with a child. A parent who fears abandonment or rejection might try to force connection (which really can't be done). Making a child *be* near you is not the same as fostering a relationship and will probably only build resentment instead. Some parents feel entitled to gratitude for the endless love and resources they've poured into their child, and that entitlement is enough to strain a relationship to the breaking point. When a parent stews over this, it can come out sounding angry and entitled. "All I'm asking is for you to want to talk to me sometimes. I took you to every single baseball game, and paid for all your equipment, and sat on those hard bleachers for years because you loved playing baseball. And now you're at a great college because of a baseball scholarship. And I just feel like you don't care that I did all that to make this happen for you. Can't you just take a few minutes every week to call me and talk?"

Perhaps you're wondering why the son in this hypothetical situation can't just call his mom. From a time-management perspective, of course he can. In terms of motivation, he might not want to for any number of reasons: His mom gives him a guilt trip and keeps him on the phone longer than she said she would. He's loving every minute of college life and doesn't want to be reminded of what he "owes" his mom for making it happen. He's a student athlete and has very little time for anything outside baseball, classes, and a little social life.

The mom sees the phone call as a duty. The son is overwhelmed by duty. If calling home is an obligation to please the parent, he isn't going to find the time, even if it's just a few minutes. A younger child might feel obligated to meet their parent's needs while they still live at home because it makes things easier for them (less nagging from the parent). But once a child leaves home, they can ignore a parent's pleas and be unburdened from making that parent feel better. In the same way that people shouldn't give gifts expecting anything in return, parents shouldn't raise children expecting to be paid back, not even in the form of gratitude. It's lovely when it happens, but not mandatory. There are things parents can do to increase the odds of having a grateful child who wants to get along (see *Your Child's Bill of Rights* in the appendix), but it isn't going to happen through coercion. Guilt is not an effective glue for strong bonds.

Quick Answers to Common Questions About Ways Kids Fail to Get Along with Their Family

Q: My sixteen-year-old son gets along fine with us when it's just us, but as soon as his younger brother comes in the room, he gets instantly annoyed. Instead of folding his brother into whatever we're doing or talking about, he just leaves. His younger brother just wants to spend time with him, but our oldest won't accommodate him at all. Can I ever expect this to change, or are we going to operate like separate units instead of one cohesive family?

A: There could be a couple things at play here. Your oldest may enjoy (even be craving) more time with just you parents. He may feel he's earned that and wants to talk about and behave in more adult ways with you. If that's the case, make sure he gets plenty of opportunity to be the big kid without his sibling intruding. If you have to send the youngest to a friend or relatives for a sleepover or take the oldest out to dinner to accomplish this, do that. After your oldest son's bucket is full, you can let him know you hope for more one-on-one time with him as well as more family time for all four of you, then solicit his ideas for both.

Another thought: Maybe there's something happening between the brothers you aren't aware of. Often in sibling relationships, we don't see the needling, borrowing without asking, teasing, or what in my house we referred to as "halo polishing"* that our kids really zoom in on. It may be worth separating each child to talk privately about whether anything is bothering them about their sibling's behavior toward them. From this, you might be able to establish new family rules to help everyone coexist more peacefully.

---

* Halo polishing is when one sibling senses the other has done something bad or is about to be in trouble, so they polish their own halo, so to speak, very publicly by being extra helpful, extra cuddly, or extra kind, showing what a good little angel they are, especially in contrast to their sibling.

Q: Yesterday I was tidying the living room, and I found a vape cartridge wedged between the couch cushions. I showed my son and asked him what was going on that he thought he could do this so blatantly in our home. He yelled at me for overreacting and said it wasn't even his. His friend had it and didn't want to get caught, so he asked my son to hold it for him. My son forgot it was there and says it must have fallen out of his pocket before he could give it back. I don't want to punish my son if he's innocent, but I also don't know if he's taking advantage of me. How can I find out the truth when he's not speaking to me now?

A: It doesn't matter if the vape is his or a friend's. What matters is that your son had it in his pocket, in your house, and, voilà, it's no longer a secret. This is good. Now you can talk about possession being legal grounds for prosecution and vaping and health and any of the stuff you want to talk about, regardless of who owns or uses the device. But first, a word on the popular "this isn't mine, I'm just holding it for a friend" defense: *Assume it is never true.*

Yes, there may be a rare circumstance in which your child is just holding a vape, bong, bag of weed or edibles, warm six-pack of White Claw hard seltzers, and so on with *zero* intention of partaking, but it's hard to imagine a good reason. The only two not-good reasons I can think of are either they're too naive to realize they're being used by a friend who doesn't want to get caught but is willing to put your child at risk or they're aware of the risk but want to ingratiate themselves with a friend with more social power. Either way, possession is illegal, regardless of innocent intention. The reality is, either the child caught with the paraphernalia is making an immature decision that puts them at risk or they're using, too. I've talked with lots of parents over the past decades who found illegal substances in their child's possession and gave their child the benefit of the doubt that they were, in fact, holding it for someone else, and *every time,* sometimes years later, the parents came to realize their child was also using.

My advice is to let your kids know well in advance that it is your policy *not* to believe the holding-for-a-friend defense. If you find drugs, or alcohol, or any paraphernalia related thereto in your child's possession, you will assume those items belong to them and they are not just acting as a mule. This works best if you declare this policy before your kids reach the age of experimentation, though that's a moving target since kids try at different ages and some never do. My advice is to aim for the start of middle school to make it clear that this is your policy. First, this will position you as a parent who knows what's going on and isn't gullible. Second, it will give your child an argument against kids partying at your house. "If my parents find anything, they're going to assume it's mine and I'll be screwed."

If you haven't established ahead of time that you won't believe the "it's not mine" defense, go ahead and give your child a get-out-of-jail-free card this time. Then explain the new system going forward. So for now, pretend the cartridge does indeed belong to a friend. You can structure your talk around what you want him to know about what you want his "friend" to know and how he can help his "friend" if this is an addiction. Be calm, nonjudgmental, and supportive.

Q: My daughter is a senior in high school and now feels it's her right to opt out of family events, especially since she'll be living away from home next year. I don't mind her missing some things, but she wants a free pass on everything, including, most recently, a planned day trip to see her grandfather, because something more fun came up. I know she is ready to spread her wings, but I want us to show up as a complete family to these things. It's embarrassing to me that she refuses to participate.

A: If you're okay with her missing some things, figure out what those *kinds* of things are and let her know that's what she can choose to miss. Or, depending on how many of these types of events your family attends, choose a quantity she can elect to skip. Kids her age do deserve to experience increased autonomy, but being part of a well-functioning family and reaping the benefits of such (having her needs met, for example) also mean she has to sometimes pay into that system. So, while she may not need to attend all the things, she should attend some.

One more note: Is it the attending itself that bothers her, or is it the missing out on other fun things that worries her? Perhaps the way you're notifying her of her obligation to attend is putting her off. Some kids like a long lead time so they can plan and schedule time with friends outside family plans. Some kids prefer spontaneity because planning only makes them dread the event more. Talk with your daughter about how she wants these events added to her calendar, as well as how often.

Q: My son used to be easy to get along with when he was little, but now he tries to do everything the opposite of how I raised him. We go to church every Sunday; he says he's an atheist. We make and sell barbecue at local fundraisers; he says he's a vegetarian. Any belief I have on a political or social issue or even a show on TV, he takes the opposite. If I say something is black, he says it's white. I don't know if he wants to fight or just can't stand who I am and wants to be different. We live in the same house, but we have nothing in common. Is this normal teenage rebellion against a parent, or is this the beginning of the end of our relationship?

A: I'm not sure I can say. It could be either. It's normal for teens to make a show of the ways in which they are different from their parents, but I find it interesting that he goes the opposite direction on *everything*. If you became a vegetarian, would he start eating meat again? (Don't try it. It'll come off as condescending unless you really mean it.) I'm just wondering. Because my sense is that there is something bigger than normal teen rebellion causing him to want to separate from you so entirely. Maybe he's worried if you *really* knew him—or who he feels he's becoming—you'd reject him, so he's rejecting you first. Or maybe you're so focused on your differences you're losing sight of ways you could connect.

Back to the vegetarian thing for a moment. As a barbecue enthusiast, you probably don't want to give up meat, but could you do a

Meatless Monday dinner at your house? Maybe he could cook some of his favorites for you and eventually with you. Instead of thinking about your world as "I do X and he does Y," try changing it up for a while. "He likes Y, so I'll ask about Y." Learn more about his favorite shows, foods, even beliefs. You don't have to adopt them for yourself, but show an interest in why *he* likes them. Then just listen. I suspect this will be a strong start to bridging the gap between you.

The Silver Lining About Failing to Get Along with Family

The good news about your child not getting along with you is that this behavior, which is scary and off-putting at times, may also reflect a child who is more ready than others to be independent.

When my oldest was about two years old, she started biting other kids. Frequently. I used to dread opening her tiny backpack after preschool and finding another incident report I had to sign and send back. After too many strikes, one incident report came with a request to sit down with the director of the preschool to talk about the "situation." I had been on a waiting list for this school and was sure they were going to kick us out. They didn't need our tuition check. They had people waiting years to take my spot! My mind jumped to how I'd go to work without childcare, and I was spinning with anxiety. The very kind director of the preschool, instead of blaming my two-year-old for not having herself together, explained that kids who start biting out of nowhere, at around her age, are on the cusp of a language burst. They want to be able to express themselves, and when they can't, they get physical. Truth be told, I forget the rest of what he said! I'm sure we moved on to talk about what to do about her behavior, so no other kids went home with bite marks on their arms, their hands, *their faces,* but the conversation memory becomes a blur after he told me my daughter's behavior wasn't a sign that she was a delinquent with rage issues. She was just smart and needed more tools to express herself, and we all needed more patience until she got those tools.

Kids like Kayla, who frequently argue with their parents or caregivers during adolescence, probably aren't delinquents with rage issues. They just have a strong need to separate from parents so they can pull themselves toward independence and begin to have great ideas and do bold things; they just don't have the tools yet to meet that desire. Finding ways to see that energy as potential, then channeling it into learning instead of fighting it, will take your bright, strong-willed child in a positive direction while preserving your relationship.

Some of you are probably the Black Sheep under more difficult circumstances. While not the situation in this case study, another silver lining to being the Black Sheep is that it can show you how to build a chosen family if the one you were born into is neither safe nor supportive.

CHAPTER THIRTEEN

Failure to Believe in Oneself: The Benchwarmer

I started high school a timid husk of a girl. A rough middle school social experience, anxiety, and some unpredictability in my childhood were fertile ground for my blooming self-doubt. Mr. Farber, my ninth-grade English teacher, had a reputation for yelling and throwing things in class, but lucky for me, I had the power of invisibility. I did my thing, blending into the background, and crossed my fingers he would keep his attention turned to the kids who talked too much.

Our first assignment was to write about a childhood memory. Easy. I dashed off two pages in cursive about the day when I was six years old, lying on the living room carpet, coloring, and my mom walked in and whispered to me, "Go say goodbye to your dad—we're taking a trip to see your grandparents." Twenty minutes later, from the backseat of our station wagon, I learned we weren't ever going back.

Mr. Farber passed our stories back the next day. Mine was covered in red ink. No, no, nooo, I thought. I could feel the stress building in the pit of my stomach. As my eyes flashed over the paper, catching editing squiggles, strikes, and circles, I saw the single note he'd written to me:

"You are a writer."

There it was. A fact. About me. I had spent years wondering who I was, and suddenly I had an answer. I wasn't just a gangly, awkward, nervous, desperate-to-be-popular girl. I *was* those things, but not *only* those things. I was a writer. Someone told me who had no reason to humor me, and so I believed him, and I was instantly liberated from my role as the Benchwarmer. I felt as if I'd been asked to join the game.

This sounds as if I were telling you to just look the other way while your child wallows in self-doubt hoping that one day they'll meet a terrifying stranger who will give them a compliment. I'm not. Although, I'm not *not* saying that's an unreasonable plan, either. Letting these things work themselves out is not just okay; it may be your only choice, since teens take their parents' praise with not a pinch but a truckload of salt. Then again, I don't want your child to be vulnerable to praise from someone with bad intentions, so while being patient is a good approach, there are some things you can do to set up guardrails against someone taking advantage of your child's lack of self-esteem. And if a stranger doesn't step in and do the job, sometimes as a parent you can make that happen.

Kids who see themselves as Benchwarmers lack the confidence or self-esteem to believe they can have or be more. They're usually pleasing and don't want to cause trouble. They're happy to cheer others on from the sidelines, but they don't grab opportunities for themselves because they're sure someone else would do a better job.

What changes things for the Benchwarmers? A good coach, for sure. Supportive fans are helpful. But it takes more than that. The one thing that can make a Benchwarmer believe in themselves is being able to contribute to the team.

Exposing the Benchwarmer to inspirational content doesn't do much for them. Let's say you're watching a sports movie with your child and you're feeling excited by the main character's resolve and perseverance. You turn to your child and say, "Look at that guy! He keeps getting knocked down and keeps getting up again. What a fighter! You should remember that. Never give up!" Your child will likely agree. *Yeah! That guy is amazing. I want to be like that, too!* But will this translate into grit? No.

Real athletes learn grit through memorable and relevant moments of success. If they never outran another player when they were gassed, never made an interception after a hard hit, never won a match after an emotional setback off the court, they'd have nothing to draw on and wouldn't know that perseverance pays off. This is why athletes practice over and over again. Experience—not listening to speeches or watching other people have success—breeds tenacity and success. A lack of experience breeds helplessness.

As a parent, your job is not to make things easy. Your job is to make sure your child has ample opportunity to experience enough challenges that they learn how to be successful despite setbacks.

Let's make a quick pivot from basketball to poop. Do you remember the children's book *Everyone Poops*? It's based on the brilliantly simple concept that parents can normalize this bodily function for kids by talking openly about how animals and people digest their food and how they deal with that. I used to tell my kids when they were in elementary school, "Even your principal poops! Have a great day!" It was my way of saying there's nothing to worry about. We're all human here. I wish I could do that for every Benchwarmer kid out there about their self-doubt. *Everyone doubts themselves! Have a great day!* We all go through periods of time when we don't believe we're capable or deserving of feeling and doing better. In this chapter, we'll explore what you can say and do to help your child climb out of that hole.

As a parent, your job is not to make things easy. Your job is to make sure your child has ample opportunity to experience enough challenges that they learn how to be successful despite setbacks.

For a deeper look at how a child can grow and learn from this kind of failure, let's see how using *Contain, Resolve, and Evolve* tactics worked for one family. Then, after the case study, I'll reply to some common questions about ways kids fail to believe in themselves.

MEET THE BENCHWARMER

Case Study: How Owen "Failed" to Believe in Himself

Betsy and Erik both had traumatic childhoods. Betsy's mom had a serious mental illness and could not care for her, and Erik's dad was violent toward him and his siblings. They are open and thoughtful about how this affected them, including how it drove the values and strategies they would bring to being parents.

Betsy works part time from home as a graphic designer, and Erik, full time as a psychologist. When they had their first son, Owen, they vowed to give their own kids a strong foundation of stability that was lacking from their own early years. They are a loving set of parents who created that environment at home, but Erik recalls that as his career took off, they had to move every year during Owen's elementary school years because of his job. This made Owen the new kid again at the start of each new grade level.

By third grade, Owen had two younger siblings, a sister and then a brother. Betsy says their younger two kids were wild children as compared with Owen, who never gave them any trouble. Whereas he was peaceful and thoughtful, they were impulsive and out of control. Betsy recalls her youngest child having a tantrum so intense he flung his head back while Betsy tried to restrain him, and it nearly broke her jaw. Erik says Owen quickly assumed the role in the family of the compliant one, and as they were constantly putting out fires with the younger two, Owen just faded into the background.

When Owen started middle school, it would be his first opportunity to settle into a school for more than one year. He adopted the standard middle school boy uniform of calf-high athletic socks, sneakers, gym shorts, and a hoodie. But on the morning of the first day of sixth grade, he made a decision that would turn out to be a fatal social flaw. He used his mom's hair gel to slick back his curly hair.

Within minutes of his arrival on campus, a group of seventh-grade boys spotted Owen and made a huge scene. His nickname became Oil Slick. "They absolutely eviscerated him," Erik says. Owen, true to himself, sank deeper and deeper into the background at school as he'd been doing at home. Betsy says he also became obsessive about his hair. She was constantly buying him new products as he tore his way through them, trying to find one that would make him more confident in his looks. She even took him to her fancy hair salon and said, "Do anything he wants," but Owen couldn't get himself over the curse of being called Oil Slick.

On top of this, Owen had hit the phase of puberty where he was putting on weight before he put on height. The summer between sixth and seventh grades, at a swim meet, his younger sister walked right up to him in front of the team and poked her finger deep into his belly. Erik said he saw the look on Owen's face and knew that was the moment that broke him.

Later that week, the swim coach posted a notice at the pool before practice with the names of all swimmers who would be going to the All-Star meet. Owen, who'd worked hard all season at improving his times, was on the list. Erik saw the notice when he picked Owen up from practice and was filled with joy for his son. When they got in the car, though, Owen said he wouldn't be going. He didn't want any of the kids from other pools to see him in his bathing suit.

That was the moment Erik decided to intervene.

Control the Narrative

During Owen's crisis of confidence, his parents were always compassionate and supportive, willing to go out of their way to do so (while still having to parent two other kids and hold down jobs). They supported his interests and followed his lead when he asked to try new things, including trying out for football. But they had never addressed Owen's lack of confidence head-on until the swim meet incident.

Erik took Owen out for dinner the day after the All-Star team was listed so the two of them could talk privately. He was straightforward. "Owen, I think you think feeling good about yourself comes naturally to some people and not to others. But it's not just something some people are born with and others aren't. It's something you can learn."

As an example, Erik talked about Betsy's brother, who'd recently visited them. As a hugely successful CEO of several major brands,

Owen's uncle seemed like one of those guys who just got it. But Erik pointed out that the things that made him successful—his charm, his determination, his confidence—can be learned. "I saw how wounded you were when your sister poked your stomach at the meet, and my guess is you think you're stuck here feeling bad about yourself," Erik said. Then he explained that if Owen was open to learning how, he could change the way he felt about himself, and Erik could help.

Owen's first reaction was that Erik wanted to be his therapist. "I don't want to be your client, Dad!" But once Erik explained he'd help only by finding him someone else to talk to, Owen opened up to the idea.

Affirm Your Child

There is something incredibly affirming in Erik telling his son that he can learn to change things about himself. I'm reminded of a celebrity interview that hit me the same way. On episode 13 of his podcast, *People I (Mostly) Admire,* Steven Levitt interviewed Yul Kwon, whose name you may recognize if you're a fan of the reality TV show *Survivor,* because he won the Cook Islands season. Kwon has also been a lawyer, an instructor at the FBI, and a business strategist at Google. The point is, Kwon is highly accomplished, and if you've seen him on TV, you'll note he's also very good looking. One might assume this is a guy who was born with a winner's good genes and better luck. But in this podcast, he talks about being the son of immigrants, always feeling like an outsider and a misfit, and being bullied in middle school. He had no self-confidence until his older sister told him he could change. He could take inventory of the things he didn't like about himself and focus on changing those things, one at a time.

Affirming a child can mean telling them the things about them you appreciate, but when you're working with a teen who is full of doubt, this might backfire. Their inner voice can argue back, if not out loud, with rebuttals to all your points. So sometimes the most affirming thing you can say to a child is "You can change. You're smart and strong enough to do this."

I highly recommend listening to this podcast with your child sometime if you are concerned about their failure to believe in themselves.

Take Action

Once Owen agreed to hear more about how he could change the parts of himself he didn't like, Erik and Betsy worked quickly to find someone to help Owen develop the tools he needed to change. They knew from observing him that *education* would be the best action they could take to keep this failure from derailing their son. Unlike other anecdotes in this book, Owen didn't need consequences, to rebuild trust, apologize, or any of the other options I've laid out. He needed to learn more about what resources were available to him so he could gather up the tools that would help him build the image he wanted but didn't have yet.

Educate

Erik felt he and Betsy had done a disservice to Owen when he was younger by simply accepting the gift of his compliant and gentle nature while they learned how to parent his younger siblings through many trials and tribulations. He knew that the key to resilience for young people is having one person who is fully invested in their success without distraction. Fortunately, Erik knew someone who would be a great match and mentor for Owen.

Gabe is a pediatrician, a neighbor of Erik and Betsy's, and the father of two preschool-age girls, and he is generally seen as the nice, fun, sporty dad in the neighborhood. Erik asked if Gabe would be willing to shoot baskets with Owen every so often, as his schedule allowed, and go over some basic skills in how to convey and feel confidence. Erik knew being forthright with Owen was important, so he explained to his son that Gabe had a lot of experience in helping teens at his medical practice and that he could offer Owen practical advice on ways to feel better about himself while they played basketball. Owen liked this idea much better than sitting in a therapist's office, and he wanted to feel better, so he agreed. Gabe texted Owen with the idea of meeting in the driveway on Saturday mornings for about fifteen or twenty minutes to shoot hoops and talk.

During their meetups, Gabe talked a lot about body language as well as verbal communication. He got Owen to open up about his thought process during social encounters. To Betsy and Erik's surprise, Gabe casually mentioned that Owen's ADHD was probably contributing to his feeling left out of conversations at school. Betsy was floored by Gabe's assumption that Owen had ADHD because his behavior was nothing like his younger siblings', both diagnosed and both eventually treated with medicine. Where they were wild, Owen was calm, so Betsy and Erik had never imagined Owen might have ADHD, too. But Owen's form of ADHD showed up as an inability to focus, and that was affecting his social life as much as his academics. When a group of guys were talking and one said something that might have been an invitation—*I gotta see that new Marvel movie*—Owen was too distracted to focus on that thread and pull it. He was missing chances to connect with other kids and blamed it on his being who he was, without ever realizing they wanted to connect but he wasn't taking the bait.

Betsy and Erik regretted waiting to medicate their younger children for too long, they say with hindsight. When first presented with the option to use ADHD medicine, they had thought, *We just need to be better parents and we can fix this.* Eventually, they realized they were at an impasse and gave the medicine a try, relying on a whisper network of friends to talk about the pros and cons of their experiences with medicine. Having experienced the benefits of treating their younger children's ADHD with medicine, they were quick to try it with Owen. All three of them were thrilled with the results.

Owen and Gabe continued to shoot hoops off and on during the summer before ninth grade. By the time he walked into his freshman homeroom, Owen felt and looked different. At Gabe's suggestion, he'd also gotten a weight bench and started working out in his garage. High school Owen was a far cry from the Owen of a couple years earlier. It was important to both Erik and Betsy they never talk to Owen about needing to change the shape of his body. Betsy said, "We didn't want him, or anyone else in his life, panicking about his body." Still, feeling confident with body language led to feeling confident with body movement, and as Owen discovered the ways in which he liked to move, his physicality began to match his emerging self-confidence.

Soon, Owen was making friends and eventually connections with other adults, from coaches to his friends' parents, and they informally began to add their mentoring to the foundation created by Gabe.

 Evolve

Triage Your Fears

Erik and Betsy were both relieved by and proud of how Owen rose to the challenge of focusing on himself and developing the tools he needs to be a confident adult, but this didn't wipe away all their fears. They worried about several things:

> Was he safely past this failure, or could something happen to trigger a relapse of self-doubt for Owen?

Did their decision to move so many times during Owen's early
years give him an unhappy childhood, exactly what they had
fought to stave off after their own traumatic childhoods?
Would Owen resent his siblings for the ways they changed both
the family dynamic and his own sense of confidence?

The first fear, about whether Owen would relapse into his former
self, is one of those fears parents have a hard time putting down. There
isn't reason to worry that after a person experiences personal growth,
they're in danger of slipping back into old ways, unlike the expected
setbacks that occur with addiction. I think Erik and Betsy can feel confident that Owen's trajectory will continue to move in the same direction as he collects more experiences that reinforce his self-confidence
and when he can, from a distance, see that his painful middle school
years created an opening for him to learn more about himself and an
appreciation that that kind of knowledge is more valuable than easy
success without effort.

Most parents wonder at some point in what way they damaged their
child and how they could have done a better job not messing things up.
But every child can—and should!—face adversity growing up so they
learn how to cope with it. Parents don't need to—and shouldn't!—
manufacture adversity. It will show up on its own. They simply need to
let their kids learn to face it.

Barring the absence of real trauma, the kind Betsy and Erik both
saw as children, it seems to me that most kids view their childhoods
with a pleasant and proud nostalgia, rather than a critical assessment.
Betsy got the relief she needed on this issue when she overheard Owen
talking to some friends on his football team about the cool places they'd
lived when he was younger. If you share this fear, and you aren't lucky
enough to overhear a contradictory story to the one you're carrying
around in your head, you can simply ask your kids how they would

describe moments from their childhood: hardest, most fun, most playful, most humorous, most boring. Throw out some superlatives and their answers may surprise you.

Face One Fear First

Of all their concerns, Erik and Betsy's biggest was that Owen might resent his siblings. They knew they needed to talk with his siblings first, about what Owen had gone through, and as a family second, to be sure his younger brother and sister understood how their behavior affected others. As a therapist, Erik is a pro at negotiating emotional family dynamics, and by using a family-meeting-style approach to the conversation, he and Betsy made sure everyone spoke respectfully (these kids are well versed in using "I" statements instead of making accusations) and had the opportunity to be heard without judgment. There were awkward moments, but overall they believe Owen felt validated and his sister better understood the emotional ramifications of teasing him in front of friends.

Uphold *Your Child's Bill of Rights*

Right: Practice Making Informed Decisions About Their Bodies

Normally, I'd think of this right as pertaining to decisions of a more permanent nature: medical decisions, piercings, or playing a dangerous sport, for example. But for Owen, it's important that he explore and keep flexing (weight-lifting pun intended) his right to feel ownership of his body and the way he chooses to style himself, without fear of social consequence. Owen's parents might worry that without their continued affirmation of his appearance, or guidance on choosing clothing or hairstyles that won't invite criticism, he will once again become victim to his peers' taunting. His parents should fight any urge to be controlling of their child's choices about how he presents himself to the world. For Owen to move forward and not get stuck in this area, especially as an older teen, he will need full access to this right of bodily autonomy. Even if he chooses to dye his hair, or slick it back, or wear an outfit that makes Erik or Betsy cringe. The more Owen does this, the more his peers and parents will know this is just a part of who he is, and as they accept this, they will stop giving him feedback. From there, his confidence will untether itself from how other people react to his appearance.

Right: Receive the Benefit of the Doubt

The other right Erik and Betsy should keep front and center in their parenting is Owen's right to the benefit of the doubt. Any parent who has seen a child suffer from self-doubt, or struggle to find their sense of self among a peer group, will know how difficult it is to let that pain go, for fear that if they assume Owen is okay now, they won't be tending to his wounds in a caring way. In actuality, by leaving that experience in the rearview mirror, they'll show Owen that he's okay and capable of taking care of himself without their constant tending. Remember when your child was young and they skinned a knee, once you assessed the damage and nursed what needed care, if you distracted them from the embarrassment, anger, and pain of the moment by getting them up-right, assuring them they were fine, and moving them along to the next task, they'd believe you. Don't skip over the step of providing the care they need—in Owen's case it was asking Gabe to help teach him—but once that part is complete, it's time to move on. This is the benefit of the doubt kids need after a fall.

See New Things

Owen's right to the benefit of the doubt ties directly to the importance of his parents seeing new things in him to help him evolve past the feeling of failure to believe in himself. As the children grow and the family dynamic continues to evolve, Betsy and Erik are forward thinking about how they see Owen as both a member of their family and a member of his peer group. Funny enough, what helped them do this was a revisiting of the past. On a family vacation to the mountains, Owen bragged about the fun the three of them had the year they lived in the mountains before his younger siblings were old enough to remember. Stories of his old tree house and the stream where he fished with his dad were more Mayberry than mayhem, and Erik, who had been filled with guilt over moving so much, was filled with the same relief Betsy felt overhearing Owen tell his teammates about places they'd lived. Sometimes seeing new things can apply to what you see in yourself as much as in your child. Erik realized it was time for him to let himself off the hook for the family moves and to join Owen in appreciating what those moves gave the family instead of focusing on what they took away.

Quick Answers to Common Questions About Ways Kids Fail to Believe in Themselves

Q: My daughter has always been an overachiever when it comes to school. She is in the top 10 percent of her class and runs track. Both her dad and I went to college, and we've always assumed she would, too. She's in her junior year of high school, so it's time to start touring potential schools. As soon as I mentioned getting her list together of where she wants to visit, she freaked out. Now she says she doesn't want to go to college. What?! When I pressed her, she said she's afraid of being away from home. How can I convince her she needs to take this next step and can't stay at home forever?
A: If this freak-out is unprecedented, it's possible she was so busy

grinding out her achievements that she never took time to step back and think about what they were all for. The thought of leaving home can be scary, understandably so, especially if it hit her all at once. If that's the case, you can take a little heat off her by suggesting you go look at a college that's an easy drive away—bonus if it's one she'd never even consider her style. Position this as a chance to see what a campus feels like with zero intention of ever going there. Watch a club quidditch match or soccer game, eat lunch, take a stroll around campus, and then go home. Zero talk about her going there—or anywhere—zero comparison to other schools, zero hype about how fun college looks to you, a forty-something-year-old. Once she sees that college isn't a big, scary, unimaginable, distant universe, she could come to her own conclusion that she'd like to see more.

If, upon reflection, you see that there were some other signs leading up to this freak-out, you may need to take a more clinical approach. Has your daughter shown tendencies toward perfectionism? Has her need for control ramped up over the last couple years? Has she changed her habits (eating, sleeping, exercise) even in ways that first seemed healthy? If, in retrospect, you can start collecting other changes that preceded college denial, it may be that this college freak-out didn't come out of nowhere but was the most obvious in a series of transformations. Make a list and then I'd suggest you talk with a counselor who specializes in anxiety among teen girls to figure out how you can help your daughter develop coping skills for when she feels overwhelmed. Also, remember that timelines can create undue pressure, and yours doesn't need to look like everyone else's. It's okay to start this process later than her peers.

Finally, we live in a society that generally sees four-year college as the obligatory course of action after graduating from high school, especially after graduating with an impressive résumé. It doesn't have to be, and it can be quite liberating to talk about life less as a narrow series of predetermined steps and more as an open field of choices. Gap years, community college, trade programs, internships, volunteer service, military service, and full-time jobs are all options your daughter can consider pursuing.

Q: My child (pronouns they/them) has been infatuated with musicals since they were a toddler. They love singing at home and in our church children's choir. The middle school posted on Instagram about auditions for the musical The Little Mermaid, *and my child was so excited to try out for the part of Sebastian. They practiced constantly. (If I hear "Under the Sea" one more time, I'll drown myself.) Now the auditions are a few days away, and they're saying they aren't going because they're too nervous. Do I let them skip the audition, even though they practiced so hard, or do I force them to go, knowing it's just jitters and they'll regret not trying?*

A: If you can figure out how to easily force a middle schooler to do something against their will, email me and we will co-author my next book.

At their age, dangling a carrot is usually more persuasive than threatening with a stick. Even if you carry them into the audition room and pull down their jaw, you can't make music come out of their mouth. I understand where you're coming from, though. If you think they'll regret not trying out (it sounds as if they may), offer to take them to do something fun after. Don't pressure them this way, but see if floating a counterbalance to the discomfort gives them a nudge.

Since this sounds like a classic case of the jitters, let's think about what causes nerves and what calms them. Performance anxiety creates a visceral reaction: rapid heart rate, dry mouth, sweat, trembling. Talk with your child about whether any of these things happen when they imagine the audition. Then practice ways to calm down your body when it starts to betray you. Deep breathing, clenching fists, shaking out the jitters—movement puts you back in charge of your body.

Incidentally, it might also help to understand that many successful performers still get severe anxiety before going onstage and they say the nerves ultimately help them. Reframing nerves as a tool, not an enemy, could help.

Nerves can also be caused by the Great Unknown. There are so many unknowns about this situation. It can easily be overwhelming. How will the audition room look? Who will be there? Will they sing onstage or on the floor? Will they get immediate feedback? If they mess up, what should they do? If someone interrupts, will it derail them? What if they forget the words? What if they trip walking in? Maybe your child can investigate ahead of time by talking with the drama teacher or an older student, and you can help out by practicing the audition with them. They might have sung the song hundreds of times from their bedroom or shower, but now it's time to practice how to introduce themselves, what to do if someone interrupts, and so on.

Q: My daughter has always been sensitive and a follower in her friend groups. She's fifteen and is good friends with one girl who has a dominant personality. Her friend says things like "You should wear more makeup because you don't have a naturally pretty face." One time she told my daughter, "Guys don't notice you because you're so shy." My daughter told me this because she wants me to buy her new clothes and makeup. She really believes this friend. I don't know if I should let her try on a new persona, or if I should refuse and hope she figures out this friend doesn't have her best interest at heart. I'm afraid my daughter's self-esteem is sinking, and I want to help her feel better, but I don't think a makeover is the answer.

A: A fifteen-year-old girl trying on a new look and experimenting with new makeup and clothing is totally in line with normal adolescent development, so even though this friend sounds not nice and possibly deeply insecure herself, I don't see any harm in taking your daughter shopping (without the friend) to see what ways she might want to start expressing herself through her personal style.

"Yes, and" I think this is a good time to explore your daughter's feelings about herself and her friend through gentle, open questions. If you attack the friend, your daughter will defend her, and you don't want to drive her to that. Instead, ask things like this:

How does it make you feel when she says that?
Do you feel better or worse after hanging out with her?
Whom do you spend time with who leaves you feeling good?
Do you trust her opinion?
What makes you feel best, happiest, most confident?
When during the day do you feel most content?

Instead of pouring your attention into what this friend is doing wrong, pour your attention into your daughter and her interests. Appearance is a part of who we are, and your daughter wants to get comfortable with hers. That makes sense. What she may not recognize at her young age is that appearance is a product not just of what she puts on her body but of what shines through her vessel to others. Hair, makeup, and clothing can be fun to play with, but they aren't what people form bonds over. You can't hit her over the head with this, but you can start pointing out the qualities people have that make them attractive: a great laugh, an ease of conversation, a sly sense of humor, a positive outlook. There is no formula, and once she understands this, she won't spend her life chasing one or believing a friend who says there is.

The Silver Lining About Failing to Believe in Oneself

In the book *Get It Done,* Ayelet Fishbach concludes that people need two things to be able to learn from failure: the ability to tune out what this says about you as a person, and the ability to tune in to what you can learn from it. When a child experiences a failure to believe in themselves, if they tune in to what this says about them, they may get stuck there. But when a parent reframes the circumstance as a learning opportunity instead of a deeply personal flaw, the child can experience tremendous social and emotional growth. On the contrary, a person who never experiences self-doubt is probably not a nice person to be around. The silver lining to being the Benchwarmer is simple and pure. You're not raising an arrogant, narcissistic future world leader. Chances are you're raising a thoughtful person who, once they evolve through this rite of passage, will likely be a positive role model and mentor to friends, family, and colleagues in the future.

Before You Go

Being There for Each Other

I asked every parent I interviewed for this book if I were to offer them a magic wand that would wave away their child's difficult experience, would they take it? All but one said no.

Not for the child who ended up in the hospital after binge drinking. Not for the one who went years without a close friend. Not for the one who was suspended. Not for the one who was labeled lazy in school. Not for the one who lost all his confidence. Not for the one who was impossible to live with.

If I'd asked them during the hardest part of their child's struggle, I'd bet all of them would have said, "Give me that wand." But from the other side, each parent saw that the growth that came out of the pain was worth it after all. For the one parent who said she'd love to wave it all away, she also thought maybe she was still too close to it to say otherwise but from where she sat it was an easy yes.

If you are in the middle of the storm, be patient. Remember to follow your steps: Contain, resolve, evolve. Remember that you, and your child, don't have to do this perfectly. Just take it one step at a time. Sometimes that will be several steps forward, and sometimes you'll take a few steps back. It's all part of the process.

And remember, I'm still here to help even after you finish reading. You can find me on my website, on social media, or in my Less Stressed Middle School Parents group on Facebook. I can also visit your school or organization for a pep talk.

My hope in writing this book was to initiate a shift in how we think about childhood failures, rebellions, and setbacks, as well as how we support each other through them. I'll leave you with one last thought on this in case you find yourself in a position to support someone else in their struggle.

Nice things to do for a parent whose child is struggling:

- Ask them to go for a walk. Offer to listen, and tell them you won't probe with questions. Just let them do a brain dump.
- Promise to be a vault. If they tell you details, keep them to yourself unless you have permission to share.
- Take a chore off their list. Walk the dog or drop off food. A meal or even some groceries to make packing lunches easier can be a huge relief.
- Offer to talk with the child. Don't push—but offer once.
- Help them find their whisper network of parents who've had a similar experience.
- Tell them that even if you don't know the right thing to say, you want them to know you're on their team/thinking of them/in solidarity.
- Say explicitly, I would never judge you or your child. This is a normal part of life.
- Remind them which of their child's qualities you like best.

- Remind them you are there to listen and commiserate if they need to vent about their child's difficult qualities to you.
- Normalize setbacks: Everyone hits bumps in the road. Yes, something upsetting and unexpected has happened, but that's just a part of life, not a reflection on who you are.
- Don't overdramatize your friend's experience. Don't "press the bruise" and bring it up every time you see them. Talk about other things.
- Don't ask them to share other people's experiences in confidence.
- Don't treat their child any differently.

I hope this book has inspired you to think about children, yours and others', and the failures they pass through as they grow up, in a new way. Failure doesn't have to be the dreaded F-word that no one wants to talk about because it's scary, negative, or stigmatizing to bring it out into the light. If we support each other, and each other's children, through the challenges failure brings, together we can build safer spaces for kids to learn and grow from their experiences in ways that benefit not just them individually but all of us as a community.

Acknowledgments

I don't know how I got so lucky to have this many friends and colleagues who are smart, funny, and kind. I might sound like a broken record, but I can't change the fact that you are each all these things.

With gratitude to:

Anna Sproul-Latimer, my brilliant literary agent, who helps me see the point whenever my vision is blurry. I don't think I'll ever write anything as clever or clear as you do, but I am better for having that bar before me.

Marnie Cochran, my editor at Penguin Random House, who is lightning fast on replies, supportive beyond measure, smart, down-to-earth, and thorough. Really, how did I get so lucky?

Quinn Davidson, my work partner for nearly twenty years, who keeps me organized and supported and, most important, whose subversive sense of humor keeps me sane.

Betsy Thorpe, my longtime local editor, for being available, flexible, wise, and enthusiastic. You are my Magic 8 Ball. I'll always ask you first.

Rosie Molinary, for being with me for the long haul, book to book to book, and demolishing my writer's block each time it stands in my way. You are my wrecking ball.

Jill Dykes, my publicist, for her warmth, creativity, and brilliant ideas. When I'm totally tapped out and can't see the angle, you are my protractor.

Chuck Heuer, my dad, for the support and advice throughout my life.

Dawn O'Malley, for sixteen years of friendship, free therapy, book feedback, and not least of all, for the totally inappropriate skits. I couldn't have survived raising teens without you.

Haley Weaver, for the designs in this book, for all the beautiful art you put into this world, for your vulnerability, humor, and friendship.

Kate Weaver, for the writing retreat that got me back on track, for the years of your support and friendship, for being my role model in more ways than you know.

Tammy Jones, my social media manager, and my dear friend, for being not only my twin in appearance but for being of the same mind. Middle school me is calling . . . what should we wear tomorrow?

Melissa Miller, for bringing your perfect balance of sincerity and humor, adventure and grounding, ease and excitement into my life. I actually would join a cult if I saw your name on the list first.

Loren Neus, for being my nonjudgmental sounding board, for reminding me to take care of myself, and for helping me figure out this parenting thing in both directions.

Stacey Yovanoff, for your generosity, your kind heart, and your nurturing spirit, evidenced by always offering to bring me coffee or a smoothie when I am in need.

Kristin Daley, for your willingness to share your big brain and relatable takes with me on both the science and practicality of being human.

Billy Simone and *Jeff Langone*, for the marketing advice, the built-in focus group, and the comedy clinic. It was a long con that started back in ninth grade. Now you're doing most of the heavy lifting without any of the royalties.

Jenna Glasser, for the Zoom writing retreats, the consistent check-ins, and the friendship of a lifetime. You make me feel sixteen in the best possible way. To many decades more of playing.

Sarah Connolly, for being my friend longer than anyone else on Earth, and for all the benefits that come with that, including being able to borrow on your wisdom, humor, strength, and incredibly kind heart. Thank you for being the collective memory keeper. Sleepover soon?

Tracy Curtis, for writing across the table from me, making me laugh, and then making me get back to work. No one is better at word play and you make me sharper.

John Duffy, for your insights and contributions to chapter 11 as well as for your excellent detective work on Twitter.

Mary Crowe, Kari Beery, and *Krista Hays*, for knowing that nothing matters more than longevity. I love being eighteen and fifty with you, all at once.

Clara and *Jack Herron*, for coming to the rescue and walking Bert and Levi when I was glued to the stool at my kitchen island for weeks trying to wrap this book up.

Most important, to:

Declan Icard, for being the best son I could ever wish for, for reminding me to be less productive some days and for cheering me on to the distance others, for being the voice in my head saying, *Why not today?*, for explaining things without ever condescending, for always being down to hang out, and for keeping the family open-minded, curious, and fully pranked.

Ella Icard, for being the best daughter I could ever wish for, for keeping my references relevant, for being so tenacious you never quit and so soft-hearted you cry at movies you've seen fifteen times, for being grateful, for being the preserver of traditions, and for keeping the family organized, informed, and well-gifted.

Travis Icard, for growing old with me. There is no one with whom I would rather raise children, walk the dogs, travel the world, do the crossword, share a cocktail, try new recipes, talk about trying new recipes, never try new recipes, than you. I love you. Meet me at the mountain house.

And finally, *Sheila Heuer*, my mom, who passed away while I was writing this book. I don't have the words yet for this one. I'm working on it. Wherever you are, I hope the blueberries are ripe, the elections are going exactly the way you want, and all the dogs are curled up at your feet.

Appendix 1:
Actions You Can Take to Resolve a Failure

Educate—Sample scenario: You found out your child's friend was busted for underage drinking. Now your child is freaking out because they like this person a lot and don't want you telling them they can't hang out together anymore. Your plan may include reading together about the effects of drinking on a developing brain, learning the signs of addiction, googling and then practicing ways your child can say no to substances without feeling dorky, or researching ways to support a friend through a tough time.

Define Consequences—Sample scenario: Your child has crashed the family car twice due to distracted driving. Your plan will likely include limiting access to car keys as well as a plan to repay some or all of the costs associated with your insurance deductible or rate increase.

Foster Connection—Sample scenario: Your child is increasingly withdrawing from family and friends, refusing to interact with peers in person or online. Your plan may involve helping them find opportunities to forge new connections where old ones have broken.

Rebuild Trust—Sample scenario: Your child has a 10:00 p.m. curfew on weekends, and they've been coming home on time then sneaking out at night through their window to spend time with their friends in the park. Your plan will probably include a list of things they can do to rebuild your trust in their ability to make safe decisions.

Seek Perspective—Sample scenario: Same as above, different curfew. Your child has a 7:30 p.m. curfew on weekends, and they've been coming home on time then sneaking out at night through their window to spend time with their friends in the park until 8:30 p.m. Your plan may include seeking new perspectives on what can reasonably keep a child safe and to what degree your rigid rules may be driving their rebellious behavior.

Enable Interventions—Sample scenario: Your teen has been engaging in sex with her older boyfriend without using protection and while under the influence. Your plan will likely need interventions with specialists in the mental health field who can assess what steps will best keep your child safe. You may need to explore residential therapy if recommended by professionals.

Reprioritize—Sample scenario: Your child tells you they don't feel like themselves in their assigned birth gender and they've had intrusive thoughts about hurting themselves. Reprioritizing may mean studying a topic you hadn't thought much about until now. It may mean spending more time and attention on this child for the time being. Education and connection with people who support and accept your child are going to show up here, too.

Apologize—Sample scenario: Your child took beer to a friend's house, where they drank when the parents were out of town and were busted by the neighbors. In addition to discipline and education, your plan should include one or more good apologies. For more on how to structure a good apology, see page 71 of this book.

Make Amends—Sample scenario: Let's reuse the same one we did for apologize, but this time make it more complicated. Your child took beer to a friend's house, where they drank when the parents were out of town, and broke a picture frame in the process. Obviously, an apology is still in order, but it isn't quite enough, since the friend's parents will be out of money to replace the frame. Ideally, the kids who were drinking would all pitch in to have the frame fixed or replaced and even for the house to be cleaned if needed.

Your Child's Bill of Rights

ADOLESCENTS HAVE THE RIGHT TO:

I. MAKE MISTAKES AND HAVE OPPORTUNITIES TO FIX THEM

II. MAINTAIN SOME PRIVACY

III. TAKE RISKS

IV. CHOOSE THEIR OWN FRIENDS AND GATHER WITH PEERS

V. PRACTICE MAKING INFORMED DECISIONS ABOUT THEIR BODIES

VI. RECEIVE THE BENEFIT OF THE DOUBT

VII. NEGOTIATE AND SELF-ADVOCATE

VIII. DETERMINE THEIR OWN VALUES

IX. ACCESS ACCURATE INFORMATION FROM MULTIPLE PERSPECTIVES AND SOURCES ON ALL TOPICS

X. SEEK INDEPENDENCE AND NOT BE RELIED UPON BY THEIR CAREGIVERS FOR PERSONAL, EMOTIONAL, OR FINANCIAL GAIN

Notes

Introduction

xiii The cupcake is an example of: Scott Appelrouth and Laura Desfor Edles, *Classical and Contemporary Sociological Theory: Text and Readings* (Los Angeles: Pine Forge Press, 2008).

Chapter One: Understanding Failure and How It Functions

5 The American Psychological Association reported: Thomas Curran and Andrew P. Hill, "Young People's Perceptions of Their Parents' Expectations and Criticism Are Increasing over Time: Implications for Perfectionism," *Psychological Bulletin* 148, no. 1–2 (2022): 107–28, doi:10.1037/bul0000347.

9 Plant ownership allowed us: "Houseplant Statistics 2022," Terrarium Tribe, June 7, 2022, terrariumtribe.com/houseplant-statistics/#hp1.

9 For me, the biggest metaphor: Ibid., terrariumtribe.com/houseplant-statistics/#hp12.

12 I think the best definition: Abraham Harold Maslow, *Self-Actualization* (San Rafael, CA: Big Sur Recordings, 1971).

13 I've long been fascinated by: Martin E. P. Seligman, "Learned Helplessness," *Annual Review of Medicine* 23 (1972): 407–12, doi.org/10.1146/annurev.me.23.020172.002203.

13 In a 2016 follow-up: S. F. Maier and M. E. Seligman, "Learned Helplessness at Fifty: Insights from Neuroscience," *Psychological Review* 123, no. 4 (2016): 349–67, doi.org/10.1037/h0024514.

13 To better understand this: M. E. Seligman and S. F. Maier, "Failure to Escape Traumatic Shock," *Journal of Experimental Psychology* 74, no. 1 (1967): 1–9, doi.org/10.1037/h0024514.

14 This experiment shows us: D. S. Hiroto and M. E. Seligman, "Generality of Learned Helplessness in Man," *Journal of Personality and Social Psychology* 31, no. 2 (1975): 311–27, doi.org/10.1037/h0076270.

16 Interestingly, research shows us: Susan Ashford, Maxim Sytch, and Lindred L. Greer, "5 Ways a Crisis Can Help You Cultivate a Growth Mindset," *Harvard Business*

Review, Aug. 20, 2020, hbr.org/2020/08/5-ways-a-crisis-can-help-you-cultivate-a
-growth-mindset.

22 The Pew Research Center reported that: *It's Becoming More Common for Young
Adults to Live at Home—and for Longer Stretches,* Pew Research Center, May 5, 2017,
www.https://www.pewresearch.org/fact-tank/2017/05/05/its-becoming-more
-common-for-young-adults-to-live-at-home-and-for-longer-stretches/.

Chapter Two: How Communities Benefit from Letting Children Fail

30 Inuit girls, at the age: Regina Franco and Barbara Hernandez, "Reaching Adulthood Through the Wintry Wilderness—Inuit Rite of Passage," Death of a Maiden,
June 9, 2016, barbbooks.wordpress.com/2016/06/09/reaching-adulthood-through
-the-wintry-wilderness-inuit-rite-of-passage/.

30 Maasai boys are taken: "Facing the Lion," Maasai Association, www.maasai
-association.org/lion.html.

30 Each sting, by the way: Rachel Nuwer, "When Becoming a Man Means Sticking
Your Hand into a Glove of Ants," *Smithsonian Magazine,* Oct. 27, 2014, www
.smithsonianmag.com.

32 The answer to this dilemma: Arnold van Gennep, *The Rites of Passage* (Chicago:
University of Chicago Press, 1960).

34 In Donna Jackson Nakazawa's: Donna Jackson Nakazawa, *Girls on the Brink:
Helping Our Daughters Thrive in an Era of Increased Anxiety, Depression, and Social
Media* (New York: Harmony Books, 2022), 40–43.

Chapter Five: Three Steps to Overcoming Failure

69 Research shows that most adolescents: Stefano Palminteri et al., "The Compu-
tational Development of Reinforcement Learning During Adolescence," *PLoS Com-
putational Biology* 12, no. 6 (2016): e1004953, doi.org/10.1371/journal
.pcbi.1004953.

74 In her book *Girls on the Brink:* Nakazawa, *Girls on the Brink.*

Chapter Six: Failure to Follow the Rules: The Rebel

81 This became a hot topic: Katie Serena, "The Bodies of Dead Climbers on Everest Are Serving as Guideposts," *All That's Interesting,* June 9, 2021, allthatsinteresting
.com/mount-everest-bodies.

Chapter Seven: Failure to Take Care of Their Body: The Daredevil

103 And the African spiny mouse: Zoe Cormier, "African Spiny Mice Can Regrow
Lost Skin," *Nature* (2012).

116 One reason we might: Ayelet Fishbach, *Get It Done: Surprising Lessons from the
Science of Motivation* (New York: Little, Brown Spark, 2022), 112.

Chapter Eight: Failure to Perform Well in School: The Misfit

127 In third grade, though: Stefan Haberstroh and Gerd Schulte-Körne, "The Diagnosis and Treatment of Dyscalculia," *Deutsches Arzteblatt International* 116, no. 7 (2019): 107–14, doi:10.3238/arztebl.2019.0107.

128 During his ninth-grade year: Dyslexia FAQ, Yale Center for Dyslexia and Creativity, dyslexia.yale.edu/dyslexia/dyslexia-faq.

Chapter Nine: Failure to Show Concern for Others: The Ego

151 In an interview on *The Today Show:* Jacob Soboroff, "Hollywood Stars Gather to Honor Beloved Drama Teacher," *The Today Show,* Aug. 29, 2022.

154 Research shows that teens: Anne van Goethem et al., "The Role of Reflection in the Effects of Community Service on Adolescent Development: A Meta-analysis," *Child Development* 85, no. 6 (2014): 2114–30, doi:10.1111/cdev.12274.

Chapter Ten: Failure to Connect with Peers: The Loner

164 This is a normal and necessary part: A. C. Hartl et al., "A Survival Analysis of Adolescent Friendships: The Downside of Dissimilarity," *Psychological Science* 26, no. 8 (Aug. 2015): 1304–15, www.ncbi.nlm.nih.gov/pubmed/2618724.

174 It's worth noting: *A Survey of LGBT Americans,* Pew Research Center, June 13, 2013, www.pewresearch.org/social-trends/2013/06/13/a-survey-of-lgbt-americans.

Chapter Eleven: Failure to Handle Their Feelings: The Sensitive One

184 Nine percent of high schoolers: "What You Need to Know About Youth Suicide," National Alliance on Mental Illness, www.nami.org/Your-Journey/Kids-Teens-and-Young-Adults/What-You-Need-to-Know-About-Youth-Suicide.

184 Since the pandemic: Marie-Laure Charpignon et al., "Evaluation of Suicides Among US Adolescents During the COVID-19 Pandemic," *JAMA Pediatrics* 176, no. 7 (2022): 724–26, doi:10.1001/jamapediatrics.2022.0515.

200 Finally, since most parents: John A. Sturgeon and Alex J. Zautra, "Social Pain and Physical Pain: Shared Paths to Resilience," *Pain Management* 6, no. 1 (2016): 63–74, doi:10.2217/pmt.15.56.

Chapter Thirteen: Failure to Believe in Oneself: The Benchwarmer

235 He knew that the key: Kathryn Ashton et al., "Adult Support During Childhood: A Retrospective Study of Trusted Adult Relationships, Sources of Personal Adult Support, and Their Association with Childhood Resilience Resources," *BMC Psychology* 9 (2021), article no. 101, doi.org/10.1186/s40359-021-00601-x.

245 In the book *Get It Done:* Fishbach, *Get It Done,* 112.

Index